gift 12/97

Dreaming of

Hitler

Dreaming of Hitler

PASSIONS & PROVOCATIONS

DAPHNE MERKIN

Crown Publishers, Inc.   New York

A complete list of permissions appears on pages 365–366.

Copyright © 1997 by Daphne Merkin

Published by Crown Publishers, Inc., 201 East 50th Street, New York, New York 10022.
Member of the Crown Publishing Group.

Random House, Inc. New York, Toronto, London, Sydney, Auckland
http://www.randomhouse.com/

CROWN and colophon are trademarks of Crown Publishers, Inc.

Printed in the United States of America

Design by Lynne Amft

Library of Congress Cataloging-in-Publication Data
Merkin, Daphne.
Dreaming of Hitler: passions & provocations / Daphne Merkin. —
1st ed./(alk. paper)
I. Title.
PS3563.E7412D74 1997
814'.54—dc21   97-11640

ISBN 0-517-70626-1

10 9 8 7 6 5 4 3 2 1

First Edition

For my mother and father, after all

Acknowledgments

My largest debt of gratitude goes to my friend and editor Elaine Pfefferblit, whose passion for language has kept my writing up to snuff and whose good humor has kept my spirits afloat. She has been a source of inspiration in this incontestably lonely business of putting words on a page. I would also like to thank my agent, Owen Laster, for drawing on years of experience the better to provide me with a steady beam of advice and encouragement. Patrick Sheehan at Crown gave cheerful assistance at every stage.

Among the many editors I have met along the way I would like to single out Chip McGrath, who believed in me from the start; Mike Kolatch, whose "tough love" approach first got me into the habit of writing on a regular basis; Pat Towers, who stayed late into the night and helped me make the leap from reviews to longer pieces; Adam Moss, for making room for those pieces; and Nancy Newhouse, for letting me be as personal and contrarian as I liked in a national newspaper column. The crew at *The New Yorker* deserves my special thanks: Tina Brown, for generously giving me the space to write my mind; Deborah Garrison, whose literary judgment goes hand in hand with an instinct for nurturing; Henry Finder, for remembering everything he's ever read; David Kuhn, for his support; and Alice Truax, for her nuanced readings. My thanks to Howard Deutsch: for being there. And especially to my daughter, Zoë, thanks for being herself—and for just being.

Contents

A Note to the Reader

To put together a collection such as this for publication—to give it the time and attention it properly requires, so it appears to have some kind of shape, however imposed or arbitrary—is to fly in the face of what the critic Roland Barthes called "the thousand forces of the world which are, all of them, disparaging forces." It requires, that is, a kind of blind faith —or, perhaps, secret conviction—that somewhere out there in the vast but ever-shrinking planet is an audience ready to pick up on your lone signal, the tap-tap-tapping of your Morse code: WRITER . . . HELP . . . STUCK OUT HERE IN MY HEAD . . . MUCH TO REPORT . . . DO YOU READ ME? The wisdom of book publishing has it that mostly there is no such audience; collections of essays are supposed to be the kiss of commercial death, and the mere mention of them is enough to elicit a gleam of desperation in an agent or editor's eye. (One publisher who recently told me of his fondness for "nifty critical essays" said it was like "having the mark of Cain upon you—they put you in a room until you repent.") It's never been clear to me why, exactly, it should be so; given the fact that our attention spans have been sharply abbreviated, the essay would seem to be precisely the form that our time, in all its channel-zapping, Net-surfing restlessness, should welcome.

I myself have always loved to read collections—whether of book reviews, like Cyril Connolly's *The Evening Colonnade* or Elizabeth Bowen's *Collected Impressions,* or more thematically significant gatherings, like Virginia Woolf's *The Common Reader* or William Gass's *On Being Blue.* There's something about this form in all its prismatic, dappled, "pied beauty" (to borrow a phrase from that inventive Jesuit poet, Gerard Manley Hopkins) that allows me to think I am getting a glimpse of the distilled essence of a given writer, the True Person behind the novelist or biographer or poet: his or her many-angled, just-arisen-from-sleep sensibility rather than a coherent professional self, dressed and ready to go. Ever since I came upon the writings of William Hazlitt and Charles Lamb in a Victorian literature class I took in college, I have been beguiled by the possibilities inherent in so personal and discursive a genre. (The catch being, of course, that even the most immediate and confiding of pieces is, at its best, a careful literary construction, assembled brick by brick from deliberate withholdings as well as timely infusions of candor.)

In the interests of readability and an overall sense of flow, every piece in this collection has been revised—some extensively. In one instance ("The Shoplifter's High"), I put more of myself in because, on rereading the article, I noticed that I seemed to be keeping the subject at an abstracted distance so as not to risk too much self-implication. In another case ("Spanking: A Romance"), I inserted details or qualifications that had been cut from the original version because of space considerations, and completely rewrote the conclusion because it did not seem to me (as well as to some readers of the piece when it first appeared in *The New Yorker*) fully in keeping with the tone—or complex intentions—of the piece.

While I'm at it, let me be the first to point out that there is a somewhat schizophrenic, "high/low" quality to this volume, which reflects not only my wildly skeetering interests but also the variety of publications I've contributed to. Still, whether I'm writing about our cultural passions for dieting and suntanning or Martin Scorsese's uncharacteristic fascination with upscale Edwardians, about growing up Orthodox Jewish without a biblical text to claim as my own or my long-standing conceptual flirtation with lesbianism, I think my impulse is always to burrow inward in hope of ferreting out what's going on under the surface. If there is any overriding theme to this collection, I would say that it is one of exposure, pulling or coaxing out of the closet some of the many skeletons we habitually shove inside it. I might mention here that it has always seemed to me that women, more than men, are collectively burdened with putting a brighter face on things, the better to keep the world going; I've always been fascinated by the ways in which truths that get whispered between women in private—about everything from the dark side of pregnancy to the eerie unreality of divorce to "unliberated" sexual peccadilloes—are rarely articulated in print. (To this end, the more literate women's magazines seem to me to be doing their readers a service well beyond the obvious one of bringing them news of clothes and cosmetics.)

In these pages I think of myself as a trench-coated spy from a forties movie, the kind of movie in which Cary Grant declares to Ingrid Bergman that he's wanted her all along: "I was a fat-headed guy full of pain. It tore me up not having you." It is my belief that in our hearts we are, many of us, daring spies, ready to spill our guts to the right listener. Although it hardly needs saying that life is not like the movies, writing in a personal voice about one's own hopes, disappointments, and fantasies requires some of the same quality of absolute trustingness that enabled Grant's character in *Notorious* to step away from life-preserving caution and into cliff-jumping abandon. I don't consider myself a particularly trusting person off the page, but somewhere along the way I decided to take my chances at being vulnerable—or as vulnerable as I was able to bear—when I sat down to write. I suppose you could call it a mediated gamble, or risk-taking at one remove; either way, it's a perfect compromise for someone like myself, made up of equal parts of fear and boldness, shyness and exhibitionism. So here I am, spilling my guts in the manner I've grown accustomed to—in the form I've always held dear. And you know what? I bet there are more right listeners out there than are dreamed of in anyone's philosophy.

"A thinking woman sleeps with monsters."
—Adrienne Rich
"Snapshots of a Daughter-in-Law"

Spanking and Other
Sexual Detours

On Not Becoming a Lesbian

Although I have preferred the company of my own sex to that of men for as far back as I can remember, I've never had a lesbian experience. I've never been close to a gay woman, either, though for a while I carried on a bantering friendship with a self-described "dyke" I met during a brief hospitalization for depression. This woman was great fun to be around; she was also very overweight and sported the kind of G.I. Joe haircut I associated with women who put their tongues in each other's mouths when they kissed instead of politely brushing the cheek. Toward the end of my hospital stay the two of us regularly signed up for passes to go out to dinner; we usually went for sushi in the next town over, but one evening we planned to have dinner at an elegant inn about an hour's drive away. On the afternoon of that evening, flowers were delivered to the nurses' station for me: They were from my friend, and I suddenly realized that she might be reading more into our outings than I intended. That night at the inn, over candles and glistening tableware, I felt other people's glances upon us. I wasn't sure whether it was because my companion was not only obese but given to an excessive style in general, or whether everyone suspected us of being lovers. As the evening wore on, I felt palpably uncomfortable and our conversation turned ever more stiff. Over dessert I decided to confront the situation directly; I explained to my friend that I had greatly appreciated the flowers but was a bit taken aback by the sheer romanticism of her gesture. She understood what I meant, and the affair was over before it had begun.

I find it striking that I don't count any lesbians among my good friends; even more surprising that over the years, I've met only a handful of women who have openly acknowledged their gayness—as opposed to having this aspect of themselves bruited about as gossip or speculation. Even so, somewhere along the way, in spite of my limited exposure, I've sensed that gay women are drawn to me. I suppose it's because I lead with my brain—something most men still react to with undisguised alarm—and because I exude the sort of attentiveness toward other women that most women save for men.

Still, I have trouble to this day imagining what it would be like to have a woman's tongue in my mouth, much less in my more intimate parts. When I say I have trouble, I mean that I literally balk at the picture: My mind closes down, resists further exploration. Perhaps this makes me a card-carrying heterosexual; more likely, it signifies nothing more than that I am a culturally conditioned woman who has tailored her erotic fantasies to fit the expectations of her time and place.

I was twelve or thereabouts when I first came upon the word *lesbian* ascribed to some unfortunate female or other; it caught my eye, like a bright red ball tossed up into the air. I can't remember any longer whether it was used about a character in one of the novels I was ceaselessly burying myself in, or was said of someone I knew in real life. I also can't recall what, exactly, I thought being a lesbian was all about. I knew it had to do with favoring the company of women over men, but beyond that I don't think I envisioned much of anything. What I do remember, clear as can be, is the *ping* of recognition that accompanied my discovery

of the term: I immediately decided that this word—this dark and elusive *she* known as a "lesbian"—and I belonged together. I was, in fact, so
convinced and terrified of what I now deemed to be my linguistically
determined fate that I immediately tried to eject it from my physical
being. The thing to do, I decided, with a child's cruel instinct for exposure, was to hang my interior destiny out to air in the bracing atmosphere of the heterosexual world I inhabited: Like a Sapphic Hester
Prynne, I would wear my perverted identity emblazoned on my chest,
the better to be cured of it.

I began by announcing to my counselor at the Orthodox Jewish
summer camp I went to that I feared I wished to sleep next to my
mother more often than was ordinary. Just in case this innocent teenager
in Bermuda shorts didn't get the message, I went on to spill the sordid
beans: I feared, I said, that I was—and then I used the word aloud for
the first time—a *lesbian.* Of course, what was really askew in my home
life had less to do with any shameful libidinal yearnings toward my
mother than with my wish to be closer to her than she allowed me to be.
(As for my father, I had given up on him early on; he was as distant as
the sky, and as impervious.) But I was a writerly young girl, and I
wanted to keep my audience interested. To this end I leaped over the
more obvious, heartrending presentation of my childhood sorrows and
landed on a sophisticated, off-center version. Who would care if I was
desperately homesick at camp for a mother I was desperately homesick
for even when I was at home? Who would understand, even if I could
have put it this way? I found it more acceptable to describe my longing
for an unavailable mother as something tainted, even unnatural—as
something wrong with me. The perception that there might be something wrong with my *parents* would come much later; in the meantime
I blamed myself for my mother's inadequacies. I particularly blamed
myself for resenting the fact that she locked her bedroom door at night,
so that even as a small child I had been unable to go in to her for reas-
surance or hugs when I woke up from a bad dream or couldn't fall asleep.

(Not one to take such inaccessibility lightly, I developed full-blown insomnia by the age of eight, but that's another story.)

The counselor was a sweet and earnest type, with a more than ordinary commitment to the Judaic principles on which the camp was founded. She took my confession to heart and immediately called up my mother, who blithely reassured this concerned messenger that my sudden interest in lesbianism was based on nothing more than something I'd been reading. And thus order was quickly restored: I learned how to wrap my hair around a juice can in order to make it straight as a stick, and continued to worry that my breasts were too big and my legs too thin whenever I took part in the endless dance-and-song fests the camp specialized in. Underneath it all I continued to pine for my mother, for her now-you-see-it, now-you-don't presence without which I floundered. Underneath it all, I felt bewildered by my bunkmates' consuming interest in the pimply, graceless boys on the other side of the camp, most of whom were idiots as far as I was concerned. What were boys to me and what was I to boys, I wondered, that I should give them the automatic edge over my girlfriends?

I wasn't completely immune to the opposite sex, however. That same summer I developed a crush on the camp's maintenance man. It helped that, at an ancient nineteen or twenty, he was some years older than the boys my friends primped for, no longer a man-in-formation but a full-fledged man. His job, menial and smelly, also gave him a masculine glamour in my eyes, especially when compared with the goody-goody boys my own age who split their day between studying the Torah and Talmud in the morning and swimming and playing tennis or baseball in the afternoon. Then, too, David F. was my idea of sexy—which is to say that he had a thin, withholding mouth and thereby suggested the essence of my mother's personality in male form. He gave me my first French kiss, or at least he tried; I screamed midway through it and scared him off. I told some of the other girls about it, and eventually my counselor heard about it. I was relieved when she came to me, full of concern about my disregard for the laws of *negiyah,* which limit physical contact between males and females who aren't married to each other. I was more than relieved, actually. I was triumphant that one identity had ousted the other: I had gone from being a potential lesbian to being a potential hussy, the genuine heterosexual article. Whatever lingering doubts I had were pushed aside. So what if I hadn't really liked the feel of David F.'s tongue, slimy and intrusive, inside my mouth? Would I have liked it any better if it had been the tongue of a girl?

I suppose somewhere along the way, however anxiety-ridden the issue of sexuality may be—as opposed to the greater chromosomal clarity of gender, of being born indisputably male or female—one reaches an intuitive decision, honors some impulses more than others. In the end, it may come down to no more than the inclination, in spite of some inner waffling, to throw one's behavioral weight behind certain norms. In the years that have passed since my blurted confession of lesbianism to my camp counselor, I have married and become a mother. These are things I wanted to do, although marriage came much harder to me than motherhood. I still look upon all men with a degree of suspicion I do not generally feel toward women, and I still feel that even men with developed sensibilities tend to be more obtuse than most women. But there is the undeniable fact that men arouse me physically—*some* men, that is, men with subtle, slightly feminine turns of mind, although I have also been captivated by men who strut like the proverbial rooster and are not the least bit interested in what I am thinking or feeling. Women, although they generally tend to irritate me less than men, do not, to the best of my self-awareness, sexually excite me. I have sometimes thought that, given my psychological makeup, it would be easier all around if they did.

As I have gotten older and observed the subject of lesbianism—as distinct from the issue of gay pride, which for the longest time translated into *male* gay pride—gain greater visibility, I note with curiosity that there still appears to be something innately dreary about the reflected image of gay women—a couple of singers (Melissa Etheridge, k. d. lang, and who knows about Madonna), a trendy bar scene, and a handful of glamorous "lipstick lesbians" notwithstanding. To feel this way is undoubtedly to date myself, or to suggest some incriminating resistance on my part, for surely the lesbian image has been overhauled and polished to a flattering sheen since Lillian Hellman's *The Children's Hour* was the operative cultural reference, with Shirley MacLaine in her Mamie Eisenhower bangs yearning silently for the boyishly lovely Audrey Hepburn.

So let me put it another way by saying that, even in the long shadow of AIDS, men loving men has an authenticity—a quality of being onto something valid that the straight world has overlooked in its heterosexual zeal—that women loving women doesn't have, at least for me. When I think of two men together, I have a sense of what they're about: the ineluctable force of it, the sidestepping of the many restrictive rules by which our thinking about sexually ordained behavior—what is allowably masculine or feminine—is governed. When I think of two women together, I think of it as the default position; immediately there comes over me a feeling of the compensatory—of dildos and harnesses and other role-playing apparatus, mental as well as physical.

Somewhere in this assessment, of course, floats a sadder, more insidious piece of reality, having to do with images of women in society at large and how we in turn assess one another. Contaminated by a cultural outlook that casts my own kind as somehow deficient or lesser than, I can see only that if straight women are not as powerful as straight men, gay women seem to be huddled together in some shabby third-class lounge. (Gay men, on the other hand, often appear to have invented a republic of their own, like ancient Greece, where women and straight men have ceased to be of much importance.) Some of this perception is based on the sense I have that the lesbian condition has not yet found a sufficiently compelling literary voice (there are exceptions, of course, such as Dorothy Allison's *Bastard Out of Carolina,* but they are generally books in which the lesbian theme barely surfaces), whereas it often appears as though anybody who grew up gay, male, and gifted has gone on to write a memoir or a novel describing how it was to grow up gay, male, and gifted.

Not long ago, in compliance with a request from a man I was trying hard to please, I went in search of a dildo. This man had pronounced that every woman's "wardrobe," as he put it, should include one, although when I asked around among my friends not one professed to owning this crucial article. So I arranged to go with a friend, who had researched an essay on women pornographers and thus was a fount of knowledge on such things, to a women's sex shop called Eve's Garden. My friend described the store as "lesbianish" and joked uneasily that the two of us would be taken for gay by virtue of crossing its threshold. The store is located on Fifty-seventh Street in Manhattan, on the upper floor of an office building, where the rents are less exalted. When we got off the elevator and walked down a corridor to a door that could have been the door to anything—a dentist's office or a public-relations firm—I remember thinking how like a woman it was to hide her erotic goods away from passersby, how unlike a man, who was wont to display his sexual paraphernalia in the full light of day in a street-level boutique on Christopher Street.

Eve's Garden turned out to be a far cry from the bawdy, Rabelaisian emporium I had envisioned; it had a dingy, slightly sad atmosphere. There were sections of books and videos, with half of these sections reserved for specifically lesbian themes, including a section on lesbian S&M. There were some cautious bondage-related devices for sale—a velvet eye mask, handcuffs, nipple clips, and a leather-fringed paddle that looked as if it might be more useful for dusting than for inflicting pain. Most eye-catching, though, was the array of dildos and dildo-shaped vibrators in all colors and sizes, dildos so big they might make a man blush for his lesser endowment.

I stood there and gaped, not knowing where to begin, other than with the conviction slowly forming in my mind that the problem of penetration—the wish to be filled by something hard and penislike and not-female—would not go away, even for lesbians. Which realization brought in its wake another thought: Given that sex requires some antiphonal tension and given, too, that sexual desire is largely a construction of the imagination, the suspension of disbelief that is required is far less when one of two men is asked to "play" a female—all he has to do is lie down and submit—than when one of two women must parody a man's role. Standing in Eve's Garden, I picked up dildo after dildo—smooth cones made of purple plastic and striated ones made of flesh-toned latex, the more ambitious the level of emulation, the more expensive—and came back to the truth as it exists, inescapably, for me: *I wanted the real thing.*

The same friend who took me to Eve's Garden described a lesbian porn film she had watched in which one woman performed oral sex on another woman's strapped-on dildo, said dildo having first been conscientiously fitted with a condom. This scenario suggests to me a stupendous muddle of issues. Why, for instance, is safe sex—which I assume is being given its due with the condom—an issue between two women, let alone a woman and a rubber penis substitute? What bothers me more is that I can't figure out who is supposed to be getting pleasure here (unless it's the dildo). And even if one were to grant that both women were getting pleasure out of their respective roles as fellatrix and fellated-upon, haven't we thereby worked our way back again to the tired conventions of heterosexuality and its reflexive power plays—its Hegelian divisions of dominance and submission?

Just as the theater of a certain form of sadomasochistic encounter requires too many props for my erotic tastes, so does the enactment of a certain kind of lesbian drama. But if the sight of two women acting at heterosexuality doesn't speak to me, the gentler, kinder lesbianism—*sans* dildos and full of mutual caresses—speaks to me even less. Perhaps it comes down to no more than that I myself am not democratic enough in matters of the libido to be able to conceive of the possibility of an erotic charge occurring in a situation in which two people lie together and neither of them has a penis. I can imagine great *emotional* intimacy developing in such a situation, but my own notion of sexual arousal hinges on an intimated imbalance of power, on someone having something that I want and don't already possess. The idea of being penetrated by a man excites me, if only because penetration promises a resolution of sorts, even if it is merely a resolution of my distrust of men.

Which comes first in the evolution of lesbianism? The desire for women? Indifference to or fear of men? Or is it something else that seals a lesbian's sexual fate, something that has less to do with emotional tugs or amorous inclinations than with a vision of oneself snug in the primordial harbor of female love?

It seems to me that women, more than men, have always run the risk of having their sexual identity defined for them by others—*this* is how arousal happens, *this* is what an orgasm should feel like—if only because so much of what transpires with women goes on inside. In Victorian times women were supposed to close their eyes and think of England, to suffer the ignominy of sex on behalf of their husbands and their country. In our own time, which is as intent on demystifying the notion of the taboo as earlier ages were on enshrining it, the touted delights of female masturbation seem to run a close second to the more interactive pleasures of copulation. (Perhaps because it has been acknowledged as a grungy compulsion all along, male masturbation has not been "discovered" as an erotic high point in quite the same way.) The proscriptive, in other words, has ceded to the prescriptive—and women are still being told what an orgasm should feel like, and how best to achieve one! In the flurry of excitement about the brave new world of masturbation we may have lost sight of the fact that a once-taboo act does not in and of itself provide sexual gratification; sometimes it provides nothing more than a

taste of the formerly forbidden, more abstract than visceral in its sense
of pleasure. Achieving orgasm through masturbation, once viewed as the
sole province of men and then as the poor cousin of the orgasm provided
for women by men, may no longer be something to hide under the covers about, but it is not the same as being touched, licked, made love to
by another human being.

There is no easy solution, so far as I can see, to what I've called "the
penetration problem." A woman has a hole where a man has a dangling
something—this penis, this odd-looking, mercurial dildo-made-flesh,
susceptible to the waning and waxing of its possessor's desire—that can
become erect and fill the hole up, thereby relieving her of her separateness, if only temporarily. (This is also why two men together—but not
two women—seem to have all the sexual equipment they need between
them.) The theory of penis envy in its literal Freudian form—which has
always struck me as misbegotten, in any case, since most women regard
the penis less as an organ to be coveted than as one to be borrowed as
needed—may have been correctly scoffed into the shadows by feminist
psychoanalytic thinking, but one is still left with the dictates, and the
limitations, of human anatomy.

Finally there is this: I have always been fascinated by women. I collect
them the way some women collect men. As a breed, I rate them more
highly than I do men, and at dinner parties I tend to talk to the female
seated on my left rather than to the male on my right. (I've often
thought that one of the problems besetting the women's movement is
that too many of its leaders seem to want to empower women without
much liking them. At a book party I attended for Alice Walker some
years ago Gloria Steinem stood talking to my then-husband—he is,
admittedly, an attractive man—without so much as acknowledging my
presence next to him.) I have never learned how to flirt properly with
men, but with women I am a practiced seductress. I like to study my
women friends, to learn their habits and their secrets. They, in turn, have

offered me the sort of sustaining affection and nurturance without which life would be even more difficult than it already is. By contrast, I have rarely been other than passingly friendly with a man I am not sexually involved with.

But if it is true to say I love women, it is equally true to say that I don't know how or, more correctly, don't wish to translate this affection into sexual terms. There is, I suppose, the option of bisexuality, but I am convinced that this is an option that rarely works well in real life, if at all. In contrast to the concept of androgyny, which has always seemed liberating, demanding no more than that one accept the existence of the boyish in the girl or the girlish in the boy, real bisexuality presupposes a flexibility and a greater tolerance of anxiety than most people have. I, at any rate, am surely not the one to give it a try. I'm sufficiently rattled when I wake up in a room not my own that the idea of waking up and not knowing on a given day whether the body beside me is male or female strikes me as a recipe for psychic disaster.

So there you have it, or at least you have what I've been able to make of my passion for women, this love that dares speak its name. Sometimes I find myself wondering whether all the interesting women I know are fooling themselves into loving men for the sheer challenge and the social endorsement of it, while each and every one of them is biding her time until she can figure out a better arrangement. Other times I wonder, had I been born into a more casually structured family or gone to college twenty years later, would I have ventured to find out if a woman's tongue in my mouth tasted better than a man's, or if a woman's fingers on my breasts could make my nipples stand up the way a man's fingers can. Meanwhile I make do with the painful strictures of being a woman who is not sure how much she likes men but knows she needs them.

Is it, for some women—for me—a dare not taken, this bright red ball suspended in the air, forever uncaught? *Lesbian:* I still warm to the word, the slow-moving sound of it, that long first syllable—*lez*—ending on an enclosure, *bian.* What would it feel like to be a woman for whom it has never been a choice, never been anything but a conviction, sending her into the embrace of another woman, a woman with a body like hers, a synonym rather than an antonym? Have I chosen heterosexuality, with its impossible anxieties, or has it chosen me? Either way, it's the closet I'm stuck in.

1995

Now, Voyeur: The Erotic Life of Movies

In 1967, the year of its release, I saw *The Graduate,* in which Dustin Hoffman breaks down the chapel door on his way to scooping up Katharine Ross, and I carried with me forever after into my own life a slightly misleading vision of romantic pursuit, of love that knows no obstacle. I carried with me as well a different, more disturbing image —an image of tassels swinging from a pair of nipples. Those nipples belonged to a stripper who performs in the all-male club that Benjamin takes a faunlike Elaine Robinson to on their first date, hoping to destroy ahead of time any possible interest he might feel in her or she in him. With pimplike detachment, Benjamin looks on as the dancer thrusts her big breasts at the couple and begins her tantalizing swirl directly over Elaine's glossy head. But then comes a response he (and, by implication, the audience) isn't prepared for, a response so virginal it ungirds his defenses and decisively shifts the plot: Elaine's big brown eyes fill up. As the tears roll silently down her rounded cheeks, Benjamin becomes contrite and then, inevitably, enamored. Having attempted to sully her purity, he now wants to claim the clean sexual slate of Mrs. Robinson's daughter for himself. As for Mrs. Robinson, with her sheer black stockings, cigarettes, and soigné airs, she is doomed to be left behind. The camera—along with Benjamin—moves remorselessly away from her, and she retracts into cinematic smallness, a haggard blur of a depersonalized Older Woman standing at the end of a long shot. As if to emphasize Mrs. Robinson's passéness, the screen suddenly seems to drain of color and freeze-frame in devitalized black-and-white.

What I was left with as I sat in the movie theater was an enlarged sense of the erotic, a glimpse of new vistas out there in the Country of Sex: Passion could be tipped with contempt, desire shot through with fury; you could sexually need someone the way Mrs. Robinson needed Benjamin and at the same time consider such a person beneath serious consideration. But most interesting of all was the triangulation of the sexual motif, a young man who slept with first mother, then daughter, and got to cast off one for the other—here were incestuous doings presented as the shiniest, most new-penny of romances!

I was thirteen when I saw *The Graduate;* a year earlier there had been the much-acclaimed *Blow-Up,* which, in its more elegantly antinarrative way, had already acquainted me both with onscreen nudity—including, if I recall correctly, a thrilling glimpse of pubic hair—and a certain quality of sexual lassitude. (I learned early on how much more morals-bending was allowed under cover of High Seriousness—Marlon Brando buttering up Maria Schneider's ass in *Last Tango in Paris*—than in the open light of Low Eroticism.) One had only to watch David Hemmings's very light but very opaque blue eyes as they met the challenge of Vanessa Redgrave's bared breasts to realize that in the universe as directed by Michelangelo Antonioni, all was not boy meets girl, boy gets girl, or even boy *wants* to get girl. Voyeurism, it seems, had its own thrills: the close but safe remove Alfred Hitchcock would make persistently sinister use of, James Stewart monitoring the world from his rear window. I was not yet a sophisticated enough moviegoer to understand that Antonioni was trying to say something about my

voyeuristic complicity as a filmgoer, or about the voyeurism disquietingly implicit in the medium itself—providing, as Stanley Cavell has
described it, "for the magical reproduction of the world by enabling us
to view it unseen." But I did glean something from *Blow-Up*'s carefully
created atmospheres of sensual surfeit about the peculiar frisson in
being an observer, of things being most interesting when they were
least obtainable.

There had undoubtedly been snatched filmic moments before that
one, moments in which I fathomed that physical desire was not always
as marmoreally sublimated as it was in the films of Greta Garbo, or as
humorously curtained off as it was in *It Happened One Night.* Of course,
the movie in question didn't necessarily have to be good, much less
artistically hailed, for me to draw my lessons. The young are infinitely
impressionable, and film, in its dazzling approximation of reality, is an
infinitely impression-producing medium: It stains the imagination,
plays to the mind's eye, like no other art. On board a ship one summer
when I was ten, I saw a screening of *Come Blow Your Horn,* a minor
coming-of-erotic-age comedy authored by Neil Simon. It featured
Frank Sinatra, Barbara Rush, and a callow Tony Bill, and its ribald,
matey flavor of sexual conquest struck me as sufficiently foreign to
make a lasting impression on me. For a while, I sized up all men according to the Frank Sinatra model—as more or less suave, more or less
casual about "dames."

I have since come to understand that I was, in all innocence, what so
many of us were who grew up on what René Clair called "the primitive
wonder of this art": a "movie-made child." To fully appreciate what I
mean by this, you'd have to go back well before my time, to 1933, when
a best-selling, furor-causing book called *Our Movie-Made Children* was
published. This book set out to demonstrate, just as the censors were
getting ready to tighten their reins, the deleterious effect the as-yet-
newish cinema had on the morals of youth—and specifically on their
amorous expectations. It cites one boy who attempted to emulate John
Gilbert's lovemaking style only to come up against brute and inadequate

reality: "I place the blame not on my inability to imitate what I have seen on the screen, but on someone else's inability to imitate Greta Garbo's receptive qualities."

As for me, I "place the blame" on any number of scenes of cinematic passion, variously shocking and tender (and, puzzlingly, sometimes shocking and tender at the same time, as in anything performed by Brando), images flickering with the refracted light of the screen, witnessed in the dark but possessed of a sheen and shimmer. It can, I think, be argued that we look upon movies, and the behavior of their stars, as road maps to our own sexual destinations; even more so, they are enactments of trips we will never take, depictions of shadow-lands we dare not visit.

Film has always been, to a greater or lesser extent, about each generation's most graphic version of the Forbidden, and thus the history of American film drags behind it the ball and chain of suppression—what André Bazin referred to as "the long, rich, byzantine tradition of censorship." Worried about those very "receptive qualities" of Garbo and her kind, the newly created Legion of Decency threatened to order its 10 million Catholic members to boycott Hollywood's films. In 1934, the studios decided to protect their product, and forestall government regulation, by amplifying and rigorously enforcing the Hays Office Production Code, which had been adopted—but not taken seriously—four years earlier: "The treatment of bedrooms must be governed by good taste and delicacy." Much of ordinary human behavior (not to mention the less ordinary, like "miscegenation" and "white slavery") was deemed verboten, including drinking and swearing, excessive kissing, adultery, and "methods of committing crime."

The inherent debauchery of film, if not of life, would henceforth be brought to heel: The relative candor and daring of early-thirties movies, such as Mae West's *She Done Him Wrong,* Joseph von Sternberg's *Morocco,* and Ernst Lubitsch's *Design for Living* (based on Ben

Hecht's sanitized version of Noël Coward's play, the script still reeked of Coward's salacious ménage à trois), would give way—up until the new liberalism of the sixties—to contingency measures. The arts of veiled allusion and innuendo were highly developed; movies were carefully screened beforehand for potentially offensive scenes and then reshot or recut to include reassuring, often narratively preposterous insertions. (Garbo's last movie, *Two-Faced Woman,* suffered from just such editorial intrusions.)

In the sense that film is both a receptacle of our most salacious fantasies and a mirror of our most stringent inhibitions, it illuminates our strange, persistently divided attitude to things sexual. The openly adulterous William Randolph Hearst, stung into action when Mae West joked about the acting ability of his mistress, Marion Davies, ran an editorial impugning West as a "monster of lubricity" and "a menace to the sacred institution of the American family." In 1893, on earliest and most primitive Kinetoscope, Fatima, the belly-dancing sensation of the Chicago World's Fair, was shown doing her coochee-coochee dance—and just as quickly censored. Needless to say, both versions featured Fatima at her gyrations under cover of heavy clothing, but the censored one disguises her movements further with a white grid.

"Sex without sin is like an egg without salt," proclaimed Luis Buñuel, with all the categorical certitude of a lapsed Catholic. Repression, in other words, is part and parcel of the excitement; without it, there is no tension, no shiver of recognition at the Other—those exciting, libidinous, threatening possibilities dormant within each of us that beckon, resplendently animated, from the screen.

Theda Bara, née Theodosia Goodman, was an early cinematic icon of Otherness: Unblond, eyes smothered in shadow, absolutely not the girl to bring home to your mother, she was the Bad Girl, the Vamp (as in Vampire). In truth she was a Jewish American girl got up to be of French-Egyptian descent so as to appear more suitably exotic. (American men had just been fighting World War I and were newly exposed to

European women.) From 1914 to 1919, Bara made more than forty films; the femme fatale territory was virgin enough that just by intimating she would sleep with a man, she could thrill. As the embodiment of the unencumbered sexual urge, she was viewed as a fascinating, if dire, model: "To understand those days," she recounted years later, "you must consider that people believed what they saw on the screen. . . . Audiences thought the stars were the way they saw them. Why, women kicked my photograph as they went into the theaters where my pictures were playing, and once on the streets of New York a woman called the police because her child spoke to me."

In the wake of Bara came other Vamps—Clara Bow, Carole Lombard, and Jean Harlow (a dentist's daughter whose homespun origins were effectively obscured under her hard-edged, studio-fabricated, satin-lined appeal), tough-talking gals who made no bones about their attraction, and attractiveness, to the opposite sex. *Red Dust*—made in 1932, before the calcification of the Code—featured a Harlow so convincing as the predatory woman that *Time* saw fit to rap the film's knuckles for its "brazen moral values." One way, then, of ducking the long shadow of our Puritan heritage has been to cast the seducer as a woman, as a smoldering, socially questionable (with the exception, perhaps, of Lombard) Vamp. The other alternative, right from the start, was to cast the woman as the unseduceable Good Maiden, as a golden-haired, sweet-featured, pregenital incarnation: Enter Mary Pickford, of whom poet Vachel Lindsay, a self-described "infatuated partisan," trilled in his 1916 book, *The Art of the Moving Picture,* "Why do the people love Mary? Because of a certain aspect of her face in her highest mood. Botticelli painted her portrait many centuries ago when by some necromancy she appeared to him in this phase of himself. . . ."

Eventually, the Bad (Sexual) Girl and the Good (Presexual) Girl would merge in the figure of the Wife as Vamp, played with winning wiliness by Myrna Loy in the *Thin Man* series of films. In the process of assimilating herself, however, the Vamp got cleaned up—her vampiness becoming more a matter of impeccable, unhousewifely style than of erotic calling. Clearly, Loy's Nora and William Powell's Nick Charles were not envisioned as anyone's idea of a real, flesh-and-blood couple. So elegantly strung as to seem exotic, they are verbally impassioned habitués of sophisticated drawing rooms rather than excitable bed partners. In Loy's wake came any number of Teasing Women—Joan Crawford, Rosalind Russell, and Paulette Goddard, among others—all very much living in the silvery continuum of Cukor et al., rather than in the world of the everyday, all slightly alien in their glossy disregard for the sanctity of sex.

And so the problem looms: What to do with eros? How to make it fit? The basic impropriety of sexual desire is a consuming American cinematic motif. The effect of this constitutional unease ranges from the discomfiting to the fatal. Interestingly, the films of the past five years seem to have embraced the more drastic approach; witness the virtual florescence of the lethal, sexually voracious female at the box office, in movies such as *Fatal Attraction, Black Widow, sex, lies, and videotape,* and *The Last Seduction,* where the Vamp doesn't quite kill the man but certainly subverts him. To the American eye, the gulf between sex and love is mostly impassable; as a result, the specter of sex may be embarrassing, or stirring, or tragic, but it is hardly ever salubrious, as it is, say, in the films of Lubitsch. In this regard it does indeed make psychic sense, when you think about it, that America invented the Western: The Western is the perfect refuge, a game for and about men, the purest genre to blow off the whole heterosexual impetus.

European cinema, by contrast, has always manifested a less prudish and more jaded attitude toward the complications of sex, exemplified by the on- and offscreen persona of Roman Polanski. This is not to suggest that European films are free of sexual fixations—the portrait of the compellingly evil Vamp, after all, reached an apogee of sorts in G. W. Pabst's *Pandora's Box,* a 1929 German film starring Louise Brooks—but that they give these images their due as part of a larger, many-angled repertoire. Where American filmmakers incline to a kind of frenzied, goggle-eyed approach to the carnal (Did you *do* it? Did you get caught?), Europeans tend to present *la dolce vita* as a coital merry-go-round, a bawdy refrain inexorably tinged (but then so is the sophisticate's view of everything in life) with melancholy and boredom. This goes a way, as well, to explaining the habitual ease with which the Europeans have slid morally ambiguous works past the censors—from Lubitsch's fractious *Merry Widow* to the bleak visions of Polanski and Ingmar Bergman—while American directors were more apt to be waylaid at the pass.

From our vantage point it is difficult to believe that as late as 1953, a thin comedy called *The Moon Is Blue* had to forfeit a Production Code Seal of Approval for using the then-taboo words *pregnant, mistress,* and *virgin.* Or that in 1959, Elizabeth Taylor set off sparks by refusing to knuckle under to Hedda Hopper's chaperoning of her offscreen sex life. When Hopper took her to task for her dalliance with Eddie Fisher— then still married to the much-loved Debbie Reynolds—Taylor is reported to have said, "What do you expect me to do? Sleep alone?"

Now that we are living in what is, to all intents and purposes, a post-censored time, the Forbidden is harder to come by. With an elasticized ratings system having replaced the Code, the days of "dream palaces," of larger-than-life stars and finger-wagging gossip columnists, may seem quaintly provincial and long-ago. I would venture to guess, however, that we still go to movies to have our sexual itches scratched, for a heady dose of unspeakable things and unviewable acts. Movies are in some sense like one long extramarital affair; they are what we imagine the unexpurgated version of our lives would look like if, one clandestine afternoon, someone were around to film it and someone else—better-looking, thinner, more physically graceful—were around to play it. We go to movies, in other words, to get lost in a dream of reality. Sexy movies offer a reprieve from the failure of our flesh, poor flesh; their continuing erotic tension offsets the inevitable slackening, with age and circumstance, of our own libidinous dramas.

It has always been difficult to predict which fantasies the public will take to—and even less easy to determine how much they know, or are willing to acknowledge, about their own desires. Then, too, one person's idea of the titillating may be another's idea of the overly clinical, which is why *Carnal Knowledge,* the first mainstream American movie to feature the onscreen unsheathing of a condom, seems to speak more to male than female viewers. What's clear, though, is that the successful sexy movies—be it *From Here to Eternity, Butterfield 8, Picnic,* or *Hud, Last Tango, Body Heat, Blue Velvet,* or *The Fabulous Baker Boys*—are those that meld with the audience's submerged fantasies at any given moment; they address themselves, with an almost prefiguring intuition, to the unstated conflicts, the shady cultural side streets of each decade. (*The Thomas Crown Affair,* for instance, coming at the tail end of all those sixties odes to the disrobed communal life, had the taste of a strange new drink. With Steve McQueen as the icy lone raider, Faye Dunaway as the remote object of his affection, and its conceit of sexual foreplay as a chess game, the movie foretold both the glamour and the hollowness of the world of the relentlessly acquisitive eighties.) Leaving room for differences of taste, a list of sexiest movies would probably have surprisingly more of the same choices on it, generation to generation, than otherwise. (We certainly can all point to the purportedly erotic movies that didn't work, and to the sleepers that worked up a lot of steam.)

It's a matter, then, of upping the ante, matching the film moment to the historical one and adding the right amount of seasoning. In this sense, repressed periods are probably better for movies: The all-important taste of salt comes through. One thinks of all those fifties movies, with their undercurrent of barely contained, brooding sexuality—of Brando, Dean, Clift, and Newman lurching toward us in their respective T-shirts and tortured manhood, always tumescent, never released. Little wonder, either, that movies so rarely portray sexual contentment: Scarlett O'Hara stretching her arms the morning after her night with Rhett is one of the few such moments that come to mind. Gable, by the way, had trouble getting his famous line of disinterest past the censors. And "Frankly, my dear, I don't give a damn" does indeed have a strange power of arousal, having little to do, I think, with its use of profanity (although it was a first) and everything to do with its sheathed rejection—its inured, masculine finality. It is the kind of line women in the audience want to seduce, to wrestle to the ground. Then, too, it would have been a different line spoken by a different actor; coming from a Bogart or a Cooper, for whom women were a diversion but not the main event, it would have undoubtedly seemed less heartbreaking.

In unraveling the crooked seam of sexual desire in American films, one must come back, finally, to that sly old master, Alfred Hitchcock. Understanding the darker dynamics of erotic tension, Hitchcock perpetually toys with sexual sadism under cover of suspense—as do his successors Brian De Palma and, more schizophrenically, David Lynch. The murder of Marion in *Psycho* takes place in a flurry of stabbings—seven or eight at least, it's hard to tell: Any way you count it, what's going on is an expression of sex as violence. If, as Pauline Kael has argued, *Bonnie and Clyde* "put the sting back in death," one could as persuasively argue that for Hitchcock the sting of sex *is* death, or at least physical danger. The closer the sexual opportunity, the more his men and women have to fear from Hitchcock. He once compared the erotic allure of his chilly blondes to "blood on snow," and there are several infamous little stories about his terrorizing attitude toward his female stars. Janet Leigh recounts that "Hitch relished scaring me," and he reportedly sent a gift of a replica of Tippi Hedren in a coffin to her daughter, Melanie Griffith (after which, understandably, Hedren never worked for him again). Given his somewhat repellent physical aspect, Hitchcock's use of all those flawlessly blue-veined beauties begins to seem like a personal vengeance on life outside the director's chair. But his directorial vision, however perverse, cannot simply be written off, as one British writer would have it, to some "slimy internal sickness." Watching Hitchcock's adroit rendering of stymied lust, we are, however temporarily, relieved of the burden of desire. His answer to the problem of eros—which is to hurt it, to *inflict* harm on the pleasured flesh—is no less than a paradigmatic response, an accurate reflection of the glint of depravity in the collective filmgoing eye.

1991

Extramarital Cravings

The possibility that we are all fated to inhabit sexual islands of our own idiosyncratic making was brought home to me at a small dinner party I attended several months ago, when the hostess mentioned that two once-prominent couples—no longer together, owing to death in one case and divorce in the other—had enjoyed sex lives that were notably "kinky." *Kinky* was the word this woman used; she smiled when she said it, as though we all shared in the recognition of what she meant. Of course, I understood the term, in some purely literal sense, as I assume did the other guests. We were grown-ups, after all, citizens of a fast-paced universe, inoculated against provincial habits of mind. I smiled back, warmed by good food and talk—but then my imagination wandered off, in directions peculiar to my history, and I felt the draft of separateness enter the room. What, I wondered, were the other guests conjuring up to go with the word *kinky*? Was it anything like the stuff I had thought of? It would be easier to talk about this subject if there were a Universal Erotic Principle—a basic theme around which permutations subtly wove themselves, as in a Baroque fugue. But one thing that stands out in the haze of confusion that surrounds the subject of sex is that there is no real consensus about what constitutes erotic pleasure. As the *Village Voice* columnist Richard Goldstein once mused, "If there's no great porn film—not even *Last Tango in Paris,* for all its value as dramatic tour de force—that's because there's no unity in people's fantasies; some of us will always think a stick of butter is for bread."

Clearly, erotic imaginations have always been as diverse as thumbprints. But sometime in the past three decades we seem to have lost our balance about things sexual. What is normal? What is off? Jeffrey Dahmer is surely everyone's idea of a sickie, and we are relieved to be able to identify him as such. What, however, is one to make of Prince Charles, longing to be Camilla Parker-Bowles's tampon? Once you put the extremes aside, where do you draw the line? How, for that matter, do you locate the center? We know only that heterosexuality has ceded its automatic right-of-way; that the dark continent of sado-masochism has been domesticated into a household state of mind; and that the gender-true convention of the man on top and all it implies no longer holds sway even in Dubuque.

Indeed, many of us prefer, perversely, the anticipation of sex to the thing itself. Or we have the opposite wish—which is to prolong the *aftermath* of lovemaking, avidly seeking out its physical aspect in lingering smells and rumpled sheets. There's a whole literature of erotic longing, with overtones of bliss and undertones of pain-in-pleasure, that has sprung up to accommodate this predilection. It's a genre written by women for women—and for men intrigued by the inner life of women. (There's also a small cadre of male authors mining this territory: James Salter, Robert Coover, and, more recently, Nicholson Baker.) French writers—perhaps because they're schooled to appreciate the theoretical, perhaps because they're not burdened by a Puritan legacy—are particularly adept at evoking these blasted-out landscapes, less romance than romantic desperation. If Marguerite Duras's *The Lover* is the purest and most literally gifted example, Pauline Réage's *Story of O* runs a close second, although the latter's reputation as a soft-core masterpiece has tended to obscure its psychological underpinnings.

Beneath their erotic feinting, these books—and the work of other (non-French) writers, such as Edna O'Brien and Jean Rhys—are about the embattled border where I leave off and you begin: the primal lure of symbiosis versus the rigorous claims of autonomy, set to a sexual beat. How much merging with the Other can one sustain without giving up the Self? The literature of longing exists on a continuum that seems to mirror the broad-ranging dynamics of this predicament: At one end is the lost-in-the-funhouse escapade, from which the two lovers emerge bruised but essentially intact; at the other the consigned-to-the-nuthouse drama, in which one of the players (usually the woman) is destroyed. Although Madame Bovarys have always existed in one form or another, the past decade or so has witnessed a heightened interest in this self-immolating romantic type, both in literature and on film; *9½ Weeks, Damage, Fatal Attraction,* and *Camille Claudel* come to mind. The prevalence of the genre suggests, among other things, that as traditional means of defining ourselves—through gender, class, and geographical origins—become more fluid, our chances of resolving our anxieties about who we are decrease.

Annie Ernaux describes the condition of obsessive erotic longing with a lighter touch than most authors: She calls it "craving through absence." Ernaux, who is French, and has previously written short, grave, and deeply affecting memoirs about her mother (*A Woman's Story*) and her father (*A Man's Place*), has now written a memoir of a sexual paradise lost. Ernaux demonstrates with an almost abjectly self-revealing candor (in contrast to the self-protective "confessional" writing of someone like Duras) that the elusiveness of the love object—the circumstantial and emotional hurdles that separate us from it—is its most powerful draw:

> As he always called me from telephone boxes, whose functioning
> could prove erratic, quite often when I picked up the receiver

there was no one on the line. After some time I realized that this "fake" phone call would be followed by the real one, fifteen minutes later at the most, the time it took to find a phone booth in working order. The first silent call was a prelude to his voice, a (rare) promise of happiness, and the interval separating it from the second call—when he would say my name and "can we meet?"—one of the most glorious moments ever.

Ernaux's book is called, with a graceful bow in the direction of irony, *Simple Passion*. It is tiny, only sixty-four wide-margined pages long, and contains the first-person account of one woman's love affair with a married man—she a divorced schoolteacher and writer, he an Eastern European stationed in Paris. The story is told in immediate flashback, several months after the affair has ended, in a habitual past tense: "I would be overcome," "He would dress slowly," "It would only last . . ." It's as if Ernaux had managed to wring a humane responsiveness out of the neutral conjugations of grammar.

The protagonist has "gotten over" the situation sufficiently to be able to recollect it in artistic tranquillity, but not enough so that we don't feel the sizzle, and the hurt. The affair, which lasted less than two years, has presumably ended because the man—"A"—has gone back to his native country. (Left unspoken is the fact that he doesn't feel strongly enough to pursue her from across the globe.) On a deeper level, the affair has ended because the protagonist has willed her "age of passion" to come to a close, out of psychological exhaustion, but also out of a need to rage—on paper rather than in her life—against the inevitable dying of sexual fixation. "So the world is beginning to mean something again outside A? The cat trainer from the Moscow Circus, the toweling bathrobe, Barbizon, the entire text assembled in my head day after day since the first night with words, images and gestures, all the signs forming the unwritten novel of a passion are beginning to fall apart."

There is perhaps in all such literature a Swinburnian wish—

implied rather than expressed—for the easeful cessation of consciousness that is the peace beyond longing, in which the disturbing vivid-
ness of carnal attraction is extinguished in the vast impersonality of
time. And curled silently behind this is yet another recognition: that
we are, writers and readers alike, temporary dwellers in the country of
speech, of squawkings on the page, on our way to permanent residence
in the universe of speechlessness—the "infinite emptiness," as Ernaux
calls it, after passion. ("Even now, rereading those first pages," she
writes, "has the same distressing nature as seeing and touching the toweling bathrobe he used to slip on at my place . . . these pages will
always mean something to me, to others too maybe, whereas the
bathrobe—which matters only to me—will lose all significance one
day and will be added to a bundle of rags. By writing this, I may also
be wanting to save the bathrobe from oblivion.")

What this slim, elliptical narrative captures better than anything
else I've read regarding the nature of erotic reverie is its encased,
nothing-further-to-be-said quality. "I would have liked," Ernaux writes,
"to have done nothing else but wait for him." (So, too, Duras in *The
Lover*: "I've . . . never loved, never done anything but wait outside the
closed door.") The book's power lies in the microscopic intensity of its
focus, a remembrance of desire past in which everything remotely associated with the loved one—all of life outside the obsession, that is—
becomes a way back into the obsession, Proust's madeleine rendered into
a whole lineup of madeleines, each more thoroughly steeped in erotic
nostalgia than the next:

> As soon as he left, I would be overcome by a wave of fatigue. I
> wouldn't tidy up straight away: I would sit staring at the glasses,
> the plates and their leftovers, the overflowing ashtray, the
> clothes, the lingerie strewn all over the bedroom and the hall-
> way, the sheets spilling over on to the carpet. I would have liked
> to keep that mess the way it was—a mess in which every object
> evoked a caress or a particular moment, forming a still-life whose

intensity and pain could never, for me, be captured by any painting in a museum. Naturally, I would never wash until the next
day, to keep his sperm inside me.

Simple Passion is transparently autobiographical. But it refuses, or gives
the impression of refusing, to take advantage of the fictional scrim that
most autobiography, from Rousseau's *Confessions* onward, has helped
itself to: the self-portraitist's crucial touch-ups, bespeaking artistic
intention or, more likely, personal vanity. This memoir falls into the
reader's lap like a steaming lump of truth, smelling of sexual hunger,
indifferent to the shamelessness or the pathos of its cause. "Having to
answer questions such as 'Is it an autobiography?'" Ernaux muses paren-
thetically, "and having to justify this or that may have stopped many
books from seeing the light of day, except in the form of a novel, which
succeeds in saving appearances."

Emaux's novel can be read in under an hour, which may help explain
why it achieved best-seller status in France—just as the brevity of
Robert James Waller's *The Bridges of Madison County* has been adduced
to explain its spectacular performance in this country. Although very
different, the two books are not unrelated literary animals. Another factor that may help explain the impact of Ernaux's book is that—though
it aches on the page like an exposed nerve—it is clearly the rumination
of someone who has imbibed the work of Barthes, Blanchot, and the
rest of the semiotic whiz kids. Her account abounds with references to
absence and presence ("I experienced pleasure like a future pain"); to the
limited province of authorship versus the unbounded terrain of the text
("Once I start typing out the text . . . I shall be through with innocence"); and to the ontological anxiety, so beloved of deconstructionists,
that besets disparate but related activities, such as sex and writing
("Living in passion or writing: in each case one's perception of time is

fundamentally different"). The lack of emotional sprawl here is entirely un-American, very much the product of a Gallic sensibility—wreathed in wine and cigarette smoke, more literate and world-weary than our Yankee one.

More shockable, too, evidently, for otherwise it is hard to figure out why this highly cerebral book caused a national controversy in France— the country of preeminent sophistication concerning affairs of the heart. Or so we've been led to believe: France, after all, is where Roman Polanski fled after romping with a girl barely old enough to baby-sit, and France is where the marriage of convenience and the ménage à trois were virtually invented. It is we Americans who are reputedly naive when it comes to the realm of the senses—we who expect our Presidents to be faithful husbands as well as faithful citizens, with any evidence to the contrary likely to ignite a major contretemps. National tastes in reading are apparently as opaque as individual sexual preferences—once again the old conundrum of what your brain sees when it is shown a stick of butter. This is not to suggest that *Simple Passion* isn't memorable—it is, in fact, a work of lyrical precision and diamond-hard clarity—only that it would be inconceivable for such a contained, literally self-conscious work to achieve a wide readership in America.

The French, on the evidence of their embrace of this book, have an admirably high tolerance for postmodern complexities, which make it difficult to tell a story—even as elemental a story as this—without an acute awareness on the storyteller's part of the creaky contraption of story-telling. That *Simple Passion* is a book—a "text"—about an affair is part and parcel of its self-perception; we are not for a moment to be fooled into thinking that this modest, hedged-in artifact is the *Ding an sich,* the affair in itself. A contemporary sensibility such as Ernaux's is defined in part by a refusal to treat her readers as unsophisticated latecomers to the literary dance: The illusion of verisimilitude that was once art's finest offering has been disavowed, and in its place is a general tentativeness about the larger reality that art is supposed to be imitating. Whether you like this kind of writing or not, it certainly isn't trying to give you the rush of immersion, the "you are there" feeling that much of American fiction still aims for. In other words, it certainly isn't *The Bridges of Madison County,* written to entertain the late-twentieth-century descendants of those cave dwellers who were lulled by the first storyteller into forgetting the howling wolves in the darkness outside.

And yet, curiously, the shock value of the woman's predicament in Ernaux's book—its readerly seduction, if you will—is not, at its core, very different from the appeal of *The Bridges of Madison County. Bridges,* of course, was the publishing surprise of last year, catching even marketing-savvy Warner Books off guard. Waller writes like a mediocre balladeer—although when he tried to make like Willie Nelson, and issued a recording of songs, he struck out. Now he has written a second novel, *Slow Waltz in Cedar Bend,* with a print run of a million and a half copies. It is very nearly a clone of the first, and given the sales record of *Bridges*—more than half a year as No. 1 on the *New York Times* best-seller list—who can blame him? It is a chestnut of the book business that romance sells, that mass-market paperbacks of a specific sort—featuring a woman in décolletage, an Alec Baldwinish male, and prose that manages to convey tumescence while at the same time primly veiling any intrusion of the phallic—do well. But "literary" fiction has never sold on the basis of love triumphant. When *Bridges* performed spectacularly, the surprise was not that a romantic story sold at this stratospheric level but that a small-size, *hardcover* love story—packaged by its publishers to look serious in its intentions, the jacket done up in smudgy, greige colors—found so many readers. (*Bridges* has dropped to No. 2 on the list, edged out by—what else?—*Slow Waltz in Cedar Bend.*)

What both of Waller's books have in common with Ernaux's book is that they reassert—in the face of AIDS, and the concept of marital fidelity, and even of premarital chastity—the perception that the heartland of eroticism lies outside the confines of marriage. In their puffed-up, clumsy, yet somehow canny way, Waller's novels sniff out the great valley of discontent between the sexes; his randy, unattached protagonists smugly observe the slow drip of calcification that occurs in even the best of domestic arrangements. Their author has figured out that at the heart of every long-suffering wife is an underappreciated wench, whose submerged glory is just waiting to be rediscovered. Here is Robert Kincaid, the peripatetic photographer in *Bridges,* on first spotting Francesca, the Iowa farm wife whose husband pays more attention to his prize steer than to her: "She came off the porch toward him. He stepped from the truck and looked at her, looked closer, and then closer still. She was lovely, or had been at one time, or could be again."

Waller's depiction of self-regarding loners with amatory talents (narcissists, if only they and he knew it) who pine for women already claimed by stalwart but unworthy spouses depends for its effect on the reader's tacit agreement—and there seem to be a lot of willing readers out there—that marriage is not good for your sex life. Possession, it seems, is nine-tenths of boredom, and the daily grind will do the rest. (Perhaps, too, this explains the sustaining pull—in and out of literature —of the Inaccessible Love Object.) Just as the imperatives of domesticity are not conducive to passion, so the imperatives of passion are not conducive to domesticity. Affairs, by their very nature, preclude taking out the garbage. Most of us know this instinctively, and yet many of us spend our adult lives making an end run around this incontestable fact, trying to have it both ways. We marry for—among other things—the simple certitude of it, the sustenance of a warm body to curl up against on a leisurely Saturday morning. We have affairs because we crave the unexpected, the quick illusion of physical congruence on a rainy Thursday afternoon. No one has ever titled a movie *A Marriage to Remember,* and for good reason: It would bomb at the box office. Marriages endure, but they're not, generally speaking, memorable except to the parties involved.

At the opening of *Slow Waltz in Cedar Bend,* the leather-jacketed, motorcycle-gunning professor who is the novel's hero spots his married prey, the gray-eyed Jellie Braden, and spends "a restless night" agitating about "primal things versus rectitude." The conflict could apply just as well to the woman writing her way out of sexual obsession in *Simple Passion*. Ernaux's narrator would willingly drop everything and light out for amorous territory, if only her man would stay in her field of vision long enough: "I knew that nothing in my life (having children, passing exams, traveling to faraway countries) had ever meant as much to me as lying in bed with that man in the middle of the afternoon."

It's odd that Ernaux, who so scrupulously records the impact of an extramarital relationship, says almost nothing about the institution of marriage itself. One can take this as an indictment—or, more simply, as a reflection of the postmodern view of connubial love. To live with a man or a woman on an ongoing, intimate basis is to grow jaded, weary of the imaginative possibilities. (In this sense, extramarital affairs offer an artificial brightening of the mundane: The habit of pressing crumbs from a plate with an index finger, which so annoys one about one's spouse, becomes an eccentric, lovable habit in one's paramour.) At some point, our husbands and wives fail to live up to a long-ago sensed potential; they become to us who they have become to themselves, and it is hard to envision them as promising more than they currently yield. An affair brings with it a reclaiming of one's own dimmed hope for oneself. Men look for the erect stalk of their youth, women for something more amorphous, something close to that moment when their erotic capacities were first ignited.

The very form of Ernaux's book—the narrative as a revisiting of a passion eclipsed—suggests that all eros is redux: a magical reading backward against the inscribed flow of history, a temporary reversal of that infinite regress, of that long unfolding wherein the flesh softens, the teeth decay, and passion wanes. If paradise is but a memory of paradise, then perhaps we are wiser to stay in our own beds and leave it to other people—writers, that is—to have their messy or bittersweet affairs and come back and report on them to us. On the last page of her memoir, Ernaux presents us directly with the purpose of *Simple Passion:* "an offering of a sort, bequeathed to others." We should be grateful for the small, comforting indiscretions of her prose—even for Robert James Waller's ungainly, strutting croonings. They relieve us for a while of our unmet curiosity, articulate for us—in neatly packaged narrative—erotic byways we have thought about while feeding the cat or reading a bedtime story to a child. Then we can close the book, turn off the light, and dream.

1993

A Taste of the Stick: Joel and Hedda, 1988

Once upon a time, they must have seemed like just another couple: he a New York lawyer, fierce-eyed, attractive in a slightly sinister way, and she a children's-book editor, pretty, contained, a bit remote. One can imagine seeing them at a cocktail party, turning around with glass in hand to be introduced: "Have you met Joel and Hedda yet?"

To write about the Lisa Steinberg case other than to denounce its horror or to indict a callous network of neighbors, colleagues, and teachers is to implicate oneself. Still, I would argue that the case occupies the press and the public imagination not only, or even primarily, because it is an instance of child abuse, however egregious. What separates this case from others is only tangentially its extrastatistical nature—that the couple was white, Jewish, and upper middle class. What marks it as special, whether we are prepared to admit it or not, is what we perceive to be the chilling example of psychopathology, of dehumanization, that the couple confronts us with: the potential for bondage that is inherent in any human bonding. Beneath the overtly acknowledged agenda of crime and punishment, of individual responsibility and collective guilt, lurks a scenario not as readily admissible into our conscious awareness. It has less to do with the tragic death of a sweet-looking six-year-old named Lisa than with the doings of the two adults who raised her.

The unacknowledged fascination of Lisa Steinberg's story lies in the lure of its murky psychosexual drama. Ever since the case broke open a year ago, we as spectators seem to have adopted an uneasy stance—part unqualified condemnation, part secret absorption—toward the tormenting and tormented pair, who brought not one but two children into their midst. All dreams, including bad ones, have actual plots as well as symbolic content. If the filthy apartment on a beautiful street, the successful professional couple and their family masking a fetid shadow existence, seem like the stuff of a living nightmare, it would appear useful to talk about Joel Steinberg and Hedda Nussbaum not just as themselves but as metaphors, as fatal archetypes.

To the extent that the issues of dominance and submission are, however disguised, issues we all live with, the Steinberg case is of interest to men and women alike. To the extent that issues of power most conspicuously show up in the arena of sexual politics, this is a case that I think particularly invokes the fears—and fantasies—of women. We all know women who we consider to have questionable taste in men—women who regularly pick or are drawn to men who are puzzlingly "not good" for them. Reductionist as it may sound, on the simplest of levels Hedda Nussbaum did no more than exercise remarkably bad taste in her choice of a partner; the consequences of this choice may have been destructive for her, but it is only with the added factor of her adopted child's death that the situation takes on a truly tragic dimension.

The two were live-in lovers for seventeen years, longer than many marriages. Although it may help to detach ourselves from the dark subtext of their mangled erotic life ("Once you taste the stick," Hedda is reported to have said, "you don't want to give it up") by envisioning the

dynamics of the couple as similar to those of a mini—concentration camp
—brutalizer and brutalized—the image is more dramatic than accurate.
Dazed and zombielike as Hedda appeared on the day of their arrest, hers
and Joel's was, after all, a *voluntary* bonding; somewhere in the depths of
the degradation she suffered there were also needs being met. The alarms
must have gone off, unheeded, at the very beginning of their relationship,
long before it had accelerated into the drastic duet it became.

In a way, our amorous choices are our only real exits from the selves
we present to the world, from what others take to be our "true" selves;
they provide the strongest clue to the mystery of who we are *inside* ourselves, away from the glare of other people. The whole truth about Joel
and Hedda, even after the case resolves itself, will go with them to
their graves. Pieces of that truth are embedded somewhere in their
joint limbic systems, in the chemistry as well as the malfeasance of
love. For some women, the man of their dreams comes dressed in
black; for some men, the woman comes dressed in bruises.

Our interpretations of what we call love vary so much as to be mutually exclusive a good deal of the time. Undoubtedly, Joel and Hedda's
idea of love had much to do with their cravings and frustrations. Almost
certainly the hostile symbiotic connection that their involvement hinged
on provided an emotional trade-off: Whether he was making love to her
or beating her, Hedda remained at the center of Joel's attention.

I suppose, too, if a relationship is kept at a high enough pitch, at a
constant and extreme level of tension, chances are it will never get bor-
ing. Joel and Hedda may well have considered their punchy romance a
higher form of communication than other, less toxic couplings. The fact
that they attempted to create a family indicates just how viable they
believed their offbeat domestic circumstances to be. In spite of the
rumors of cultlike influences and perverse child-rearing practices, I can't
quite imagine that the two of them (illegally) adopted a girl and then a
boy as part of a larger scheme of physical and sexual abuse: The original
intention must have been a normal, even a constructive one—a wish to
cement their union and act on a parenting impulse.

Perhaps it is best—it is certainly easiest—to regard this couple as popular sentiment would have it: a fiendish man, a victimized woman, a degeneration abetted by massive drug use, and the tragedy of a dead child. The trouble with this view of the case is that it sidesteps the possibility that Hedda, at least to begin with, *liked* being abused—that she was, moreover, sexually aroused by the violence inflicted on her. It is a dynamic we cannot much bear to look at.

The mutual psychic kinks that led to the matching of a Hedda and Joel are not what the trial is about. After almost a year of intensive psychiatric care, Hedda Nussbaum may well be freed of that vision of salvation that includes in it a large dosage of cruelty (or, as is more likely, may want to save her own skin) and be able to testify conclusively against her former lover. It may be that Joel Steinberg will attempt a belated insanity plea and spring us from the need to place his furies in a recognizable context. Still, I wonder if somewhere in Hedda Nussbaum is a woman waiting to be beaten again—to be pummeled out of her senses and into incarceration. The shadow of Steinberg may have fallen across her path, but certain fates require hefty assists in order to unfold.

In the dire appetites of this couple I think we can locate a broader cultural appetite, an appetite that some have argued is innate to our species: a hunger for hostility. The line separating acceptable cultural sadomasochism from the intolerable real article is thinner than we imagine. (It is interesting, but a subject for a different piece, to note how much more open the homosexual community is about its fascination with pain in the name of pleasure.) Morton Downey, Jr., whose instinct for the primitive and regressive is impeccable, has taken a show with an "original edgy feel of impending violence" nationwide, in media columnist Edwin Diamond's phrase—and the pleasure it yields its audience is all in the manipulation, and relieving, of hostility. In "Under My Thumb," arguably one of the most erotic songs ever written, Mick Jagger sneers at "this squirming dog" of a girl, "the sweetest pet in the world." $9^{1}/_{2}$ *Weeks,* a sleek treatment of sexual enslavement, is one of the most widely rented videos in New York. The examples litter the landscape. The point is that there is titillation to be had here, the sort of excitement that more mature and less debased versions of sexual bonding can't sustain.

In a controversial book that appeared some years ago, *Sexual Excitement: Dynamics of Erotic Life,* psychoanalyst Robert Stoller baldly stated his theory: "In the absence of special physiologic factors . . . and putting aside the obvious effects that result from direct stimulation of erotic body parts, it is hostility—the desire, overt or hidden, to harm another person—that generates and enhances sexual excitement. The absence of hostility leads to sexual indifference and boredom."

Even if we don't subscribe to so bald an equation, we should recognize that what Hedda Nussbaum and Joel Steinberg suggest to us is the paradoxical relationship between love and loss of self, between erotic possession and release. I hope I will not be understood as condoning the one or blaming the other if I say that the intricate mechanism of self-hatred that enabled Hedda to cling to a man who battered her also enabled Joel to cling to the woman he battered. In this sense they turn to us equally dark faces of the moon.

Most of us lead lives in which there is a patina of civilization: The lights work, there is fresh milk in the refrigerator, a reasonable amount of care is taken with those we are close to. Most of us, in other words, fix what we can about the past and then forget it. To be successfully socialized into adulthood means to give up on compulsively reenacting the dramas of humiliation or rage that we bring with us from our childhood years— the years in which we were captive to other people's wishes and demands. What sadomasochism, the bloody rituals of a couple on a tree-lined block in Greenwich Village, implies is that some of us have pasts that won't let themselves be forgotten, that rise up in debilitating form in the present.

"Every woman," Sylvia Plath famously declared in her corrosive poem "Daddy," "adores a Fascist, / The boot in the face, the brute / Brute heart of a brute like you." Some women think if they lick the hard boot long enough it will turn soft. It could be that the draw of sado-masochism is that it dangles the possibility of relief, the promise of a vast tenderness to come after the violence is done with. Perhaps it contains within itself the idea of submission to a curative pain that will resolve all past hurts. Or perhaps the constant threat of punishment obscures the larger, less controllable threat of imminent departure—of the inevitable withdrawal or moderation of the Other's affection. What is clear is that sadomasochism can be understood as a bizarre, even arcane effort to circumvent ordinary boundaries: life's limits, the fading of love, the passing of time, the softening of the flesh. Its roots are in the past, and its continuum is with the past. It is a pathology, but reassuring in some terrible way, as are all pathologies.

Here is Dr. Stoller again: "The hostility of erotism is an attempt, repeated over and over, to undo childhood traumas and frustrations that threaten the development of one's masculinity or femininity. The same dynamics, though in different mixes and degrees, are found in almost everyone, those labeled perverse and those not so labeled." To dismiss Joel and Hedda as aberrant or alien is to miss the real point: Once upon a time, they were just another couple at a cocktail party.

1988

Desperately Seeking Torture: S & M on the Internet

All of us know—or think we know—how to tell the difference between fantasy and reality. Our workaday functioning selves call on this ability constantly; it is what distinguishes children from adults and the psychotic from the merely neurotic. It's also what gives an enjoyable titillating quality to thrillers and horror movies—allowing us to sit with racing pulses on the edge of our seats, secure in the knowledge that the blood being splattered isn't real and that the rampaging dinosaur is a computer-generated special effect.

In our erotic lives, however, the realms of fantasy and reality are less firmly delineated, the better to ignite our imaginations: We call upon fantasy when a given reality disappoints (the wife is too fat, the husband looks nothing like Mel Gibson) or when the demands of ongoing intimacy—which require us to be aroused by people we've come to know in all their grubby particulars—outpace our emotional abilities. When you add to this the further qualification that few of us grow up with unambiguous messages about the value of our own sexuality, it's no surprise that our erotic fantasies are often a compromise between affection and hostility—or that the sadomasochistic impulse flows under the surface of sexual life like a dark current. Indeed, given the nature of contemporary culture, with its embrace of the transgressive and its transmutation of once-taboo behavior into a hip lifestyle variant, a touch of S&M is being used to sell everything from overcoats to underwear. More disturbingly, an identification with the sadomasochistic ethos has created a mushrooming cult of devotees, with clubs and newsletters and, thanks to the arrival of the information superhighway, Internet chat rooms all their own.

But consider this: What if the line between reality and fantasy becomes so blurry as to be all but indiscernible? What if you could displace your own identity—leave behind the depressing actuality of a failed marriage and a run-down trailer, with its jumble of dirty dishes in the sink and rusty toys littering the lawn—and take on the alternate persona of "Slowhand," a dominant male into sexual bondage, torture, and death? And what, again, if you could leave behind your doldrumy existence as an overweight, isolated woman living in a small tract home on a cul-de-sac, cut off from other houses by a thick row of trees, and become "Nancy," a submissive also into kinkiness and danger? What if the two of you got so into "master-slave" role-playing that it overran the confines of the "virtual" and resulted in a very real dead body?

It began with six or seven weeks of electronically transmitted computer messages—the contents of which were "raw, sexual, and violent," according to the investigators who examined them—and ended on a deserted stretch of road in a remote part of rural North Carolina, where police found Sharon Lopatka's asphyxiated corpse interred in a shallow grave in Robert Glass's front yard, not far from his children's swing set. As is often the case, the victim and her accused killer struck the people around them as more or less normal. But both were loners, and if one looks closer, it becomes clear that there are other anomalies as well. Robert Glass, a bearded and bespectacled forty-five-year-old, is the introverted scion of a respected, civic-minded family (his sister is a church organist); he lived in a mobile home a half-mile away from the white-columned antebellum mansion in which he grew up. A county computer analyst with a "good work record" over sixteen years, Glass was separated from his wife, Sherri, who had left six months earlier, taking their three young children with her; although she describes him as "a nice, gentle person," she was sufficiently alarmed by the contents of her husband's E-mail sessions to confront him about them.

Sharon Lopatka, a matronly looking thirty-five-year-old, was a rebellious product of the Orthodox Jewish world. The daughter of a longtime cantor of a prominent Baltimore congregation, she had once performed Hebrew musical standards with her father and three younger sisters. To other people she appeared to be a "free spirit" even while adhering to the religious observances of her background. And she is remembered as never quite fitting in: "She was a little more hippie than everybody else," recalled a high-school classmate. "She didn't have a lot of friends, and if she thought you would be friends with her she'd leech on to you. But most of the time she was alone." Sharon eventually put distance between herself and the insular world of her family by marrying outside the faith and moving to Hampstead, Maryland, where she ran a variety of on-line businesses (including a "how-to" newsletter offering budget decorating tips) from her home. Neighbors, quoted in news reports, say she was rarely seen with her husband, a construction worker: He rode his bike and ran with their black Labrador retriever while she was often spotted alone in her car, with rock music blaring from the windows. The couple, whose frame ranch sits behind a row of pines at the bottom of a steep hill, "did not socialize and . . . weren't involved in any neighborhood activities."

What transpired between October 13, 1996, when Lopatka boarded a train in Baltimore, and her strangulation three days later in Lenoir, the small mill town at the foot of the Blue Ridge Mountains where Robert Glass was born and raised, is anyone's lurid guess. (Glass, through his attorney, claims that Lopatka was accidentally strangled by a rope they were using during sex.) But it seems disquietingly clear that a fatal encounter was what the corpulent, quiet woman—who, under the alias

"Nancy," had exchanged detailed descriptions with "Slowhand" of the torture to be inflicted on her—had in mind when she headed out the door that day. She left a note for her husband (who thought she was visiting friends in Georgia), informing him that she would not be returning: "If my body is never retrieved, don't worry, know that I am at peace." She had, in fact, for some time been openly advertising her wish to be killed. According to one woman who frequents a chat room for bondage and discipline enthusiasts, several men had engaged in conversations with Lopatka but backed off when they realized she was deadly serious in her intentions. "Want to talk about torturing to death?" asked one message posted August 22 to a chat room dealing with necrophilia, by a sender who turned out to be Lopatka. "I have a kind of fascination with torturing till death. . . . Of course, I can't speak about it with my family." She also wrote: "I want to surrender completely. I want to die."

Who of us has not had moments of desperation, moments in which we'd like to hand over our hard-won autonomy to someone else? The need to exercise volition—from shampooing one's hair to choosing a child's school—is a wearying constant of adult life, and one of the promises of sadomasochism is that in return for abdicating power within the context of a ritualized relationship, the submissive (or so-called bottom) will cede the burdens of choice and its attendant responsibility to the dominant (or so-called top) for the duration of the encounter. This scenario usually goes along with certain negotiated ground rules, including designated "safewords" that are meant to return the participants to the reality of the non-S&M arena.

There is no denying that a case like this—in which people act on disturbing but not entirely alien impulses—fascinates as much as it repels. Even the most well adapted among us sit on fantasies, be they infantile, grandiose, or rageful in nature. Indeed, it is safe to say we all have a little perversion in us waiting to come out, given the right opportunity. But a real danger of the S&M universe is that the chasm between the urge to add some spice to one's sex life and a consumingly self-destructive wish like Sharon Lopatka's can be crossed more rapidly than one would think. This is especially true in an electronic age, where "Slowhand" and "Nancy" can up the ante on their real-life counterparts without anyone being the wiser—until it's too late.

It is, I suppose, a grim twist of justice that the very mode of communication that cloaked the protagonists' dire plans eventually led Maryland police, assisted by a five-year-old Computer Crimes Unit, to unmask their true identities. I suppose, too, one salutary outcome of this otherwise dismal case is the discovery that anonymity is provisional even for cybermeisters; although Glass had sent his E-mail partner a disk that was meant to erase the sexually explicit messages and directions for meeting they had exchanged, computer sleuths were able to retrieve this information from Lopatka's aging Packard Bell computer. (One detective who works in this unit was quoted as saying that most people don't realize that, unless extraordinary technical precautions are taken, 99.9 percent of things done on the Internet can be traced.)

Still, the assumption of anonymity is surely one of the lures of communicating via clicking keyboards and coolly lit screens. What seems increasingly apparent is that the twilight, mediated world of the Internet is a perfect breeding ground for victims and their victimizers. (It has led people to forge relationships that turned deadly in at least four instances.) Denuded of the human aspect and shielded from scrutiny by an impersonal atmosphere, how easy it is to reinvent yourself and to objectify another person. As a sex chat room user observed of her fellow users: "Because of that anonymity, they feel a greater freedom to explore their darker side. They just feel totally liberated. It's almost as if there's no moral constraint on them anymore."

Of course, without all the restricting interpersonal paraphernalia of guilt, shame, and repression, there would be no civilized society. Perhaps the saddest aspect of this case is that, notwithstanding its up-to-the-minute, high-tech angle, it reeks of the loneliness that is part of the age-old human condition—a loneliness that finds ever more extreme outlets with the advent of cyberspace. What happens if, like Sharon Lopatka, you want to duck out of the real world—not for the duration of an escapist piece of entertainment but for the duration of forever? Though one can draw a distinction between raving pathology and the carefully orchestrated scripts of sadomasochism, sometimes the two intersect in the psyche of one person, and that individual has a better chance of going undetected on the Internet than in a roomful of people you can see and hear. Click on, click off. Even the cybercop unit had trouble deciphering whether 870 pages of E-mail messages were "reality, or are we talking about fantasy?" Click on, click off. Careful, now.

1996

Spanking: A Romance

On the bookshelves abutting the desk at which I write is a seemingly haphazard collection of volumes. These shelves, of honey-colored wood becomingly scarred by age and relocation, contain classic writerly guides; a variety of dictionaries, thesauruses, and compendiums of quotations; texts on depression, spanning the popular and the esoteric; and a selection of favorites like Cyril Connolly's *The Evening Colonnade,* an out-of-print edition of *The Widow's Children,* by Paula Fox, and worn blue galleys of Andrew Motion's biography of Philip Larkin. Pride of place, however, is given over to books on a subject that has been a source of secret fascination to me for as far back as I can remember: sadomasochism (S&M, or S/M, in the jaded shorthand that's current). This group, a changing exhibit with some permanent installations, includes a mini-library of the vast psychoanalytic literature surrounding S&M, ranging from Theodor Reik's classic *Masochism in Sex and Society* through Jessica Benjamin's *The Bonds of Love* to the entire oeuvre of the psychiatrist Robert Stoller. And then there's the fiction: two paperback copies of *9½ Weeks,* which has not lost its hold on my imagination since I first bought it in hardcover, seventeen years ago; *Story of O,* although this stalwart piece of porn has never given me quite the frisson it seems to have elicited in so many other women; *Nothing Natural,* by Jenny Diski, a 1986 British novel in which the depressed heroine finds herself responding to the tastes of a violent lover, its relevant pages ("He delicately edged her knickers down using the tips of his thumb and forefinger") carefully folded over, and some cheesier stuff, like *The Story of Monique* and *Half Dressed, She Obeyed*—books that get straight down to the business at hand without indulging in any niceties. (From the foreword to *The Training of Mrs. Pritchard:* "Dolly knew that her husband had a violent temper, but she rarely provoked his anger. She knew that if she did, she'd wind up with a burning, red hot ass!")

Perhaps my favorite of the lot is *Spanking the Maid,* a slim novel by Robert Coover, which obsessively recounts the daily life of an eager but imperfect maid who is forever being ordered to pull down her flannelette drawers and bend over for a variety of corrective measures from her master. ("Sometimes he stretches her across his lap. Sometimes she must bend over a chair or the bed, or lie flat out on it, or be horsed over the pillows, the dresser or a stool.") I suppose I love the Coover because it speaks both to the literary snob in me and to my baser—my debasement-*seeking*—sexual self. There is something mesmerizing about the novel's repetitiveness, the way it veils its randy core with tireless wordplay and Talmudic inventories: "Sometimes he uses a rod, sometimes his hand, his belt, sometimes a whip, a cane, a cat-o'-ninetails, a bull's pizzle, a hickory switch, a martinet, ruler, slipper, a leather strap, a hairbrush."

The fact is that I cannot remember a time when I didn't think about being spanked as a sexually gratifying act, didn't fantasize about being reduced to a craven object of desire by a firm male hand. Depending on my mood, these daydreams were marked by an atmosphere of greater or lesser ravishment, but all of them featured similar ingredients. Most important among them was a heightened—and deeply pleasurable— sense of exposure, brought about by the fact that enormous attention was being paid to my bottom, and by the fact that there was an aspect of helpless display attached to this particular body part. This scenario, in which my normally skittish self was reduced to a condition of wordless compliance via a specific ritual of chastisement, exerted a grip that was the more strong because I felt it to be so at odds with the intellectually weighty, morally upright part of me. Although I tend to be loquacious bordering on confessional with my friends, the discomfort I felt about my interest in erotic discipline and what it might suggest about me necessitated a degree of privacy that I was otherwise disinclined to observe. But even as I write the foregoing I feel a sense of relief (as well as shame) at finally giving voice to this confession, at putting down on paper, under my own name, what I know to be true of myself.

When did it get started? And why?

How long has it taken me to progress from fantasy to actually playing my own version of *Spanking the Maid*? I am not an adventurous person—far from it. I shy away from going to movies alone, much less traveling by myself, and I managed to get through college and two years of graduate school in the seventies without inhaling and with my virginity intact. I am so wedded to the familiar that I hold on with the tenacity of a bulldog to objects that have outgrown their usefulness. And yet I am drawn to the psychic hang-gliding that is implicit in the enterprise of sadomasochism, to its brute strictures of submission and dominance. What is still more curious is that allowing myself to be treated as a naughty girl (albeit one with womanly breasts and pubic hair) who must be punished not only arouses me but actually soothes me—enables me to jump over my own shadow, across the inhibitions that impede me, and to land on the other side of sexual pleasure, at a place where the body takes over and the mind leaves off.

On the surface, it seems incongruous that I, a conscientious Upper East Side mother, who avoids corporal punishment of her young daughter in favor of more enlightened approaches to child-rearing, should be attracted to the stuff of Victorian nannies and their charges. I don't think I have ever seen any of my friends spank their children, and I am always astonished by the blind "what was good for me is good for them" vehemence with which corporal punishment is sometimes espoused as a virtue capable of curing all social ills, from teenage pregnancies to drug abuse. How had it come to be that an expensively self-aware (thanks to decades of therapy), putatively independent-minded woman like me had managed to cultivate an impulse toward sexual humiliation alongside an impulse toward normative life? It was a conundrum. But, as with all puzzles, the clues were strewn everywhere, if one only knew where to begin looking and had the courage not to deny what turned up.

I don't remember myself being spanked as a child, although I know that I was. The family I grew up in was more Victorian than not: Its atmosphere was formal and rule-ridden, and a strict sense of hierarchy—of observable difference in power and privilege between adults and children —prevailed at all times. (I recall being acutely conscious, when I visited friends' houses, of the more casual relations that existed between many parents and their children—a state of fluid near-parity rather than constantly delineated inequality.) Some of this was attributable to the fact that my parents were European—Orthodox German-Jewish, to be specific—but other circumstances were at play as well. There were six of us children, and very little attention to go around. My father was terrifying and distant, surrounded by a moat of professional and worldly concerns—his business, the synagogue, philanthropy. I don't think he ever came to see me in a school performance or to discuss my progress with my teachers; the only occasion on which I definitely recall his being present was my high-school graduation. My mother was mercurial, and there was a cruel streak to her character that showed itself particularly when I became too emotional or needy. I sensed, early on, that there was something hardened in her response to the inner lives of her children—

some way in which she failed to take in our distress and make it her own but, rather, stood outside, coolly observing it.

I have often noticed that one of the redeeming aspects of households with difficult or inaccessible parents is the existence of a benign stand-in, a nurse or governess who connects to her charges with all the warmth that is otherwise lacking. (I think of Winston Churchill, who addressed his adored governess by the all-embracing nickname "Woomany.") My family had no such happy mother substitute; instead, there was an over-worked nanny, who was herself one of an alarmingly populous brood of sixteen, and was not inclined to respect the individual natures of the many children in her care. But even had she been so, she was under orders to keep us quiet, especially after my father returned home from his office. The nanny had an odd relationship with my mother, whom she seemed to regard with respect verging on fear (in later years, I came to read their dynamic as itself having an S&Mish quality about it), but with me and my siblings she was given carte blanche to do what she saw fit to ensure good behavior. Her means included spankings, which were administered sometimes with her very strong hand and once in a while with the back of a Kent hairbrush, one of those indestructible wooden instruments of English vintage. And though I seem to have blocked out any precise memories of being spanked myself, I do remember being scared of the nanny and of her considerable physical force, evidenced by the muscles in her forearms. I remember, too, the slow motion way in which she used to pull one of my younger brothers over her knees and then spank him for what seemed like hours.

Was the nanny herself excited by the spankings; does that explain the magic circle I drew around the activity? I can't say for certain, but when I look back on my young self standing in the doorway and watch-ing my brother being punished, I think I construed those spankings to be a form of love. The humiliation was safely someone else's, as were the tears, but there was something to be envied in all that attention and energy applied to a little boy's round, bare bottom. Spankings involve physical contact, after all, and there was very little touching in our house; they might even be said to be no more than overly vigorous caresses, resulting in momentarily reddened flesh but no great harm. There was something else as well: The spankings had a distinct beginning and end, after which life went back to its usual contours. By contrast, my mother's punitive style was much less succinct: She could go for days without talking to me, and even after we made up there was always the danger of another fight, so that nothing was ever clearly before—or after—the moment of transgression. The psychological discomfort I felt with my mother was immense because it was so unpredictable: Would she be in a good mood or a destructive one toward me on a particular day? The limited physical discomfort of receiving a spanking seemed a freedom of sorts when set against the specter of emotional pain that might go on forever and ever.

Like anyone who expends a lot of energy in keeping his or her passion a secret, I always longed for company. For years now, I've kept a mental list, spanning the centuries and various levels of fame, of people who go in for amatory discipline: Jean-Jacques Rousseau admitted to being a committed spankee in his *Confessions,* and Swinburne swooned for a good flagellation. In Hollywood, Peter Lawford apparently wanted to be beaten, and Jack Nicholson is reputed to like giving spankings. Kenneth Tynan, according to both his wives, was famously obsessed with what's often been called "the English vice." (Although it might just as well be called the French vice, or the Transylvanian, the addiction to it having less to do with geographical than psychic boundaries. It's unclear to me whether the British, with their upper-class traditions of all-powerful nannies and boarding schools where bare-buttocked canings have been honed to a fine art, actually have a greater penchant for this form of sexual play—or have simply referred to it in print more frequently.) I was constantly on the lookout: When I watched late-night TV, even a quick preview shot of John Wayne—an actor who has never remotely appealed to me—landing a smack on the upturned, fully clothed bottom of some flailing actress was enough to stir my erotic soul. "Bottom," "ass," "rump," "behind," "rear end," "tush," "fanny," "nates": None sufficiently evoke for me the orblike vulnerability of that area—how the image of a woman's presenting it, her underpants pulled down to somewhere below the knees, thrilled me. (Technically, the complete rather than the partial removal of underpants has always been less stimulating to my imagination; this has something to do, I guess, with the implicitly temporary nature of the act of submission, and with the potential for retrieval of both coverage and dignity.)

Curiously, over the years I've devoted to therapy, I've rarely discussed this crooked byway of my psychological being—maybe because I cannot conceive of mentioning the subject without envisioning the therapist in question, male or female, immediately envisioning *me* in the position under discussion, overturned on some disembodied knee, the white expanse of my bottom exposed for a flurry of reddening slaps. (This aspect of blushing skin has always seemed to me to be crucial to the spanking fantasy, suggesting skin that's been warmed out of its usual pallor and into visible heat.) Although a woman therapist should be easier in this regard, I have not found it to be the case. Perhaps it's because I suspect all women of having the same secret longing: to be spanked as a facilitating prelude to the enactments of lust.

Feelings of embarrassment nestled inside shame nestled inside excitement that the subject of spanking arouses, like a set of Russian dolls. . . . Not long ago, I finally disclosed my furtive yen to my current (male) shrink, who opined that "violence isn't foreplay": He's right, of course, but, as I tried to explain to him, a certain degree of forcefulness lubricates my mind, slackens the reins of my superego. Even more strangely, it releases me, if only for a moment, from my vigilant distrust of men. He did concede that the number of women patients who over the years have confided their fantasies of being spanked with a paddle or a badminton racquet (!) was, in his words, "mind-boggling." (Perhaps the *Belle de Jour*–like fantasy of being tamed by a lover—which men are reported to share, in large numbers—grows all the stronger in times that encourage sexual parity: Equality between men and women, or even the pretext of it, takes a lot of work and may not in any case be the surest route to sexual excitement. Or perhaps its origins reside in some basic developmental tension that is never completely resolved, arising from those immutable differences between boys and girls which begin with brute anatomy and proceed from there.)

When was it that I finally edged forward, peered over the rim of fantasy and into the clear-blue possibility of acting out the carefully conceived rituals of my imagination? Alone as I may have felt with my fixation, I dimly intuited already as a teenager that there were people besides myself caught up in these embarrassing longings. Somewhere along the way I rebelled against the tawdry closetedness of the whole thing and began toying with the idea of airing my wishes in the outside world. For starters, I found it increasingly difficult to move among members of the opposite sex. I couldn't encounter anyone—from my flirty Shakespeare professor to the irritable pharmacist who filled my antidepressant prescriptions—without wondering whether he silently yearned to turn me over his knee. (I cultivated what I imagined to be a suitably provocative manner, half brazen and half diffident, the better to catch gleanings of this intention wherever it smoldered.) I was in my early twenties when I finally made friends with another would-be spankee. She was several years older, a literary type like myself, and between discussions of favorite movies (including, among others, *The World of Henry Orient* and *The Parent Trap,* both of which have an underlying theme of "naughtiness") and parallel mother obsessions, we stumbled upon our shared romance with erotic discipline.

Although K. had acres of sexual as well as extrasexual experience on me (including an intimate acquaintance with all manner of illegal drugs), she was a virgin as far as spankings were concerned. We excitedly discussed the probability of getting a man to "do it" to us, which seemed slight given that neither of us seemed remotely like the sort of young woman who would tolerate such a practice, much less invite it. It was

with K. that I went to a porno store on Eighth Avenue in search of top-
ical literature; I kept watch outside while she ventured in and eventually
exited with several thin paperbacks, which we perused with greater
application than was warranted. What we were looking for was something that didn't exist—a key that would open the door, a path that
would link our social presentation of ourselves, as autonomous female
beings, with our latent existences as penitentially inclined subordinates.
At the time, K. was going out with a man who seemed up for anything:
threesomes, anonymous pickups, on-camera sex, and the like. She and I
planned a scenario in which she would leave a hairbrush lying next to
the bed and would somehow get her boyfriend to understand, in the
course of an evening, that he was to use the back of said brush on her
bottom. We endlessly revised the dialogue that would enable her to pro-
cure the fulfillment of this dream; the trick of it was that her speaking
part had to be suggestive without her having to ask directly for what she
wanted. (One of the problems with this fantasy was that its gratification
seemed to preclude a sense of irony, which we were both saddled with in
spades. The idea of actually announcing to a man that one wanted to be
spanked struck both of us as compromising beyond words.) The brush
lay there invitingly, inches from where K. frolicked between the sheets
with the man to whom nothing erotic was alien, but it—the "it" toward
which we schemed and plotted—never happened.

As time passed, the question loomed with increasing urgency: Would
my desires have to remain in the realm of fantasy forever? (It had started
so long ago; I remembered the mother of a childhood friend issuing the
warning "I'll cook your goose!" It excited me to hear her say that, with its
implied threat, its vision of scorched flesh.) The world as I knew it during
the seventies and early eighties was the brave new postfeminist one of
equal sexual opportunity; women were as likely to be the initiators as to
submit docilely to the imprecations of their male partners. Still, I couldn't
see how I would ever be able to ask for what I wanted. Under cover of
being attracted to men who admired my brain and took their cues from
the culture at large about treating women as real people rather than

embodiments of arrested male desire, I was all the while moving ever further back into a puerile daydream of my own. I couldn't imagine that "nice" guys—the kind I tended to meet, lawyers and their ilk, solid citizens in the making who molded their careers and their love lives with equal caution—gave much thought to spanking as a pastime. Would they recoil in disgust if they knew that this was what I wanted? The men I dated saw me as a formidable—if not to say bristling—adult woman. How were they to know that I was still a child, still transfixed by the past?

There was something else holding me back, and it had to do with my fear of wading in too deep even before I took the first step. From the start, the boundaries of my sadomasochistic wishes had never been clear to me; I maintained that they were confined to spanking and naughty-little-girl stuff, but this didn't explain my fascination with the further ends of enslavement and pain. What worried me was that fantasies, however extended and baroque, were safe, whereas enactments of fantasy, however limited, were potentially risky—if only because the question of where to stop would always arise. How hard it was to put parameters around this subject, to delineate the border beyond which sexual games turned into something rougher—not just a bit of fun but a near-lethal dose of harm. Did one proceed, inevitably, from hands to paddles to whips to chains to being strung up on pulleys? Within the flexible context of the sadomasochistic universe, the margin of error struck me as enormous. Where did you draw the line between mutually agreed upon love play, however aggressive, and domestic abuse? (Hedda Nussbaum and her smashed-up face had haunted me sufficiently to write about; when I look back on that essay I see it as an effort to ward off what I feared about my own proclivities.) Adding to the confusion was the fact that, beginning sometime in the eighties, the S&M subculture had come out into the open with almost evangelical zeal, presenting itself as yet one more option among a smorgasbord of sexual courses. This culture discoursed learnedly about "tops" (sadists) and "bottoms" (masochists).

Paradoxically, the "bottom" is viewed as having the greater degree of power in the relationship, because of the opportunity for having his or her wishes more directly met—and also because the "bottom" is supposed to have the ability to control the degree of violence in a given encounter by using a previously arranged code word, called the *safeword.*

Another term repeatedly alluded to by serious S&M philosophes—who often appear to consider themselves in the vanguard, striding toward new horizons that the rest of the population has yet to glimpse —is consensual. This word contains the kernel of their rationale, such as it is, because it posits volition as the crucial differentiating factor between being tied up and clobbered for the pleasure at the end of the pain and humiliation rather than for the inherent abuse. All this struck me as problematic at best, and I used to think often of Groucho Marx's famous self-hating chestnut about not wanting to belong to any club that would accept him as a member. The idea of consorting with people who base a significant part of their identity on their proclivities for being whipped or put on a leash seemed inconceivable to me, as inconceivable as joining a Tuesday-night bowling club.

So, despite my intense curiosity, I never frequented an S&M bar or thought of answering S&M-tinged personals. I could see why many women confined their adventures to reading about S&M or bondage and discipline (B&D, for the initiated). My own cautionary example involved a woman I knew briefly who hung out with an S&M club downtown called the Eulenspiegel Society: When she ended up being beaten black and blue (even on her face), I realized that she and I were talking a different language of aberrant desire.

All the while, I continued to read and dream, feeding my appetite. In my mid-twenties, I met a man who had fairly advanced sadistic skills, albeit of a psychological rather than a physical variety. His wish to control me—to offer and then withdraw affection on an erratic and hurtful schedule of his own devising—coincided with my secret wish to be mastered, but it never occurred to him to spank me, and I never asked. (I was undoubtedly afraid of what I might unleash: I had visions of being splattered against the wall.) Our relationship may not have taken on an explicitly S&M aspect, but it was riddled with the impulses—including, most important, a demonstrated disparity in power between two partners—that physical sadomasochism seeks to accommodate. Once, after a fight, he ordered me to get down on my knees before his standing, undressed self; another time, he lay on the bed and languidly suggested that I crawl across the floor in order to win back his favor. Although these were not things I wanted to be told to do on a regular basis, my mind read both of these demands as a signal for arousal. I experienced degradation (or, at least, a degree of degradation) as a thrill; there was no mistaking it. I wondered with growing anxiety how I would ever make do with less dubious forms of sexual engagement.

Somewhere on the graph of my autobiographical map, halfway between rage and fear, was the locus of my attraction to this kind of erotic dance—more of a last tango in Paris than a Fred Astaire–Ginger Rogers waltz. Although I thought I had acquired some abstract understanding of its derivation, I wasn't sure I could change the outcome. Then again, I wondered: Could it be that it was a preconditioned taste, like the one for spicy food, in which case it would have less to do with my personal history than with some encoding in my genes? I read tirelessly in the psychiatric literature and noted that Robert Stoller, an American psychiatrist who specialized in writing about gender and perversion, had reached the conclusion that there was more to sadomasochism than mere pathology: "Erotic deviance," he notes bemusedly in *Perversion*, "is as specially human as are murder, humor, fantasy, competitive sports, art, or cooking."

Finally, in my late twenties, I admitted my wish to be spanked to a man who seemed distant from my world, and thus not in a position to assess how fitting or incongruous this wish might be with the rest of me. He was from the West Coast; to my intractably Manhattanite sensibilities, he might as well have hailed from Sri Lanka. Whereas I was accustomed to the edgy New York style, this man's way of looking at things seemed slower and less driven by the need to evaluate. He also had a receptive quality that made me think I could trust him with my fantasy, and after we'd been going out for several months, I did. He appeared delighted at the prospect of implementing my wishes, and so it was that I found myself in the position I had been dreaming of for years: thrust over a man's knee, being soundly spanked for some concocted misdeed. (How much I liked those adverbs—"soundly," "firmly," "roundly," "thoroughly"—leading up to the most resonant verb I knew of in the English language.) The sheer tactile stimulation of it—the chastening sting—would have been enough to arouse me, but there was also, at last, the heady sense of emotional release: I was and was not a child; was and was not a sensual being; was and was not being reduced; was and was not being forced into letting go; was and was not the one in control. I had fantasized about this event for so long that in the back of my mind there had always lurked the fear that its gratification would prove disappointing. I needn't have worried: The reality of spanking, at least initially, was as good as the dream.

I eventually married this man, after dillydallying for six years. By then, sex between us had lost some of its sheen, and somewhere along the way I had begun to tire of the spankings; I found them too hard, and then again not hard enough, to excite me. If, as I have come to think, mine was an addictive personality, kept in line by the tight parameters of my upbringing and by some exertion of will, then spankings were my drug of choice: They were meant to blunt the edges of my existence. But the edges kept springing back into sight again, resilient as weeds. I had veered in and out of depression since adolescence and had also begun to wonder whether my depression wasn't intimately linked to the whole spanking thing. (What I actually suspected was that I wanted to be spanked to death—transported out of my sorrow into a state of numbness, of permanent *un*feeling.) Then, too, I found that domesticity, with its dirty dishes and regular hours, didn't mesh particularly well with the role-playing agenda of erotic discipline, which required the sort of imaginative space that was compromised by the grind of daily life. A year after we married, I gave birth to a daughter; I was now a parent myself, attending to the needs of an imperious infant while fighting off freshly ignited feelings about the lack of mothering in my own childhood. The fantasy receded, its urgent claim on my imagination muted by the realization that I had to look toward the future, for my child's sake if not for my own. I had tussled with these impulses for a long time; I knew they still exerted a sway over me, but it was time to turn my back on them.

And then there it was again, the familiar urge come back to vex me. I had been separated from my husband for several years and was on a first date with a man. We had talked a lot and sparred even more (my defenses were up, as they always were when I was attracted to someone), and while I was looking in my study for something I wanted to show him, he said idly, "It seems to me that what you really need is a good spanking." Bingo. I continued to search through a file drawer, but inside I was lurching, drunk with excitement at being recognized. (I wondered what signal I gave off—a special pheromone that only certain men could smell?) The remark passed into the air, electrifying it. I was afraid to break the spell, afraid to respond to the comment, afraid to ignore it.

A day or two later, the man called me, and I referred to the comment by coy indirection. We played a guessing game—I told him that something he had said during the evening intrigued me, involving a word beginning with s—and I couldn't decide if he had genuinely forgotten or was feigning ignorance. (My embarrassment about the subject of spanking has never faded even slightly; I might as well have been back in my twenties with K., one of those overgrown schoolgirls asking for trouble.) In the days that followed, I could think of nothing else: At a perfume counter in Saks Fifth Avenue, I heard a passing comment by one saleswoman to another as "male bondage" when what she had actually said was "nail varnish"; I met a friend at a tearoom famous for its homemade jams and suddenly noticed, with a flush of delight, that the strawberry-and-apple preserves were called Rosy Cheeks. I would say my interest was comical, if it didn't feel so consuming, and, underneath it all, so sad—this fascination with having my bottom spanked, this willingness to suspend my hard-won adult identity for the pleasure of being disciplined by a man as part of foreplay.

In any case, I confided in him, and we quickly became involved in a fairly conventional romance that included some light S&M. What we were doing may have been moderate by hard-core standards, but there was some danger in it: Our forays left me hungry for more radical sensations, and their tone began to permeate our relationship in disturbing ways. Some months into our affair, during a lengthy car ride to a country inn, I found myself engaging in a bizarre exchange. The man had been regaling me with his own initiation into bona fide S&M, with a woman who liked to have her nipples "pulled" ("Pull them off!" she told him), and with whom he enacted baroque, carefully orchestrated dramas involving belts and riding crops and immobilization. He finally left her because she wanted to be mummified, which scared him. The disaffected manner in which he told the story threatened me, and when he was finished I launched—impulsively, a bit crazily—into a gothic tale of my own, in which I had purportedly been whipped and then left chained to a bed with only a tin can to relieve myself in. He questioned me closely about the details: Did I like it? Was I in a lot of pain? Did we, my demon lover and I, have sex? Anal sex? Threesomes? Were there other people watching us? (I'd noticed, with some unease, that this kind of voyeurism—the degrading of a woman in front of an audience —seemed to be of tireless interest to him.) Who *was* this man? he wanted to know. I paused—the fabrication had begun to run away with itself—and then claimed that he was someone I knew only tangentially, through book publishing. As we drove on for a minute or two in silence, my anxiety mounted; he seemed lost in thought and then, sounding aggrieved, remarked on my failure to tell him about this episode before. The truth was that I had wanted to admit the story was a lie even as I was concocting it, but I felt trapped in some inchoate, defiant need of my own. Our relationship had become a kind of competition —a bitter race, in which I found myself compelled to "top" him with my story. A little later, we stopped for dinner, and soon after we sat down I leaned over and confessed that I had made the whole thing up. He looked bewildered, and then angry. For a moment, I felt as though I had exposed him, made a mockery of this sordid little world of S&M.

But whom was I really exposing—him or myself? It occurred to me that underneath my own limited participation in this world I felt enormous resentment; I was following the steps in a dance I couldn't control. Spanking and its accoutrements may have helped to subdue my simmering rage toward men—as well as theirs toward me—but it also demonstrated how far I was from healthy intimacy, from the real give-and-take that makes a relationship viable. (The sadomasochistic dynamic exists, at least partly, to shake things up—as a prophylactic against the sweltering possibility of too much closeness. Here's Stoller again: "I would guess that only in the rare people who can indefinitely contain sexual excitement and love within the same relationship do hostility and secrecy play insignificant parts in producing excitement.") Besides, there was something innately troubling about such a hierarchical mode of interaction, with its partly parodic lexicon: "I'm not the bottom in this relationship," my companion retorted at one point, when I asked him to apologize for some perceived wrongdoing. The remark made me uncomfortable, and I realized that I was growing impatient with the confining grid of "top" and "bottom," with the tableau in which tenderness always had to be mediated by hostility. During our time together, the mechanism of my own compulsion had started to grate on me; in fact, it had started to bore me. (It had started to bore me, that is, with this particular man—which suggests to me that too much repetition in anything erotic is counterlibidinous.)

I have no doubt that there are people who are into S&M—or believe that they are into it, which comes to the same thing—for the sophisticated experimentation, the "gourmet sex" of it. I suppose, too, that sadomasochism can be dispassionately viewed as a heightened paradigm for the discrepancies in power and control that run in a more diffuse fashion through all human relations. One can class such behavior as pathological or, with greater poetic license and less clinical judgment, as part of the infinite human variety, but I have come to believe that for me it was about nothing less gripping than stating and restating, in an adult arena, the emotional conditions of my childhood, where accepting pain was the price of affection. I believed in a magic trick, an impossible reversal: If you chose of your own free will to let someone hurt you, then all past hurt would be wondrously undone.

"The desires of the heart," Auden observed, "are as crooked as corkscrews." I don't, in all honesty, expect my own desires to ever straighten out completely. It would be nice to say that sweetness and light are what do it for me now, but that would be stretching things; I know there's something about a "normal," low-key sexual atmosphere that I find inherently claustrophobic.

Will it ever be enough for me to be desired by a man without having to go through my *Taming of the Shrew*–like paces? Or to desire a man without his having to jazz himself up with the artifices of domination? Will my need for sexual spiciness always outweigh my yearning for affection? The maze that brought me to this place is decipherable only in part, but it's interesting to note that my cherished spanking fantasy, once acted upon, began to induce the sort of ennui most people associate with going through the same old sexual moves in the same old connubial bed. I'm not sure where this leaves me, or what's in store on the erotic road ahead—but I'm hoping that my destination lies somewhere between boredom and bruises.

1996

CODA

Although there was some speculation at the time of the trial that Hedda Nussbaum would crumble on re-encountering Joel Steinberg in the courtroom, she did not and did, in fact, testify against him—thereby guaranteeing herself immunity from prosecution. Nussbaum was transformed, briefly and improbably, into a feminist cause célèbre, seen as an iconic instance of vicious domestic abuse. (Her collusion with Steinberg —at least as far as the death of their six-year-old adopted child went— was conveniently forgotten in the process.) I was asked by two publishers whether I was interested in writing a book about the case, but feared immersing myself to the extent necessary to write at that length. Several books did eventually appear; one, a novel by Susan Brownmiller, attempted to explore the psychological demons that impelled Nussbaum into Steinberg's arms (I reviewed it, favorably, for a magazine called *New York Woman*). Another, a nonfiction book by Joyce Johnson, took a much more condemning view of Nussbaum's role, and included the speculation that she was jealous of Steinberg's attachment to little Lisa and may herself have been abusive to the child.

My own long-standing interest in the emotional logistics of sado-masochism—which was the real point of departure for my piece about Hedda and Joel—eventually led to my decision to write more personally about the issues of dominance and submission. This article, on my ongoing fascination with sexual spanking, appeared in a special women's issue of *The New Yorker,* under the title "Unlikely Obsession"; it has generated more response than anything else I've written. I have received an astonishing amount of mail—some of it very intelligent, and much of it quite moving. This correspondence includes a priority letter from an urbane-sounding reader in Loury, France, who discerned "some sadness between [those] lines on a topic that, after all, concerns love and his games"; any number of cards and notes applauding my "courage" in publishing the piece; a furious, single-spaced letter of Marxist derivation decrying my "undercurrent of class bias"; and a home video from a happily S&M-embracing couple in Columbus, Ohio, who urged me to

ignore the phumphutings of my rational self and "GO FOR IT." (The
Midwest—and this is the least scientifically adduced of demographic
generalizations—seems to be especially full of closeted spanking enthusiasts.) I have received confessions from art-history professors and
anonymous, increasingly indignant missives from a member of the Yale
Club and invitations to get together for the purposes of mutual exploration from as far away as Alabama and Toronto. Women as well as men
have written me, almost in equal number, and with an equal level of
intensity; interestingly enough, only men have presumed to actually
look me up in the phone book and call me. Only men, that is, have managed to ignore the existence of the piece as a literary *objet* in favor of reading it as one long personal ad. Will they never learn?

In the wake of publishing "Unlikely Obsession," it sometimes
seemed to me that everyone and their mother was sitting on a beating
fantasy—everyone, that is, had a little S&M inside them ready to
emerge. One ponytailed male book editor who had never seemed particularly intrigued by me or my writing came up to me at a party and
thanked me, with a look of newfound reverence in his eyes, for revealing
the content of my erotic character. As is true of all fixations that are
deemed unmentionable or, at the very least, embarrassing by society at
large (although it's worth noting, as I did in my piece, that homosexual
culture has always been fairly open about the allure of corporal punishment as part of sexual foreplay), this one seems to draw a lot of people
who are ardent to the point of exhaustive in their interest. Thanks to my
article, I discovered (I hand on this information for those who might find
it useful) that there is a glossily produced magazine for spanking aficionados called, punningly, *Stand Corrected,* as well as a regular "personals" newsletter to which one can subscribe. And a very polite young man
from Buffalo called to tell me that someone had ripped my piece out of
The New Yorker in his local library, and then went on to inform me that
there was a deluxe edition of Robert Coover's *Spanking the Maid* (which
I had referred to in my piece) available for a hundred dollars. He also
wondered whether I knew that there were three (going on four) videos

at large of something called "Cinema Swats"—compilations of hundreds of scenes of, well, cinema swats—and urged me to check out Paulette Goddard being turned over Ray Milland's knee in *Reap the Wind. . . .*

Then there was the friend of mine who called from the West Coast a day after my essay appeared to let me know that I was being impersonated on the Internet by someone who had opened a discussion by calling him- or herself "Daphne@TheNewYorker"; he kindly faxed me some of the E-mail, which passionately addressed the pros and cons of my coming out with my interest in spanking in a "mainstream" publication—where, it was generally felt, I had been pressured into taking too apologetic/moralistic a stance. (There is no group quite so avid in their sense of being misunderstood as a self-annointed bunch of deviants.) My friend hastened, in turn, to explain that he had happened to amble on to this spanking group only because he was looking for information on "spelunking." Yeah, and Elvis lives.

Sometimes it felt as if I had opened a spigot that couldn't be turned off, all those letters and confessions and spanking arcana falling into my lap. In one of those odd congruences that could make one wonder whether all of life is hopelessly overdetermined, I received a message on my answering machine one day from a man who had written a warts-and-all account of the time he spent in the employ of John Lennon and Yoko Ono. (I had acquired his book years earlier when I was an editor. The book was eventually canceled because of legal problems, but not before I put up a ferocious fight for it and as a result lost my job.) The author wanted me to know that he had read my piece and that I should add John Lennon to my list of spankees. Seems he had liked his paddlings fairly savage. I must say it all made some kind of sad sense to me in retrospect: my irrational investment in a book that revealed Lennon's need to be dominated by an evil mother figure, my own fascination with punitive love, all of us hurtling backward in time to nursery land, where "the little piggies" need "a damn good whacking."

My most recent—and perhaps most obsessive—communiqué arrived just as I began to write this coda. It came from someone who had written to me half a year earlier and was trying to pique my interest with a printout entitled "The Definitive (Provisional) Annotated Bibliography of Spanking Scenes in Novels." Composed of four single-spaced pages, the list included page citations and brief descriptions of spanking scenes in books by authors from A to C, everyone from Margaret Atwood to Pearl Buck to Anton Chekhov. (If I was interested in receiving the rest, I was to drop him a line.)

And then came the ultimate accolade: A friend in the Midwest sent me an item gleaned from the personals column in his local newspaper. In case I missed it, he had circled the ad: SWM was seeking "Daphne Merkin type" for mutual involvement and pleasure. Somewhere along the way I had become an unwitting symbol—not quite what I had in mind when I bared my soul, but nakedness is always risky.

1997

First Person Ambivalent

Ready, Willing, and Wary

And so it was that I arrived at what I consider to be a dramatic new understanding of the concept of change. Although I have always been intrigued by the idea of change in the abstract—even of radical self-transformation—and am very much open to the untried and untrodden on an intellectual level, I have pursued a rather mollusklike course in my personal life.

Thus while the rest of my peers left home, set up apartments of their own, and eventually married, I seemed to do everything at a distinctly tardy pace. For an extended period during my twenties, I engaged in loverlike convolutions with my mother while my friends were engaged in similar convolutions with real lovers. I shared a rambling apartment with two roommates and eventually moved into a subterranean little domicile of my own, only to find myself fleeing backward into the atmosphere of childhood whenever possible. And then came that period in my late twenties and early thirties when I watched with horror as the last of the marriage holdouts succumbed and I was left alone, clinging to the reef of my intractable fear, refusing to *move on*, preferring to *stay put* until I felt ready.

The truth is, I've never really understood how people move on, ford-
ing the chasm between one "life passage" and the next. I keep thinking
they're hiding something from me, some crucial bit of information that
would explain how someone who seems torn between two pairs of shoes
one day can up and choose the person she wants to undertake matrimony
with on the next. What do they do with the ambivalence inherent in any
decision? How do they quiet the voices of doubt and anxiety? Where do
they draw the glimmer of certitude from—that glimmer without which
no forward motion is possible? *Why do they want to move on?*

There, I might as well admit it: I have never approached anything
new with other than negative anticipation. I cling to the skirts of stasis
the way other people chase adventure. Deep down, I know I'm Gustave
Flaubert; I want to stay home forever, under a maternal wing, and assess
the world as it passes by with a cynical and astute eye. Stuck in the
amber of domestic familiarity, I would find nothing human alien to me
—as long as I could remain unyieldingly the same.

But isn't it the case that creatively inclined people are often the least
risk-taking, once you get them away from their pens and paints? Think
of those eternal homebodies, Jane Austen, Emily Dickinson, and Alice
James, the future-resistant sister of William and Henry; think in more
recent years of Joseph Cornell, the artist who tried to stay the rush of
time with his evocative and imaginatively far-ranging boxes. Cornell
was the Homebody Extraordinaire, living, working, and dying on the
same street—called, fittingly enough, Utopia Parkway—to which he
moved with his mother and siblings when he was twenty-five.

Ah, but all this protesting is just another form of my inveterate nostalgia, for change has come and claimed me in all my recalcitrance and there
is no going back. In the past six months I've done what I thought only
other people did: I've gotten married. The man in question is handsome,
humorous, and blessed with a capacious ability to disregard my obsessive
broodings. I can't say I did it with the blithe aspect of readiness many of
the women I know seemed able to call upon; I did it in conflict and panic.

I spent my honeymoon in Hawaii in a tailspin of distress, trying to figure out how I had come to this next phase of my life when I was still trying to create Cornell-like boxes of my past. I left my husband to his snorkeling and exploring while I sat on the beach in front of our hotel reading a just-published tome about dysfunctional personality styles, thinking that in it I would find clues to my own. (I turn to such works for escape the way other people turn to romance novels: Something about the human spectacle in all its malformed variety infinitely soothes me.)

If I never expected to get married, I expected to get pregnant even less. Although I knew I wanted children, I envisioned the path toward procreation as thorny and infinitely delayed. Everything in my life—including the fact that I had been diagnosed as having polycystic ovaries—seemed to suggest that I would get pregnant (and there was always the fear that I wouldn't) in the same laggardly fashion that I managed all *next steps*. But nature—or God, if you listen to my mother—had something else in mind, and a week or two after my honeymoon I found myself in my gynecologist's office discussing means to boost my presumedly tenuous fertility, only to be given the unexpected news that I was pregnant!

So here I am, sitting in my old room at home with my mother, entertaining names for my prospective child. I am the same indecisive, backward-looking person I've always been, only now I'm married and pregnant. And here's what I think I've discovered about change: Whereas I used to think it was something absolute, something hard and durable that you could touch, like a bump on your head, it appears to me now that change—at least in its internalized form—is a proximate condition at best. I am reminded of something a maverick and gifted psychiatrist once told me when I explained that I didn't feel the requisite positive emotions to get on with my life: "Fake it," Dr. Albert said, with a cunning smile. And so, indeed, what I am doing these days is a benign form of faking it, practicing a willing suspension of disbelief on my own behalf. Instead of my old conviction that you have to be absolutely prepared for it ahead of time, I have started to toy with the notion that change can also make you ready *after* the fact.

Of course, with even the most cautious acceptance of change comes

the shadow side—the fear of being cornered, of being inextricably rede-
fined. With choice also comes entrapment. It may well be that nothing
is forever, as the adventurous like to declare, but some things cannot be
undone easily (marriage) and others cannot be undone at all (children).
There is a closing off of certain avenues when one moves forward; the
arena in which to play out one's fate may not necessarily get smaller
when marriage or childbearing is elected, but it undeniably takes on a
different form. And then there is the other specter: We all make new
choices in the hope that they're for the better; but what happens when
they prove to be for the worse?

I can't say, then, that it surprises me much to find myself dreaming
of late about other men, the men who preceded my husband; I call them
"Divorce Dreams," but in truth I think they are marriage dreams,
dreams in which I keep coming to terms with options that have passed,
paving the way for the present and the future. Nor does it surprise me
that I gravitate to music that reminds me of the music I loved in my college days—the wistful, Dylanesque lyrics and mournful harmonies of
the Indigo Girls. We humans are a conservative bunch, after all, and
have trouble adjusting to the shock of the new.

What does surprise me, however, is how much more tolerant we are
of men in this regard, how much more understanding of a man who's not
"ready" to marry or be a father than of a woman who balks at similar
junctures. "He's just a boy at heart," we say of such men. It's little girls,
after all, who already chant gaily of adaptation in the playground,
singing "First comes love, then comes marriage, then comes junior in
the baby carriage." Can it really be that we expect women to mature
with greater ease merely because our culture would have it so?

So here it is: Deep down, I know I'm still Gustave Flaubert. Meanwhile, my belly keeps getting bigger and, in the change-embracing way
of the seasons, the summer is here again. From the outside in—and that
may be more important than I used to grant—I'm ready.

1989

Secrets of a Pregnant Woman

Sometime during the eighth month of my pregnancy, in the fetid days of late August, my anxiety about the impending birth of the baby I was carrying transposed itself into a pair of black Alain Mikli sunglasses. As anyone who has so much as stuck his or her nose into the vast literature of childbirth can tell you, absentmindedness is a frequently cited symptom of the last trimester of pregnancy. In other words, not only do you begin to resemble a small car—a small, continuously out-of-breath car —but you may also find yourself losing objects of greater or lesser significance. After the Alain Mikli sunglasses, I went on to misplace a watch in a beach house and to leave a new and quite beautiful maternity nightgown, as well as a novel by Fay Weldon (about a pregnant woman!), in a hotel room. Still, nothing so encapsulated—and displaced—the terror of futurity for me as the loss of those sunglasses.

They were a black matte frame, the height of chicdom circa two years earlier. For several days after I lost them, I obsessed over them the way one might expect to obsess over the loss of something incalculably dear, something irreplaceable. I made countless phone calls about them, and, after I was embarrassed to make yet another call to the same unyielding source, I had various people make calls on my behalf. The glasses never did turn up, and I eventually overcame my grief enough to order a new pair.

What is most striking about this minidrama is how it conveniently usurped the larger ongoing drama being played out in my life. For those several days when I attempted to track the glasses down, the fact of my being pregnant got blurred—pleasantly so. I almost forgot about it, just as I often forgot about it at night in my dreams. My husband, who is given to a certain dryness about my emotional upheavals, asked me, after listening to the saga of the sunglasses, if I didn't think it was trying to tell me something. And, of course, it was: Somewhere deep in the web of feelings I had about becoming a mother, I both did and did not want to lose the baby growing inside me. This is not to suggest that I was always equally alienated from my own protuberant physical state; I had grown attached to the froglike kicks of the fetus (kicks that always made me think of a diver's fins), and there was one dream from which I woke up desolate, a recurring dream in which I looked down at my belly and suddenly realized it was no longer swollen with child but had become, rather, a flat, Cher-like stomach. Far from feeling relieved, I would wake up from this dream mourning the child I would never know.

The mythology surrounding pregnancy is immense, rivaling the mythology of virginity. The cultural halo placed upon the subject has little to do with its complex reality and everything to do with the wish of both men and women to make an adorable, sweet-smelling bundle out of a fearsome and extraordinary process. Perhaps because pregnancy, once under way, precludes men to the same extent that virginity, while intact, relies upon them, it has been the female condition to invite the most beatification. What men get out of this (largely unconscious) arrangement is a cleaned-up procreative model, running smoothly and without too much trouble, requiring little in the way of maintenance except an occasional sympathetic back rub and obligatory attendance at Lamaze classes. Women, as is their pacific wont, collude with men in this conspiracy—in hopes, I can only think, of earning male esteem for their good sportsmanship and, in the process, a tacit sense of superiority shared with all women since Eve. (If telling the truth about marriage would serve to keep most women single, as Carolyn Heilbrun argues in her irreverent and witty book *Writing a Woman's Life,* how much more damaging the effects of telling the truth about pregnancy.)

What we are left with, then, is an untroubled image of luminescent expectation—glowingly complexioned, thickly maned—that not only defies emotional logic but serves to obscure the genuine physical distortion that is taking place, replete with such unpretty indications as nausea, constipation, and heartburn. This subterfuge is all-embracing. Even friends to whom I had ascribed qualities of subtlety and unconventionality reacted to my pregnancy with the most cookie-cutter of inquiries, as though I was no longer my old, ardently conflicted self but some new, immaculate version: the mother-to-be, blessed be her name, joyously stocking up on stretchies. Everywhere I looked, with one or two exceptions, I met with the same claustrophobic, velvety response; most disappointingly, the man I had thought of as a keen and eccentric mentor stunned me by penning a letter of congratulations that displayed the utmost sentimentality about incipient motherhood, right down to the stuff about shining skin and hair. I wondered nervously what he'd think of me in my unradiant actuality, all ballooning breasts and waterlogged ankles. . . . Pregnancy, I came to discover, was a lonely place to be—a frontier from which a genial haze of misinformation issued forth, leaving you to your own devices.

In my thirties and a mother-to-be, still I hardly count myself among those women—much described and analyzed in the media in recent years—to whom the idea of childbearing came in a belated epiphany or as the latest expression of self-evolvement. After all, I descend, on my mother's side, from an awesomely fecund line: My grandmother at her death had more than one hundred great-grandchildren, and one of my uncles welcomed his fiftieth grandchild into the world just this summer.

As one of six siblings myself and an attentive aunt to ten nieces and nephews, I have always had an attitude toward children that has been, of necessity, more casual than many of my peers': I have always taken the presence of children in adult life for granted, rather than seeing them as a decision to be suspended until the right confluence of career, finances, and longing occurs. At the same time I have always been less than convinced of the transformational aspects of motherhood, the wish of all daughters to do their mothers one better notwithstanding. It seems to me, for instance, that if you're a fairly unconscious person, you will be, for better or worse, a fairly unconscious mother. Just as the lowly rattle, almost alone among the traditional icons of babyhood, has stayed the same, so, I would argue, has the number of "good enough" mothers (in the phrase of the British child psychoanalyst D. W. Winnicott) from one generation to the next. Although it would be nice to think that the late-eighties, yuppified approach to pregnancy and child-rearing—exemplified in the plethora of books on prenatal and postpartum and post-postpartum care, as well as in the fertile crop of stores carrying the latest in bottles, pacifiers, gender-coded diapers and geodesic mobiles—guaranteed better parents, a large part of me is in agreement with the Russian cabdriver who lectured me as I lay splayed at my full nine months' amplitude in the back of his taxi: "You fulfill your fantasies, not theirs. . . . You buy all those fancy accessories, the baby doesn't care. About babies and pregnancy everyone becomes a sage."

Indeed I discovered these last months that pregnancy is a screen on which people play out their fantasies, their unsatisfied lifetime roles. Something about the dependent, captive *waitingness* of the condition—its aura of visible receptivity—provokes strangers into telling you their unsolicited, projected feelings about children ("You'll never have a care-free moment again") and the universe in general ("What a shitty place to bring someone into, don't you think?"). Women, in particular, are a strange hybrid of supportive murmurings and ominous warnings; the closer one's due date—i.e., the bigger one's belly—the more likely one is to elicit the bare-boned, brutal truth about the pain, fatigue, and plain terror of childbirth. While I am waiting in a bookstore to have a memoir wrapped, the woman in front of me starts up one of those friendly "how much longer do you have" conversations. Within seconds she has compared going through labor to going through a war. The man wrapping her books looks up, alarmed, and I give him a beseeching look: *Tell me it isn't so.*

Let the truth be known: What I have felt during much of my pregnancy is fat, panicked, and resentful. No matter where you come from, no matter how fertile the strain that spawned you, to be pregnant, at least the first time around, is to be in a state of future shock all one's own; short of being catapulted into outer space, it is one of the most emotionally surreal experiences a human being can have. It is difficult, especially during the early months of carrying a child, to actually conceive of conception: that what is inside, contained, quiescent, will one day become external, autonomous, and given to bawling in the wee hours of the morning. At the same time, pregnancy also qualifies as one of the most wholly *uninvented* circumstances of self—an incontestable physical event the like of which you couldn't imagine beforehand if you tried. For a contemporary, urban woman like myself, it suggests, as well, a not entirely comfortable sense of animal continuity, a return to mammalian beginnings. With all those hormones kicking in and the evidence of one's senses alerting one to the fact that the female body has been biologically programmed (the late-twentieth-century executive in a skirt be damned) to species-preserving ends—to releasing milk through the nipples, for example—it is possible to find oneself feeling peculiarly *bovine,* caught up in some impassive, cud-chewing state.

And here's another truth I'd like to bruit about: I'm not quite sure I get the point of husbands during pregnancy. Although it has become almost mandatory in the past decade to include them at every step, from early ob-gyn visits to ultrasound screenings to elbow proximity at the delivery itself, I wonder if this is done more out of a certain wishful denial of the unshareable essence of the experience—its being an exclusively female province—than any real kinship the condition itself allows for. The agitprop of upper-middle-class pregnancy is formidable, from the excessively detailed information provided at the amniocentesis to the excessive prepping at childbirth classes, where hair-raising scenes of an actual labor are shown, complete with close-ups of the mother's face contorting in pain and the crimson slash of the episiotomy.

Part and parcel of the agitprop is that all this shared knowledge will create better "partnering," a stronger bond between man and woman. And perhaps it works for some. As for me, I have this to say: During my childbirth classes (I opted to take them privately, so as not to have to deal with a gaggle of zealously breathing mothers-to-be and their attentive "coaches"), the person I bonded with was my Lamaze instructor. A woman with great powers of consolation, she was more in touch with my torrential fear and anxiety than my husband. My husband, who has two teenage daughters, likes to present himself as an old hand—even something of an expert—in matters of babies and child care. As he lectured both me and the instructor on my inability to relax and breathe properly, I became somewhat irritated. "Who's teaching this," I groused at him, "you or Deborah?" Finally, when he saw fit to propound one of his theories about labor pain while I huffed and puffed away like the big bad wolf, I had enough: "Don't come to the hospital!" I shrieked. "I want Deborah there with me, not you."

As long as I'm going on about the extraneousness of husbands in this period, I should make mention of the issue of sex—or the lack thereof. Pregnancy might well be subtitled "The De-Eroticization of the American Wife," to listen to most men talk. A business associate of mine who described his feelings about his wife's body during her two pregnancies with a vivid sense of recoil, kept constant track of my husband's libidinal interest in me. In a bizarre twist, I found myself bantering about my husband's purported lack of responsiveness whenever this man and I talked, for fear he would find anything else heterosexually deviant. In all fairness to my husband (who is less drawn to the anorexic, tautly worked-out late-twentieth-century female prototype than most men), I was far more put off by my rounded form than he. The problem became one of ironically mediated disinterest: I found it impossible, as the months passed, to believe that he could still find me erotically appealing even as he tried to convince me that he did.

As to men other than my spouse, I grew ever more invisible as a woman the more visible I grew in my pregnancy. No loud whistles or appreciative glances came my way as I lumbered down the avenue; the one time I discerned a man looking at me with what I considered to be sexual curiosity, I actually stopped and checked myself out in a passing store window with amazed, wallflower-at-the-dance wonder: Could he possibly have meant *me?* Big ole me? Even my most sexually vulpine male friend, who regards no one of the feminine persuasion as off-limits, admitted that he considered pregnant women "not to be tampered with."

What should be left after all this, in the absence of erotic heat, is a sense of the chivalrous. Or so one would think. But no, these are stark, postmodern times—a far cry from the pampering days of my grandmother, who took to her *Wochenbett,* a bed accoutred with special linens and nightgowns, for a month after childbirth. The only chivalrous gesture made toward me during my pregnancy occurred in the last two weeks. One of New York's finest, a cop with a mustache and twinkling eyes, asked if he could help me get a taxi. It was rush hour on Madison Avenue and I had been walking up and down fruitlessly for fifteen minutes when this knight in blue stepped into the street, put up his hand, and pointed with the other one at my belly. Minutes later I was on my way home.

I am writing this within days of my due date and have been told it can happen anytime, which has given me the aspect of a human time bomb. When I try and envision the onset of labor, I think of the pounding music from *Jaws* and of myself clenched in the grip of huge forces outside of my control. I look down the long valley of pregnancy and remember certain scenes from the past nine months: having dinner with friends, a doctor and his fiancée, at which we discussed the color of placenta and my husband offered up authoritatively that it was green . . . listening to Rod Stewart's "You Wear It Well" piped in over the coffee I am drinking with a svelte friend and remarking to her that I once wanted to be Patti Smith . . . lying in the sun and reading a book about *Horizon*, the magazine founded and edited by the English literary critic Cyril Connolly—he who opined that "there is no more somber enemy of good art than the pram in the hall"—and musing about the women who moved in Connolly's orbit, most of whom seemed not to have children . . . thinking about the things I would have liked to do before assuming the mantle of motherhood: travel more, look at art, learn Latin, live a wild life. . . .

I'd like to conclude by saying I take it all back, the sentimentalists are right: I've had my kid and it's love at first sight, instant relief from the ball of anxieties I've been carrying around all these months. I'd like to, but I'd be fooling you. The secret life of a pregnant woman has in it an almost unbearable sense of possibilities lost: Gone forever is the vision of oneself dramatically alone on a stage, preparing to leave one's idiosyncratic mark on the planet, unencumbered by anything except one's own inhibitions. And that sense of loss is, in the main, accurate. To give birth to a child is to see oneself on that stage, but this time a small paw is clutching at one's arm or leg, demanding to be fed or snuggled or changed. The lighting has softened imperceptibly, from a high-intensity beam to something duskier and less egocentric. Sure, you can go on to take over the world, to negotiate deals or write a masterpiece, but a part of you will always be hovering around the crib, making certain no harm will come, your ear cocked for cries.

It's been several weeks since my daughter painfully tunneled her way out under my hospital gown, to emerge looking like a gray kitten streaked with blood. Placed on my belly, warm from the womb, she blinked up at me and I thought, What have I done? And who are you?

Sitting on a park bench with a baby carriage (a scene which has a certain placid charm), I often find myself startled by the fact of her existence. But there is something else I am startled by, something my secret life of pregnancy didn't prepare me for—and that is the sense of possibilities to come. Who will Zoë be when she grows up? The fierceness of my hopes for her astonishes me.

1990

The Knight in Shining Armani

Just the other day it happened again: I was sifting through a rack of charming but inflationary baby clothes together with my friend Susan when she said, sotto voce: "I talked to my cousin yesterday. She saw *Pretty Woman*. She said she loved it, too." Although I doubt Susan's cousin loves the movie as much as Susan does (she's seen it three times), the list of suspects keeps growing. My friend Willa is up to four viewings. I myself have gone twice so far and have devoted several phone conversations to rapt discussions of the movie—one of which concerned the motivation of the Richard Gere character, at the sort of esoteric level of discourse more usually to be found in a graduate seminar on Henry James.

It's a small but noteworthy phenomenon, this illicit affection for a glossy cinematic tale about a prostitute and a high-rolling businessman that's gripped the hearts and minds of a surprising number of the women I know. Independent-minded women all, ranging from twenty-year-olds to a friend's eighty-three-year-old aunt, most of them admit to their fondness abashedly, as though they've been caught indulging a taste for something unworthy or sickly sweet. There are those who have confessed only under duress, in the line of direct questioning; I have found this to be particularly true for women in their early twenties. Inheritors of the feminist mystique, they are peers of the women who felt compelled to protest the choice of Barbara Bush as a commencement speaker.

For self-aware young women such as these, owning up to the pleasures of a retro, gender-structured movie like *Pretty Woman* verges on the politically incorrect—and thus is even more of a statement, a sign that you dare think for yourself. "Not only did I enjoy the movie," says a twenty-two-year-old writer, "I don't like the people who don't. They disturb me. I think they lack humor and perspective."

Others, like my friend Deborah, a decade older and more bemused, have less personally at stake but still concede the issue with a foreordained defensiveness: "I liked it," she says. "I liked it completely."

Another voice pipes up: "It's been a long time since I've thought about a movie so much, since I've actually found myself wishing for the sequel." So speaks Sara, a skeptical-to-the-bone woman, divorced, a family therapist, relatively immune to the myth of The Redemptive Male— the right man will provide you with the right life—that women have historically lived by. Or is she? Are, indeed, any of us, with or without husbands or lovers? Judging by the response to this brightly shellacked and cannily updated Pygmalion story, the answer is no. If it weren't already a movie, it could be a book, one of those best-selling syndrome books purporting to explain the inexplicable behavior of the female of the species: "Pretty Woman: Why Smart Women Still Long for the Knight on the White Horse."

It would be foolish to suggest that the popularity of the film disproves any of feminism's claims or offsets criticism of it, including the fact that the movie glamorizes prostitution. Still, it does point to certain gaps—fissures, I should say—in the women's movement's re-envisioning of the world, as well as in its perception of the female imagination. For one thing, it seems to me that feminism has never paid enough attention to the intractable nature of fantasy life, its pervasive hold on our more adult selves. Along with that oversight, in focusing on the hostile or infantile tone of many of the patriarchal images of women, it fails to take note of the fact that fantasies—however primitive and unenlightened—aren't exclusively the domain of men.

This is especially true of romance, where the rational and the prescriptive don't hold nearly as much sway as we'd like. For every man who dreams of the hooker with a heart of gold, there must be a woman who dreams of the lost little boy inside the ruthless tycoon. Just as certain prototypical male fantasies—of sexual domination over women and women's emotional submission to them—seem to linger on no matter how disapproving the culture, so, too, do certain crude female scenarios —of sexual submission to and emotional domination over men—continue to flourish.

Would *Pretty Woman* have been possible—would it have been the box-office hit it has become—in the seventies or even the early eighties? Somehow, I doubt it. As the conceits of our society—those notions it deems valuable versus those it deems antiquated or, worse, inimical— change, it is to be supposed our attitudes toward those conceits get revised, too.

Not so very long ago, about the time of Paul Mazursky's then-hip *An Unmarried Woman* (winter '78, to be exact), we seemed to want our romantic horizons contracted, brought closer to the ground—as reflected in a new stringency about the sexes. So we warmed (albeit a tad incredulously) to Jill Clayburgh sniffling red-nosedly into a handkerchief, choosing the succor of self-definition over the succor of Alan Bates. I suppose one fantasy is as valid as another, although in that era of newly raised consciousness, we were probably in real danger of mistaking the glamorous cinematic image of the uncoupled, unencumbered woman for the reality. Enough water has passed over the dam since then, however, for us not only to be able to reconsider some hitherto rejected fantasies—the knight in shining Armani who rescues the damsel in distressed jeans—but to recognize their enduring appeal.

Pretty Woman is about a fetching prostitute who, in the course of teaching a driven corporate raider how to feel, earns not only a whole new wardrobe culled from Rodeo Drive, but also his love. From what I can tell, the movie is far more popular with women than it is with men; it seems only to bewilder or anger the latter. And small wonder: As far as fairy tales go, this one not only has a Prince Charming, but it also has an audacious, instinctive, principled heroine who reforms the Prince—getting him to take off his shoes and walk barefoot in the park—before she will have him. In other words, the only one who has to do any real self-examination is the man! The hooker may learn to dress up and to distinguish one fork from another, but it is the corporate raider who learns to look at life differently and is humanized in the process. What we have is the myth of the redemptive male, but with a shrewd fillip, Hollywood's bow to the New Cinderella, who has the movie's last line: "She rescues him right back."

Of course, so fluffy a piece of moviemaking as this works at least as much on its charm as its subliminal message. *Pretty Woman* is set in Los Angeles at its glitziest, and half the fun of the film is getting to watch beautiful people wear beautiful clothes as they move around beautiful settings—the racetrack, the opera, and a baronial hotel suite—saying beautiful things, such as "Strawberries help the taste of champagne." Yes, the premises of *Pretty Woman* are improbable from the get-go: It's hard to believe, in these AIDS-ridden times, that any successful businessman, even so insouciant a one as Richard Gere, would hazard sex with a hooker who works the Strip, even so fetching a one as Julia Roberts. (The movie gets around this with the briefest of acknowledgments—a visual gag involving a rainbow-colored assortment of condoms.) And yes, there is something unsettling about its glib appropriation of old and new themes, as well as its fudged sense of morality. But it appears that in the postmodernist, postfeminist, closing decade of the twentieth century, we still need our myths, our amatory fictions; they help us endure. We are ready again to try on the mad, implausible embrace—and even to wear it for a while.

1990

My Kingdom for a Scarf

Several weeks ago I briefly considered risking my life—or, at least, a limb or two—in order to retrieve a scarf I had left in the taxi that was just pulling away. I was with a friend, and the two of us had become engaged in a conversation about politics with our opinionated and well-informed driver. The scarf in question was newish, one of those vast challis paisleys that are meant to be draped, shawl-like, over (rather than under) a coat. I might add that it was the first such scarf I owned; prior to it, I had only a drawer full of haphazardly gathered, skimpy silk squares, most of which I never wore.

I am in general not the sort of person to go in for elaborately conceived fashion, but having admired for some time the effect of almost military elegance that was achieved when women wore scarves this way, I decided I was ready to try it myself. I had just the coat for the purpose, too: a simple but well-styled black cashmere with a shawl collar. The scarf had been purchased in one of those tiny, exquisitely organized stores that can seduce you into thinking it matters less what you wear than how you accessorize what you wear, and the scarf came in just the noncolor colors that I like: mustard and khaki and taupe, shades of dun, nothing too vivid, yet subtly enlivening.

I have traced the etiology of this object the better to convey the irrational significance of its loss. I ran after that cab for a good long stretch —across Seventy-ninth Street and over to Fifth and then down a few blocks; I got honked at and sworn at as I raced heedlessly, without regard to red lights or oncoming traffic, toward my fast-disappearing scarf. I gave up only when I lost track of the cab in a sea of yellow. As I hurried back to my waiting friend, the foolish bravado of my effort struck me: my kingdom for a horse, maybe, but my life for a scarf? It didn't, on the surface, make sense.

It continued to not make sense when I, a native and therefore cynical New Yorker, hung on the phone the next day trying to get in touch with the taxi lost and found. The ways of this establishment, for those who have never dealt with it, are labyrinthine: When the Muzak finally stops and a living person comes on the line, it is only to inform you that there *is* no longer a general lost and found; anything left in a taxi has to be brought in to the police station closest to the drop-off point by a driver who is presumably not only honest but deeply enterprising. Short of this highly unlikely sequence of events having taken place, I was welcome to arrange to come in to look at a photographic lineup of drivers.

No, I didn't make an appointment to study the physiognomy of thousands of Manhattan cabbies. I did, however, wend my way back to the store where I'd bought the scarf to check first if they had another in stock, and then, with fading hope, if it could be reordered. (It couldn't.) If time is money, as the saying goes, the worth of my scarf had been expanded tenfold. Then again, it should be clear at this point in my minisaga that its true subtext has nothing to do with scarves. What it has to do with is loss, the disappearance of anything—big or little, inanimate or human—that helps moor us in what George Eliot in *Middlemarch* called "the largeness of the world." To grieve over such a loss, one might say, is to grieve over all losses. I think what I must have had somewhere in mind as I bounded toward the taxi that sped along, oblivious to my scarf resting on the backseat, was an act of redemptive hara-kiri: If I could undo this one loss, even if I had to die in the process, I could undo all the losses I'd suffered. If I could have my scarf back, in its generous, enveloping softness, it was possible that nothing else was gone forever, either.

A list of the losses I've incurred in the past year or so would include, in no particular order of importance: a job; a pair of earrings; a piece of my work (the paperback copies of my novel were recently shredded); a literary mentor; that damn scarf; and one of my most kindred-spirited friends. It could be argued that some of these were ordinary losses and that others were necessary, but what I know for certain is that sooner or later all of them—people and objects alike—will turn up, deep at night, scattered across my dreams. In dreams my friend is sitting on a beach chair again, discoursing avidly about books in his dry, humorous voice, and I am back in my office again, under the fluorescent light, juggling calls, and there, plain as can be, folded neatly on a shelf, is my challis scarf. I have yet to have the perfect dream of retrieval, in which everything is found in one blissful spot, but there is always tomorrow.

For as long as I can remember, I have been an assiduous counter of losses—the sort of person who remembers, with a stab of pain, that which is missing. I realize, of course, that this sort of raging about a scarf strikes many people as incomprehensible. In the mental exercise whereby we try to divide people into arbitrary categories, I suggest a valid division would be those who cut their losses versus those of us who keen over them. For those of us who fit the latter category, every loss is tinged with mortality: The valence of a scarf, as weighed on the scales of the psyche, is not all that different from the valence of a worthier object; both are eligible for the Pantheon of Losses. Listen to one such implacable soul expound with poetic intensity on the loss of a pin—a pin, she is at pains to point out, that she bought for thirty dollars at a "junky, secondhand shop": "I loved that pin. From the day I found it to the day I lost it, I was the happiest person. Ever since I lost it, I wander around looking for it." Given such longing, who's to argue the source?

As a rule, I tend to gravitate toward people who don't take even minor losses lightly, who fight and kick and scream. It seems to me that there is something admirable about their defiance. And yet, although there may be greater health in adapting to loss than in becoming fixated on it, in the end we have one loss self-protectively in mind. And which of us, to put it bluntly, would be happy to have our own deaths gotten over too quickly?

The world is full of wisdom—folk and otherwise—about how best to respond to loss, much of it hortatory in nature. And with good reason: The human condition is so full of spilled milk that if we cried too much each and every time, we'd never move on. Most of us have learned by adulthood to reserve our feelings of desolation for the really tragic losses—the deaths of loved ones most signally. It is only in very small children, who haven't yet caught on to the fact that losing and more losing is, as the poet Gerard Manley Hopkins said, "the blight man was born for," that we catch glimpses of our uninured primal selves, inconsolable over the most trivial of privations.

Some years ago, when I was a graduate student, a professor quoted a writer as follows: "The true paradises are paradises we have lost." I later discovered that the reference was to Proust—who, God knows, is unbeatable as far as the plangent evocation of loss goes. In any case, liking the sound of it, I immediately wrote the quote down in my notebook. It's a line I recall often: I'm always looking for antidotes to my inborn nostalgia, and this seems as sprightly a perspective on the matter as any. Still, I'm not sure I believe it, or how much difference it makes. When I am dead and buried I suppose I shall not care at all about the red suede glove I dropped in Central Park fifteen years ago. Meanwhile, I want everything back.

1991

A Complicated Friendship: Remembering Diana Trilling

I first met Diana Trilling in what I could have sworn was the summer of 1977 but turns out, upon my checking the date with someone who was there, to have been two years later. (My memory is a fairly reliable instrument, but since it's Diana I'm writing about, who was such a rigid and exacting chronicler of her own time and place, it seems important to pin these facts down and not let them scamper about.) So it was the summer of 1979: I was staying with friends on Martha's Vineyard, and Diana —who hadn't yet vacated Chilmark, and the uncomfortable proximity of Lillian Hellman, for Wellfleet—invited us all for dinner.

There were other guests that evening, including Daniel and Pearl Bell and the drama critic Robert Brustein, and there was a rather formally served and very tasty meal, but what I recall most vividly was the magisterial presence of Diana herself. I was immediately struck by the apparent ease with which she moved between what I thought of as mutually exclusive roles: that of the facilitating hostess, provider of sustenance and comfort, and that of the dominating, muscular conversationalist—a wittier and far less maternal persona. Being given to a somewhat Manichaean view of the world and still very much torn between the conflicting pulls in my own life—I had recently fled graduate studies at Columbia because of a vision of myself growing as dry and dusty as the stacks in Butler Library—I was fascinated by Diana's Hydra-like ability to straddle different realms. For someone who had come of age just as feminism was heating up its claim that a choice had to be made between being a woman in the restrictive *Kinder, Küche, Kirche* sense of the term or being a woman who was like a man, Diana Trilling came across as a daunting model, suggesting that it was possible to keep the baby while analyzing the problematic nature of the bathwater. There was half a century between us, and yet Diana, who turned seventy-four that August (she had already been a widow for several years), exuded a dazzling energy, a life force that would put a much younger woman to shame.

I had encountered her once before, while I was still a student at Barnard, when I crossed over to the Columbia campus to hear her give a talk on George Eliot's *Middlemarch* (and here again, Diana's corrective spirit hovers, bidding me to check this passing reference for accuracy, but our complicated friendship hinged as much on my spirit of resistance as on anything, so this one will have to stand). She spoke with great authority, with an asperity that didn't allow for sentimental accountings or ideological projections—in itself a relief, back in those days of nascent political correctness—but also, or so it seemed to me, with a discernible air of vulnerability. The subtext of her discussion was the generic condition of the female writer, and she was, after all, a woman with vast intellectual ambitions of her own, who not only had trouble jump-starting her career but had been married for forty-six years to Lionel Trilling, a more accomplished and famous literary figure. There was little she didn't know about male-female trade-offs, wives who played the muse versus wives who polished the silver versus wives who themselves shone with bookish brilliance while their husbands lingered obligingly in the background. (Indeed, two of these luminaries, Mary McCarthy and Hannah Arendt, had exchanged snickering notes about Diana's efforts to obtain cultural eminence beyond her existing reputation as a peerless hausfrau and fiercely protective spouse.)

From the 1940s on, when she began her writing career as a fiction reviewer for *The Nation,* she persisted in airing her outspoken views on everything from the big novels of the day (she deemed Saul Bellow "talented and clever" but *Dangling Man* "not the kind of novel I like"; George Orwell's *1984* led her to observe that "one is disturbed by the book's implacable tone and the extremes of pressure it exerts upon the reader," while of Nabokov's *Bend Sinister* she notes that "by my count the book has four successful moments") to the psychedelic culture of Timothy Leary to the Jean Harris murder case. For the next fifty years, on up through O. J. Simpson and date rape, she continued to render her judgments, in a style that was distinctly cadenced and weighty—sometimes stentorian, but always morally commanding—yet also capable of the odd imaginative leap. Still, there would always be those among the New York Intellectuals—that backstabbing, self-enamored tribe whose members she described (*Commentary* cofounder Elliot Cohen was "a genius of hostile intimacy") and whose customs she documented with bristling affection and no small amount of skepticism in her last book, *The Beginning of the Journey*—who thought she did better at cooking than cogitating.

As our friendship deepened over the next fifteen years, the fears, conflicts, doubts, and even rage that simmered just under Diana's formidable (a word that seems to have been invented with her in mind) surface became clearer to me—and in some paradoxical fashion contributed to my seeing her as a truly valiant character. I think of the two of us talking late into the night after having had dinner together, often as not something curried or a chicken potpie or transcendentally good meat loaf, always accompanied by Diana's monogrammed pink paper napkins. (I note with embarrassment that on the few occasions I tried to return her hospitality, fiasco generally ensued; once I brought over Chinese takeout, but since I didn't own a microwave and Diana rarely resorted to using hers, we heated up the food *in* the plastic containers and had to trash the whole gloppy mess. Another time I arrived at Diana's in the late afternoon with six fresh quail and my culinarily gifted boyfriend in tow. She watched with visible disapproval as he and I proceeded to bicker over the next three hours on the right way to do everything, and when we finally sat down to peck at the bony birds, the atmosphere was grim beyond telling.) It was only after I moved from a ninth-floor apartment—which her fear of heights had prevented her from visiting—to one on a lower floor that I succeeded in entertaining Diana on my own turf.

I remember sitting until past midnight in her small, L-shaped kitchen, with its tall white cabinets and red linoleum floor, at a table with an array of pill bottles on it, and usually a section or two of that day's *New York Times.* Everything was orderly and neat; she was one of the tidiest people I knew, from her desk drawers to her bookkeeping to her dishes. I suppose you could say that this was an extension of her domestic side, except that an almost visceral need to impose precision and logic on the chaotic material of the world was at the heart of her approach both to writing and to life. It seems to me that Diana was afraid of any kind of mess—perhaps because she was on intimate terms with the disorder and darkness that lay in wait on the other side of vigilance. I always thought that her acute interest in emotional problems derived as much from the streak of unhappiness in her own personality, with which she did constant battle, as from having suffered through her husband's bouts of depression. (For all her attachment to the psychoanalytic point of view, Diana was an eminently practical person. At a period when Prozac was still a gleam on the pharmaceutical horizon, she would patiently listen to my arguments that medication could not undo the past and then call to inquire the next morning whether I was taking my antidepressant prescription as I should.)

Diana's passion for order was expressed in any number of habits, some admirable and some less so. She loved ceremony, and although she showed little understanding of the religious impulse, she was a sucker for secular rituals. Her Thanksgiving dinners were planned to the second, with drinks and hors d'oeuvres scheduled promptly for four or five; the appearance of her son, Jim, bearing a golden turkey on a platter into the living room, was the signal to come to the table. She was a crack organizer, with a martial sense of timing and a keenly developed spatial instinct: To watch her instruct her good friend Quentin Anderson on how to position her luggage in the trunk for the annual car ride up to Massachusetts was nothing short of awe-inspiring. But her managerial skills and inflexible standards sometimes precluded an understanding of other people's needs; she could be a terror to work for (Diana was always looking for better, longer-lasting secretarial help) and she could be highly intolerant of even slight deviations from her own routine. On the several occasions I stayed with her on the Cape, we inevitably got into arguments—as often as not about trifles, where I'd placed the jam in the fridge or some such, but also about more basic things, pertaining to a tone I took or the regard I held her in. Diana had a consuming quality to her, and although others may have learned how to negotiate a medium-cool relationship with her, I never did. Still, she was always amenable to making up, and she did not consider it beneath her to broach a reconciliation if we had fallen out. The phone would ring and it would be her plummy voice on the other end, calling me "dear" or "darling," or a note would arrive on her familiar stationery, pale gray or white paper with the letterhead in royal-blue type.

I haven't mentioned how much fun she was, her delight in amusing and being amused. Her more sober side notwithstanding, she adored gossip and a good juicy indiscretion could send her into gales of laughter. Long before the high/low split became a hot cultural topic, Diana had a robust appreciation of the less exalted aspects of life: diets and movie stars and who was sexy and how rich or powerful so-and-so was reputed to be. Although she was a political liberal in the classical sense of the word, she was temperamentally a royalist. (I think it was this latter "grande dame" aspect, reflected in her adherence to bourgeois standards—her insistence that maids wear uniforms, for instance—even on unbourgeois Claremont Avenue, that rubbed certain people, such as

Gore Vidal and Cyril Connolly, the wrong way). She was intensely curious about the English monarchy (she kept a Christmas card from Queen Elizabeth in her bedroom) and liked the glitter of celebrities. Yet she was also genuinely interested in the lives of ordinary people (Diana was the sort of woman who would chat with great ease with her butcher and elicit personal details from her cleaning woman) and she was disinclined to call upon the service of others—continuing to cook and do the dishes into her eighties, when her vision was beginning to fail.

I was always surprised by the fact that she entertained crushes on certain kinds of swaggering men, and that while her eyesight was still good she liked watching macho TV shows, such as *Starsky and Hutch* and *Hill Street Blues*. Her flowing cursive suggested a less restricted person than the one she appeared to be, as did the flowery perfume she wore. Sometimes I had the feeling that buried deep inside her was a wild woman clamoring to be let out, the sort of woman who would stand on top of the piano in the middle of a party and belt out a song. She was laced through and through with contradictions, capable of great pettiness (a mutual friend of ours once remarked that Diana was "always gaveling people out of society") and equally breathtaking acts of generosity.

As old age steadily crept up on her, Diana became thin and frail. She eventually depended on either a cane or the firm arm of a companion to help her walk, but at a time when most women are content to move toward greater disengagement or passivity, Diana retained a psychological hunger—a craving for recognition—that was astonishing to observe. Like many insecure people, she felt chronically undervalued by the world at large; she was never convinced that she had achieved the "life of significant contention," of "public weight," she wished for. "Our heyday seems to be behind us," she told an interviewer shortly before the publication of *The Beginning of the Journey,* referring to what she called "the loss of intellectual glamour" that existed at Columbia when her husband taught there. Perhaps because she feared obscurity most of all, she refused to be shoved off the stage, continuing to write well after her vision had faded and her health declined.

It's hard to believe she is gone, that the snapping vigor of her presence will no longer serve as a reminder to everyone to sit up straighter in their seats. At her funeral last month (at Diana's specification, there were no eulogies, perhaps because she preferred not to be the subject of a conversation she could not preside over), the evident sorrow of her two young granddaughters was a testament to the warmth and charm she exuded when she knew she was loved. It occurs to me, sadly, that my own ferocious love for her became strained over time by an equally ferocious ambivalence that prevented me from responding to her in the last year or two with the wholehearted devotion she so wanted—and needed. I'll miss her in all her splendid difficulty.

1996

On Not Attending My College Reunion

I graduated from Barnard what has come to seem like oh so many years ago (sixteen, to be exact) on a bright day in May. The guest speaker that year was Lillian Hellman, a woman of granite features and obdurate convictions; her certitude about the choices that lay before us seemed at an impossible remove from the clamorous reality not only of Morning-side Heights but of the world as I knew it. I remember myself as a thin-ner, brisker version of my current self—shinier, somehow—standing among my peers, all of us decked out in the solemn vestments of com-mencement: dusky blue robes and those stiff, funny-looking, squared-off caps. Remember this moment, I told myself, trying to imprint its significance on my brain. But it was difficult to focus on the occasion at hand when I was busy worrying whether my mortarboard would fall clownishly askew on my freshly washed-and-cut hair. And maybe it is in the nature of such moments, white-hot as they are, to be pushed to the sides of our lives—to evade direct emotional scrutiny. Perhaps we are afraid that to look too closely at them might prove dangerous, like staring into the sun.

After graduation, as we all know, life goes on. In my case, I went on to a flirtation with graduate school, a variety of jobs in book and magazine publishing, and an intermittent dedication to the notion of myself as a writer. At the close of my twenties, I was saved from an unregenerately tentative grasp of my literary identity (in spite of the fact that I was reviewing for *The New York Times Book Review* and *The New Republic* as well as writing a regular books column for *The New Leader*) by the support and interest of a publisher. He offered me a contract and more money than I was then making as an associate editor at a women's magazine on the basis of no more than a dare and a promise—*his* daring and *my* promise.

I promptly took the opportunity to rid myself of my duties at *McCall's,* which included writing such pieces as "What Your Voice Says About You" and composing copy for what were referred to as the "service" sections of the magazine—food, beauty, and fashion. I can't say I felt much regret about quitting a job where I sat around and mulled over the chirpiest way to open a summer food section on meat loaf ("Ground meat again? That old stand-by of the American table . . ."). Still, it wasn't easy to go from these prefabricated tasks to the more daunting, self-propelled one of writing a novel. When the publisher had gently inquired in his large office high above Third Avenue what I was planning to write about, I had answered that I wanted to write a novel about sexual obsession. After the contract arrived, with nothing to do but write, I stared out the window of my apartment and sat in coffee shops for six months. Then I finally started a novel about my mother.

I tell you all this by way of coming to the somewhat thorny main point of this piece. I would like to explain why I have made it a habit (thus far, at least) not to attend class reunions and why, in a similar vein, I peruse the class notes that appear regularly at the back of the alumnae magazine with a mixture of rabid curiosity and an apprehension bordering on dread. Although I don't doubt that there are some large-hearted Barnard graduates out there, cut from a less competitive—or perhaps more self-contented—cloth than myself, my hunch is that this is the way many of us read them. Here's my friend Bethanie on the subject: "I know too many real stories," she says, "that never translate into notes of achievement, that have no currency in that magazine. I only allow myself to read up until '64 and then again from '88 on, because anything in between them is like standing in a stiff wind. You have to hold on." Behind this feeling, of course, is the not readily acknowledged sense of one-upmanship that many of us harbor toward our peers. It's not the sort of intractably envious feeling that sours one's basic social impulses or disrupts friendships. But as we move further away from the imposed camaraderie of our college years and slowly grow into the more enclosed shape of our adult selves, the urge to merge with our peers—to hang out with like-minded types at the West End or the Mill Luncheonette or Tom's Restaurant—necessarily lessens.

Most of us don't lead the sort of lives you see enacted on television. The typical *thirtysomething* scenario in which a fairly homogeneous bunch of guys and gals gather in Hope and Michael Steadman's kitchen to discuss the latest career hitch or romantic fling of one of the group—like a grown-up, ever-together Spanky and Our Gang—is a beguiling but increasingly faint vision. Take Bethanie again, whose capacity for nostalgia has always struck me as epic and whose tendency in this direction has been exacerbated by living in Milan: She admits to having "happily allowed myself to disappear into another life." In truth, after sharing the particular thrills and anxieties of the interregnum known as college, we all disappear into "another life," and the thread of connection frays yearly.

There is, underneath it all, a simple explanation for my reluctance to partake of commemorative activity when it comes to my alma mater. It involves what I can only call a Machiavellian form of emotional accounting, the sort of bottom-line, three-o'clock-in-the-morning realizations that leave one inwardly gasping: *Is this my life?* Is this really the particular set of circumstances that have come to define me? The problem with college reunions—I know this without having attended any—is that they leave room for too much soul-scorching realism, for observing that you haven't managed to retain your girlish figure like Y, and that Z's career is in great shape even though you looked like the one who was going to soar. Not to mention husbands and children, where the opportunity for invidious comparison is endless.

When it comes to one's peers it's hard not to find oneself mentally comparing life notes, and even more difficult not to find oneself at either pole of envy or smugness. I don't want to gird myself to attend my class reunion only to discover that someone I recall as unbearably flamboyant when she sat next to me in my writing seminar has not ended up a belly dancer as I had imagined, but is now married to a scion of a prominent family, has two children, and is working on her third serious novel. On the other hand, I'd feel equally discomfited to discover that someone I had once admired from afar for her flirtation skills is living alone in an apartment with her dog. Of course, the question to be asked is this: Would someone living alone with her dog be likely to show up? Reunions, like class notes, call upon the public presentation of self; in doing so, it's perhaps inevitable that they attract certain types of people over others. Then, too, there is the commonplace fact that the sharing of accomplishments is so much easier on the ego than the disclosure of failures or disappointments.

I used to tell myself I'd wait to attend a reunion until I had my book done. By the time my novel, *Enchantment,* came out, I was working as a senior editor at a publishing house and was invited to be one of the judges for the Elizabeth Janeway prize (for best undergraduate essay). I might have made my move then. I did return to Barnard to speak at a career panel on the writing business, but I still didn't have it in me to attend a reunion. You see, by that point I had convinced myself that I would be the only graduate from my year not yet married, and that I would inevitably strike others—not to mention myself—as an accomplished but lonely soul. I've since married and am the mother of a little girl, and I still haven't made it back. I guess there are always more excuses not to run out of, if that's what you're inclined to do.

Perhaps the most valuable piece of this ongoing conflict is that it does, indeed, go on, year in and year out, as reliably as Barnard puts out new graduates. You might even say it's become a yardstick of sorts, this reunion-aversion of mine, a way of taking stock—albeit from a safe distance. But one of these days, before the year 2000, I promise myself I'm going to go public: Meet you on the campus lawn.

1991

Notes of a Lonely White Woman

Once upon a time, there was a white upper-middle-class woman (although to hear her tell it she felt, if not poor, then at least strapped for money much of the time), who was heterosexual (although she has recently been made to understand that such proclivities are no more fixed than the evening tide) and Jewish (an ethnic minority historically associated with victimization and literary talent, now held to be under suspicion on both these scores). This woman was also a mother (paid lip service to as a socially useful occupation, but mostly seen as a demographic opportunity for exploitation by ever-proliferating children's stores and by new magazines aimed at parents of "advanced maternal age") and a writer. She was in the habit of ambling through the world, lonely as a Wordsworthian cloud, in search of company to pass the hours when she was not either staring at a blank piece of paper until the drops of blood formed on her forehead (an appealingly dramatic definition of her chosen vocation which she has pasted up on her computer screen), or worrying whether her child was developmentally abreast—if not ahead—of her peers.

She happened one day to come upon a group of women sitting under a tree, their heads bent together in discussion. She approached them shyly, as befitted a newcomer. One of them, evidently the leader, turned to her and asked her whether she had ever explored her bisexuality. Being an honest sort, she shook her head. The leader stared at her sternly. "Don't you read *New York* magazine?" Eager to belong, she answered happily in the affirmative. (Although she subscribed to a number of more demanding and less trendy magazines, *New York* was the one she took to bed when it arrived, happy to graze upon its smoothly ingestible smorgasbord of gossip, reviews, listings, and soft "hard" articles.) Didn't she know, then, that lesbianism was chic? the leader asked her. She allowed that she did, but no one could hear her answer above the din. The leader's voice had risen to a shout: "AND WHAT ABOUT YOUR SELF-ESTEEM, WHAT ARE YOU PLANNING TO DO ABOUT THAT?"

I will here without further ado abandon my lonely white woman to her symbolic predicament—which is in some way the predicament of being a complex person in an age of cultural downsizing—and turn to the underlying problem behind this predicament, which is the problem of "political correctness." I must say right off that although I see "political correctness" as a continuing and pervasive problem, it remains a paradoxically insular one. What I mean by this is that a large part of the world goes about its business without any awareness that the term has come into being, or if they have heard of the term, they remain uncertain as to what it signifies. (Just as the term *multiculturalism* is commonly misunderstood to stand for an old-fashioned "melting-pot" approach to different cultures, rather than the newfangled compensatory approach which looks upon all cultures as either privileged, and therefore inherently bad—or marginalized, and therefore inherently valuable.) This part of the world is privy to political correctness, if at all, in its most watered-down, generalized form—as a form of keeping up, culturally speaking, with the Joneses.

Thus, in June of this year *The New York Times* reported that a teacher's decision to show an anti-abortion film to seventh-grade students in

Westchester County outraged parents and ignited a larger community about how "politically sensitive" issues should be addressed in the public schools. (Presumably a film from a pro-choice viewpoint would not have struck this particular community as troubling in any way.) And in the July issue of *Vogue,* mention was made of a prominent New York socialite who was spotted wearing "the world's first politically correct charm bracelet" (featuring the acronym C for Choice; H for Housing; A for Animal Rights; R for Racial Harmony; and M for Money to Fight AIDS). It was also this summer that I received a note from a magazine editor telling me that an essay I had submitted was too "ethnocentric." What stopped me short was that I couldn't image the word being applied by anyone but a liberally inclined assimilated Jewish editor to anything but an essay on a Jewish theme. If it's Jewish, I thought to myself, it's the wrong kind of ethnocentrism. Next time around I'd try writing as a black Muslim and see who'd dare call me *ethnocentric.* . . .

Clearly, then, there is a whole hierarchy of pieties and subterfuges that accompanies the phenomenon, and one locates oneself according to which level of "correctness" one's antennae have picked up on. One doesn't, in other words, call blacks "Negroes," unless one wants to demonstrate a state of utter indifference to the post-sixties Zeitgeist (or is oneself a black intellectual, in which case the usage is taken to be either affectionate or parodic—and sometimes, confusingly, both). One doesn't call blacks "blacks" either, but rather "African-Americans"—which followed, in turn, upon Afro-Americans, at the urging of Jesse Jackson—unless one wants to exhibit a somewhat somnolent attitude to the more recent developments in the nomenclature of penitence. (*The New York Times,* it's interesting to note, can't make up its mind in the course of one and the same article whether to employ the former or the latter term.)

Then there is the part of the world that *has* heard of "PCism" and its attendant disturbances. Here one is either at pains to distance oneself from the host of implicit and explicit opinions that go along with being a convert to what isn't so much a movement as a singular, heavily media-influenced shift in ordinary modes of cognition (for example, "I know this is very un-PC of me, but I really think most women still want to get married by the time they're twenty-five"). Or one is caught up so firmly in its grip that one can't imagine who would choose the darkness of the pre-PC epoch over the enlightenment of multiculturalism and gender studies.

To ascertain how thin PCism really is, one has only to look at the thinness of the criticism of it. (Camille Paglia, for instance, has gotten as far as she has with her thuggish mode of antifeminism in part because the stage is otherwise empty.) Political correctness has, with a few rare exceptional instances, confounded any critique of itself; the quirky forum of talk radio has spawned its most amusing detractors to date, with Howard Stern being much the funniest. It has successfully, that is, carried off the intellectual spoils of a consumer democracy—with that system's implied promise of equal choices for all and its denial of the continuing realities of power, violence, and class. Jacques Attali, in his provocative jeremiad *Millennium: Winners and Losers in the Coming World Order,* daringly touches upon some of the unresolved imperatives under-lying a market-driven society such as ours, which includes a basic refusal to deal with the politically *in*correct fact that there will always be haves and have-nots: "To be sure," he writes, "a central conundrum remains: how to balance economic growth with social justice."

The real trouble with "political correctness" as it is played out in the media is that it so often appears to be a done deal—the triumph of cul-tural osmosis over realpolitik. What one knows and feels to be true about contemporary life—that AIDS, for example, is not only a tragic plague but also a darling of the press, attended to with an insistence other ravaging diseases (such as breast cancer or schizophrenia) have failed to garner for themselves—is not only not said but defied by con-tinual assertion otherwise. Thus, several days after a sensationalistic piece about having contracted AIDS appeared in *The New Yorker,* the author of this piece could be found declaring in an interview with *The New York Times* that AIDS was ignored by the powers that be!

I can think of no other disease-cum-cause the symbol of which—the telegenic looped red ribbon—is worn so tirelessly, pinned to lapels and collars, at occasions and events that have no connection whatsoever to the subject of AIDS. Hollywood has embraced it as a platform nonpareil, but so have less likely tribunes. "AIDS awareness" has overtaken the arts to a degree that verges on the automatic. Last year, as a judge of the National Book Critics Circle, I was handed a prepinned red ribbon to wear onstage along with the other judges, minutes before the ceremonies began. It simply hadn't occurred to the person who had arranged for this homage to inquire beforehand whether there were any of us who were disinclined to wear the ribbon.

Of course, just as AIDS is a PC illness if ever there was one, so the pro-choice movement in all its uncalibrated stridency is a perfect PC cause. When I suggested to an editor of *Mirabella,* one of the more literate women's magazines, that it would be interesting to write a piece from the "other" side—from the point of view of a woman who supported the right-to-life movement—I was told that the magazine had a policy of not acknowledging such views. *Basta.* The credentials of both the pro-choice cause and the AIDS cause are impeccable, since both imply a subversion of the conventional assumptions of the body politic without directly attacking those assumptions. Both touch, as well, on the all-important issues of class, race, and gender—that trio of analytic cudgels used, in a more academic context, to smash the daylights out of a literary canon perceived as being composed of too many benighted late-nineteenth-century and twentieth-century White European Males.

What is unfortunate is that the quality of irreproachable moral superiority which is one of PC's more insidious characteristics has effectively muffled a frank atmosphere of debate and silenced those who have qualms about its operating principles. To even begin to question the premises of any of its holy causes is to risk being branded a shrill and heartless troglodyte. To suggest, for instance, that in America, at least, AIDS continues to be a very specifically induced, localized disease largely affecting homosexuals and intravenous-drug users and has *not* passed into the heterosexual population in the manner initially predicted and might, therefore, not be the paradigmatic casualty of our times; or to suggest that the right to abortion on demand has had little effect on a large portion of its presumptive beneficiaries—i.e., inner-city, drug-addicted mothers who, ignoring the hard-won option of terminating unwanted pregnancies, continue to bear children at a breathtaking rate without the means to care for said children—is to come up against a horrified reaction to one's "homophobic" or "racist" views.

This brings me, curiously enough, to the not unconnected matter of why I fled the academy. I attended Columbia University as a graduate student in English in the late seventies. Although political correctness was not to be given its official identity for another decade or so, one could see it beginning to gain a toehold. True, the turmoil and disenchantment of the sixties had done much to restore the university to its original nonpartisan purpose of educating, but I sensed the glimmerings of a new style of repressive order in very specific ways. In the first day of a seminar on the British moderns—Samuel Butler, Virginia Woolf, E. M. Forster, et al.—my hip, cowboy-booted professor approached the writers under discussion with all the guilt-ridden hostility of a card-carrying Weatherman. How, he wanted to know, did these writers produced by the British class system account for or deal with the intransigent fact of European hegemony—the global dominance of the British Empire, with George the Sixth straddling the top and the masses of the Third World huddled down at the bottom? Although this was not the first time I had heard the Third World referred to in this way, with an almost axiomatic and curious sense of deference, it was definitely the first time I heard the free world referred to as "the 'so-called free' world." (Remember that this was still in the seventies, before "texts" took over where "novels" had once stood. Too, I had graduated from Barnard College, which, with a few exceptions, had continued to teach English literature not as an offshoot of a larger contextual ideology featuring the oppressed and the oppressors, but as a matter of mere readers and writers.) Even without further exposure, I knew I was not interested in learning how to read with the aid of this pious template that was being clamped down on a subtle and highly individualistic literature, squeezing the juice out of it.

There were other experiences: In another seminar, led by a skeptical but *au courant* Britisher, I read *S/Z* by Roland Barthes and so first glimpsed the lost horizon of deconstructionism. Although I found Barthes's writing entertaining and provocative, I immediately began to wonder whether it offered a deeper elucidation than other, more traditional approaches. (The truth be told, I found myself musing on the pity of it that Barthes wasn't born into a Talmudic family, where his close, irony-filled readings could be applied to less flimsy narratives.) What I had glimpsed, of course, was nothing less than the future—a future filled with dense semiotic murmurings, clogged with atonal words like *marginalized* and *valorized* (not to mention *redactor*), policed by rabid men and even more rabid women. I tucked my Forster and my Woolf under my arm and fled.

I ran, as it happened, straight into the arms of book publishing, which was itself about to be taken over by wave after wave of political correctness. (The furor caused by the publication of Kingsley Amis's misogynist novel, *Jake's Thing,* was just one example—as though misogyny weren't owed faithful literary representation every bit as much as fidelity, say, or uxoriousness.) But since book publishing is a bottom-line enterprise, unlike the academy, PCism is more a matter of cocktail-party patter than anything else. If a book looks like it'll sell, in other words, it makes not a whit of difference whether it's by John Kenneth Galbraith or Rush Limbaugh. (It could be argued that, a few egregious instances of campus censorship of First Amendment rights aside, the triumph of political correctness is, in the end, largely a cocktail-party triumph: a mode of social discourse which ensures that the espouser of its views— however visibly privileged—is taken to be a thoughtful, well-meaning creature, fully attuned to the baneful ways of the democratic society he or she inhabits.)

To sum it up as I see it: Political correctness is a form of specious moral one-upmanship, an unholy stew composed of some stale left-overs from the egalitarian sixties mixed together with an expedient, yuppie-style approach to age-old questions of probity. It posits a false leveling of human topography, as though everyone could be pulled back to the starting gate all the time, and there would always be a referee watching to see that no one had a head start. The bitter truth is that of course there are head starts in real life, just as the bittersweet truth is that being born into money and status doesn't ensure happiness, much less success. I find myself thinking often these days of a deeply cynical adage that used to be invoked with great relish by the publisher William Jovanovich, a self-made, politically incorrect man if there ever was one: "Life's a bitch. And then you die." It strikes me as a more useful aphorism—in its toughness, if nothing else—than what I construe to be the politically correct version: "Life's an apology. And then you go work out."

So, should we sit shiva, or is there any hope? Perhaps the very fickleness of the American psychic landscape—that vast tract filled with enough ontological anxiety and self-promotional genius to accommodate the appearance, within a short span of time, of a given cultural phenomenon and then, inevitably, a counterphenomenon—should give hope. As befits a country founded on the capitalist ethic, the process is not dissimilar to the way in which the stock market is endlessly "correcting" itself. Take, for instance, the way in which the general compulsion to discover traces of sexual or emotional abuse has been followed by the emergence of false-memory syndrome, in which adult survivors of alleged abuse discover that they have been misled by over-zealous therapists into "remembering" incidents that never occurred in the first place!

Media consultant David Garth, who began as a liberal and helped engineer John Lindsay's two mayoral victories, signed on with Rudy Giuliani, as he told *New York* magazine, in spite of an initial perception that Giuliani was "way right of center." "When I got to know him," Garth said, "I saw he was a decent guy, moderate and very smart, much

quicker on his feet than people give him credit for. His major sin seems
to be that he isn't politically correct—*and I've gotten a little sick of political correctness.*"

Many little sicknesses just might make an epidemic, if you see what
I mean. Just as there was once a pre-PC era, so there will be a post-PC
period, with new orthodoxies of its own, no doubt. I'm sure the student
radicals of the sixties never envisioned that the day would come when
Jerry Rubin would start a dating service, or that Abbie Hoffman would
spend his last years peddling fake Rolexes.

As for that lonely white woman out there looking for company:
Perhaps she should start an Anti-Self-Esteem Movement. Anyone care
to join?

1993

Dancing with My Daughter

So here I am, dancing with my daughter in the middle of the day, in my living room, in an apartment the resale value of which is dubious, in a building which gamely tries for Park Avenue jauntiness with a uniformed doorman and topiary out front, on a block marked unmistakably by tenements and a raucous public school, sending all of us spinning toward the greater grime of Lexington Avenue.

Location, location, location: Over thataway are the carriage-trade pleasures of Madison Avenue, stores lofty with imported merchandise for the wee inheritors, hand-stitched smock dresses and English Mary Janes that close with a button instead of a buckle, toys at Penny Whistle and haircuts at Michael's, where a wall of yellowing photos includes a six-year-old John-John in his then-trendsetting longer cut. Over thisaway, looking toward the river, are the Sloanses and pizzerias and Duane Reades serving less exalted needs.

I live, metaphorically speaking, somewhere between Ecce Panis and HMV, between freshly made focaccia and overmarketed new releases from rock bands I should have outgrown years ago. Like k. d. lang, I have a "constant craving" to be filled with I know not what. But something is bound to catch my eye, some gleaming, costly, unnecessary *thing* or other.

And so this is where you'll find me, a thirtysomething woman, half out of a marriage, dancing on this cold Tuesday afternoon with a three-year-old named Zoë, her hair the color of burnt sugar, hair that makes women of a certain type croon, knowing how much it would cost them to duplicate at Louis Licari. Wait just a minute, I long to say to the God of Eclipsed Moments in the Sun. I'm still here, falling off the edge of this glamorous, decaying city, but holding on. Sure, someone is bound to drown me out this year or the next in a tidal wave of achievement. Somewhere, somehow, *at this very moment,* Madonna is doing something focused and ego-building: meeting with movie producers, working out with her trainer, stenciling tattoos on a gay-looking Hispanic who might, just might, be her next boyfriend in time for her next synergistic book/video/music project.

Somewhere, somehow, all over this city, my friends are racing me to the finish line, writing books and would-be books. Will they become more famous than I? (I recognize this is not a profound question but it is a distinctly contemporary one.)

Why is it so much easier to tighten someone else's prose than to unreel my own? In the last two weeks alone, I've done enough unpaid editorial work—from rewriting one friend's flap copy to shaping another's book proposal—to set up my very own publishing house. Then again, I have a novel under contract to finish and a patient editor who can't fathom my hankering after unworthy distraction—all that is gleaming, costly, unnecessary.

Discipline is remembering what you want. I pass this wisdom on to you, noted several days ago in the window of a bookstore selling religious books. I remember what I want, but I keep forgetting where I put it. Meanwhile, I try to sort out my piles of papers, the Amex receipts, the phone bills, bank deposit slips, all the things I tore out intending to read. It is a cold Tuesday afternoon on which I play a tape I bought in Grand Central Station, featuring the undulant melodies of Antara del

Barrio, a group of street musicians who appeared before me the other evening, as if in a sunlit vision, as I made my way to the IRT between the homeless and the departing Connecticut commuters. The plaintive Latin sound of maracas, recorder, and drums sings out to me in my non-barrio dwelling here on the fabled Upper East Side, where I dance with my red-haired daughter, in this, the winter of our discontent, in the middle of the day, in my living room.

1993

In the Country of Divorce

THE LAY OF THE LAND

Who could know it would be this way—that you enter the country of divorce at your own peril and leave it a changed person? (If and when you enter: Be prepared to stay awhile, bring plenty of clean underwear and reading material, but most of all bring lots of cash.) Who could know, given the fact that divorce rolls so trippingly off the tip of the cultural tongue these days—everyone's doing it, at least one out of two couples —that you'd think it would be easy, or at least not all that hard.

Well, think again. The breakup of a marriage, American-style— especially if there's a child involved—is more in the spirit of war than you'd believe possible of a negotiation between two people who once slept side by side. Amiable instances are rumored to exist, although I have yet to encounter one. It's a rough sport, this divorcing game, and the financial bloodletting is not the worst of it. I realize that each person's experience is unique, but what I've discovered these past three long —*very* long—years is that a process that began in dire seriousness gradually took on, somewhere into the second year when my ex-husband-to-be and I sat for hours in a shabby courtroom with peeling walls while our lawyers chatted and the judge listened to other cases, an atmosphere of the surreal. What was I doing here, in a near-empty room dominated by an American flag and a feeling of grim supplication? (Once you appear before a judge, you are placing your fate in the hands of what you devoutly hope will be justice.) And how would I ever get out?

In our beginnings are our ends, only for some of us the beginnings never get off the ground. I got married in a sea of doubts, a thicket of anxieties—pick whichever metaphor of turmoil you prefer, and it would apply—and although I suppose for some reluctant brides the institution of matrimony in itself exerts a certain calming influence, in my case I remained a reluctant bride from first to last. I say none of this happily, but it seems to me that it's important to tell the truth about one's own circumstances if one is to shed some light. My marriage had its besetting problems, yet I've come to think that what distinguishes a marriage that lasts from one that doesn't isn't how good or bad the union in question is but how tolerable the partners find it to be. We all know of atrocious marriages that continue to drip, Jackson Pollack– like, across the canvas of life until the death of one of the spouses, or of wobbly but not inherently hopeless ones that topple over before you can say Raoul Felder.

What I'm trying to suggest is that there's some sort of psychic bartering that goes on within most enduring marriages—he's a bore at dinner parties but he pays for the clothes and the shrink, or she's a bitch most of the time and hasn't learned how to cook but she looks great in a strapless gown—that doesn't get articulated in public, because it's not in anyone's interest to do so. (The great Marxist theoreticians notwithstanding, most cultures are profoundly conservative in nature. Sure, there are those brief historical interims in which everything we've taken for granted about marriage, motherhood, and morals seems to be up for grabs, but stick around long enough and you'll see the pendulum swing back again.) Marriage, however it gets reconfigured from time to time, is indubitably part of the proven way of doing things: It works, more or less; besides which, no one's figured out a better way of ensuring that the male of the human species sits down to breakfast with the female on an ongoing basis.

This, at any rate, is how I've come to see it, over in the muddy marshes of Divorce Country in which I've gotten bogged down: The institution of marriage is a complex, partial satisfaction of myriad needs —sexual, romantic, and economic. It varies so radically from one couple to the next as to lack all criteria of the "norm." There are those spouses who function with an almost claustrophobic quality of togetherness; others who prefer to live in different cities. But somewhere along the way, no matter what a particular marriage looks like from the outside, the two people inside have to feel comfortable with how their respective sides of the equation tally. Contrary to advice-column wisdom, which has it that the small differences are what eventually do a marriage in, it is my belief that the big conflicts—clashing notions of intimacy, say, rather than tension over putting caps on toothpaste tubes—are what land two people in real trouble. I, for instance, married a man who left me feeling lonely not because he wasn't home but because he *was*. I found myself circling him nervously, my troth plighted to this alien presence plopped down in the middle of my one-bedroom apartment, until the day came when I stuffed two suitcases full of courage and ran for the hills. I felt like one of the Von Trapp family at the end of *The Sound of Music,* scrambling over the mountains that linked neutral Switzerland to Nazi Austria; I didn't know if I'd survive the journey, but I knew that staying where I was would doom me to a worse fate than the one that lay ahead.

CROSSING THE BORDER

I am lying in bed at two or three in the morning, a year into my divorce. My young daughter is asleep in her crib in her room with its lovingly chosen toys and stenciled border of pastel-colored ducklings. I have watched TV, read a sprinkling of magazines, and still I cannot fall asleep due to the anxiety that clutches at my chest. I begin making lists in my head, dividing categories into subcategories—an activity that has often soothed me in the past: How many divorced women do I know? Divorced women with children? Divorced women without children? Divorced women who have remarried? Failed to remarry? How long do you have to have been married for it to look like you've given it the old college try? (If I stretch things, and include the months my husband refused to move out of the apartment and slept on a chaise longue in the living room, it just makes the three-year mark. Which means I've been divorced as long as I've been married.) I look up at the ceiling and start enumerating my virtues as a marital partner for the benefit of the Great Judge in the sky: long legs, good hair, intelligence, wit, empathy, and erratic kindness. He shakes His head at me, and in my heart of hearts I know He recognizes that I am an inadequate person. Why else would I be getting a divorce?

TRAVEL TIPS FOR FIRST-TIME VISITORS

Divorce is a country that doesn't recognize the high road; once you enter it, be prepared to put aside any mainland principles about decency and fairness. Be prepared, in other words, to put on your hiking boots and forge through the mud. I'm on my second lawyer—third, if you count the lawyer I went to for several meetings before I decided she would be too expensive. The next lawyer was a partner in a less prominent firm; he was a softhearted, perennially distracted sort whom I think I chose because he made me feel less guilty about standing up for myself. (My guilt had much to do with the fact that it was I who had initiated divorce proceedings; the fact that my husband immediately retaliated by suing for sole custody of our daughter should have gone a long way toward assuaging that guilt, but strangely did not.) I had been told that this lawyer was "good for women"—and he did, indeed, seem to harbor little animus against either sex. But he also seemed to expend minimal energy on my behalf, and as the months went by and my phone calls went unreturned and my husband continued to live in our apartment even though I had already filed for divorce, loudly finding fault with my every move as a mother (his specialty was to emit a grim chuckle whenever I spoke up against his rigid ideas about child-rearing, as if to suggest that I was the last person to have any say in these matters), I realized I would have to make a change.

The lawyer I have retained since then is a smart, scrappy woman in practice for herself. My relationship with her has been tempestuous; it has survived any number of confrontations, ranging from her verdict on the tone of the message on my answering machine ("too flaky") to my verdict on her style of giving me instructions ("authoritarian"). She is involved in the feminist end of law, which alarmed as much as it attracted me: I wanted to make sure she understood that I was not getting my divorce on behalf of the women's movement, and that I was not interested in taking a rhetorical—if right-minded—position that would endanger my chances.

Truth be told, there is nothing like a divorce to make a Madonna out of a Tammy Wynette. Nothing like a divorce, that is, to make even the most accommodating and least politicized female sit up and take note of the fact that the judicial system is run primarily by men who tend on the whole to favor women who stay at home and busy themselves with *Kinder* and *Küche*—and to regard with punitive suspicion (however unconscious) those women who want it every which way, the career and the children and the divorce. In this regard, the more strident agendas of the women's movement (which include an implicit devaluation of motherhood and an insistence on equal roles at home) have done an inadvertent disservice to divorcing professional women who also happen to be passionate mothers. It's a curious phenomenon, hard to understand until you're caught in the middle of it: All the tradition-bound attitudes that men were left to struggle with in the last three decades while women were busy taking great strides forward in the workplace seem to resurface over the issue of child custody. "In the fifties," observes a psychiatrist I know, "you could shoot up heroin and you'd still get the child because you were the mother." In the nineties judges are supposed to be "gender neutral." Fathers who want to be the custodial parent tend to be given the benefit of the doubt (up to 40 percent petition for custody, the majority of whom win), and the burden of proof has been shifted onto mothers, especially if they work outside the home.

LEARNING THE LANGUAGE

A question: Why is the vocabulary so woefully underdeveloped? I can understand how, long ago in the dark ages of divorce, when unmarried women were still referred to as spinsters and the concept of "quality time" hadn't yet been invented, the need for a more fluid terminology was scant. But now that divorce has become a thing of custody suits that stretch on for years; of forensic psychiatrists who conduct painstaking interviews and pay house visits as though one or the other of the parties dabbled in serial murder; of legal counsel garnering astronomic fees by the hour, I surely can't be the first person to find herself at a descriptive loss. Who is my daughter's father to me now that we are no longer married but not yet divorced? This is pure semantics, never mind the more existential stuff: Is he, linguistically speaking, my "ex-husband-to-be," which sounds like a mangled form of Latin, or should I refer to him as my "estranged husband," which sounds even clumsier, as though he's been swallowed by a whale?

GOING NATIVE

Sex seems so far away, an island that's floating farther and farther off since I've been living alone. In the beginning of my divorce I didn't think about sex much, lost as I was in feelings that precluded erotic pleasure, feelings that had to do with ancient conflicts about the "wrongness" or "rightness" of my being. Perhaps I wasn't lovable (even though it was I who wanted out); perhaps I didn't know how to love. How to explain this abiding sense of shame, this lingering feeling that it was all my own fault? I might remark here that I find it curious that over the last two years not one person among my wide circle of friends has asked me how it feels to live alone—physically alone—after living with a man. It is as if my sexual feelings have become taboo, a link to the banished privileges of the connubial bed. (It occurs to me that this must be the way the elderly feel they're treated, as though their libidos have vanished along with their muscle tone).

I go into bookstores and furtively look at the section that carries titles on divorce and child custody, hoping not to be spotted. After I buy the books, they lie unread on my night table as I escape into the romantic world of late-night movies; it seems I am not willing to become an official part of the getting-a-divorce population. When I'm not avoiding the subject altogether, I keep trying to figure out the reasons for my unease. True, I come from an Orthodox Jewish background, where divorce is relatively infrequent, and all five of my siblings are married to their original spouses. But I gave up being Orthodox years ago, and I now move in a world where divorce is rife. So how to explain it?

Ah, here we come upon the gap—crevasse, actually—between the reality that is bruited about in magazines and the reality that is felt by one nonstatistical adult female within the context of her daily life. To wit: Divorce may not have the stigma it once had, but it is still cause for anxiety. Marriage, as one of my restlessly married friends says, is a "cover," a form of social armor: You can go to parties and announce, "This is my husband," and the world will smile upon you as one of their suitably partnered own. The divorced woman suggests, by her very presence, a threat to the status quo; she carries with her the subliminal risk of her own instability, her lack of conviction about so important a decision as whom she should marry. Worse yet, there is the specter of her singleness with its accompanying burden of emotional neediness. (Present yourself as a married woman and you are free to indulge in "safe flirting"; present yourself as a divorced woman and you are seen as a potential predator.) Worst of all, she suggests the possibility that the marriages around her may themselves fall apart. Which brings me to a conundrum: Why is it that, in the logistics of courtship, divorced women often seem older than they actually are, while divorced men seem younger?

■ ■ ■

HEART OF DARKNESS

It is the end of May, a weekend afternoon on the cusp of summer, breezy and shining. I am sitting on a bench facing Manhattan's East River, with a Walkman and a book. On the promenade behind me people amble, run, ride bikes, and parade by in a joyous celebration of family life—arms entwined, offspring perched on shoulders or gurgling in strollers. Everybody's a pair, everyone's been married for years, even the young-looking couples have an air of long-standing domestic contentment. Or so it seems to me, sitting by myself despite the fact that I am the mother of a four-and-a-half-year-old daughter, whose father I had known for six years before I married him in my parents' living room. I am a woman in the middle of a divorce that seems to have gone on forever, and today is my daughter's day with her father, leaving me to my own devices.

I lean down to pick up a page of newspaper that has landed near my bench. An advertisement in bold type catches my eye: It turns out to be for a group that meets weekly to discuss the anxieties of going through divorce. This could be taken for a sign from above, except that I am uncomfortable with the notion of divorce, painful as it is, being converted into yet another arm of the endlessly proliferating support-group industry. Then, too, I find it hard to envision talking to friends—let alone complete strangers—about my fears: Is there an amorous future after divorce? Will there ever be a second husband? And if there is, will he be better than the one I'm divorcing? How am I to define myself now that I'm no longer that solemn creature known as Wife—now that I've blown off the man I vowed to honor, cherish, and respect until death did us part? I recognize, of course, that I have other parts left to play—as writer, friend, mother, daughter, sister, aunt—but they all seem to pale next to this lapsed one: Once I was married, the wife of X; now I am not. What I've discovered is that the things people warn you about going into a divorce have to do with the time, expense, and difficulty of it; what they don't warn you about is the sheer craziness—that unique combination of outer-directed rage and equally furious self-incrimination—that the process induces. (At some point I am loaned a book about divorce called, literally, *Crazy Time*. Alas, the title seems too close for comfort and I never do more than glance at it.)

DREAMING OF ELSEWHERE

To this day I find it unbearably sad to discuss with my daughter why her parents no longer live together. Oh, I've trotted out all the *Good House-keeping* seal-of-approval phrases and explained that no, I didn't think we'd all be one family again, and yes, Daddy and I both loved her the same as we always had even though we couldn't get along with each other. But there is something in me that rebels against the whole tinny enterprise of justifying inchoate adult behavior to a little girl grappling with abstract concepts like love and constancy and sorrow. So not long ago I bought a video called *Divorce Can Happen to the Nicest People,* and on a recent Saturday night my daughter and I cuddled up in my bed to watch it. The film failed to hold our attention: The most interesting thing about it for me was that the screenplay was written by Peter Mayle —who went on to publish the phenomenally successful books about going to live in Provence with his family. The video wasn't half over before Zoë had fallen asleep, her mouth slightly open, her arms askew. I leaned over to give her a kiss, and then I lay in the dark, wondering if Peter Mayle had written about divorce from personal experience and whether my own life might change dramatically for the better after my divorce became final and whether I would create a new family with the man I loved and go on to write best-sellers, and the horrendous particulars of my first marriage, the bickering, and taunting and twisting of intimate details into weapons, would fade away. . . .

LETTER FROM ABROAD

When I think about my divorce, I keep coming back to the opening sentence of L. P. Hartley's *The Go-Between,* one of those gently cadenced British novels that is eerily familiar with the bleaker aspects of human behavior: "The past is a foreign country: They do things differently there." It could just as well apply to the permanent present tense in which the breakup of marriages takes place: *Divorce is a foreign country: They do things differently there.* If I've learned anything from my sojourn in this strange land, it's that I'm made of tougher stuff than I once thought. You're born alone, you die alone, and you get divorced alone. It's taken me a while to wrap my mind around that obdurate fact, but now that I've finally adjusted to this chilly new landscape, I'm looking forward to making my way back one of these days to friendlier climes. Somewhere beyond the horizon shimmers the vista of Life-After-Divorce. I'm sure it's a country filled with potholes and roadblocks all its own, but from where I'm standing it looks like nothing less than paradise.

1994

The Death of Private Life

O Whither Hast Thou Led Me, Egypt? — The Fate of Richard Burton

Long before his death in 1984 of a cerebral hemorrhage at the age of fifty-eight, it had become customary to speak of Richard Burton as having carried about him an aura of unkept promise, of failed destiny. He was viewed in terms that were almost cinematic: in a golden, soft-focused light. Like the Hamlet he played and replayed, Burton was understood to be a man marred by his own self-destructive urges—for wine and women—and by a tragically compromised ambition. In 1975, the cuttingly perceptive critic Kenneth Tynan, a contemporary who had called the actor one of "the young lions" of the postwar British stage, lamented that "Burton went his own way, which was the theatre's loss, and, really, not much of anyone's gain." Posthumous comments made the same point more gently. "I feel nothing but sadness," John Gielgud told *The New York Times*. "He chose a rather mad way of throwing away his theater career. . . ." Then, as if to assuage his own sense of disappointment, Gielgud added: "He was awfully good to people and generous."

Burton's oversize personality had always lent itself to other people's exaggerations: His first girlfriend admitted to his biographer, Paul

Ferris, that Burton was "perhaps a shade too stimulating for me, a bigger personality than I could cope with." Then, too, the actor seemed to enjoy conspiring in the creation of his own legend. Beginning in the late sixties, several years after he married Elizabeth Taylor and was commanding enormous fees for his film appearances, Burton spoke of returning to the stage. He offered a Faustian image for his predicament: "Everybody is offered a choice: one easy, one difficult. Most men, regardless of their craft, profession, or background, are faced at one time or another with an obvious, easy one and a difficult, more rewarding one."

Richard Burton was an odd, capricious man—a mixture of great drive and great carelessness, with a streak of Celtic melancholy and perverseness. (He would draw on these traits in one of his most powerful performances—as the pecked-at and pecking George, in *Who's Afraid of Virginia Woolf?*) One wonders if he may not have been too intelligent for movie stardom. It is conceivable that Burton, who had a reputation as a wit, was possessed of too acute a sense of irony about the fuss and stir surrounding the limelight. There is also another possibility: that the conventional myth of Success may not have lured Burton as much as the more Romantic notion of once having had it all only to throw it away. If there is truth in this, then Burton can be seen as a latter-day disciple of the Victorian pedagogue and essayist Walter Pater—inspired by the Art of Life, the moment's "hard, gem-like flame," rather than the Life of Art.

Burton appeared to suggest something of this attitude in his world-well-lost-for-love liaison with Elizabeth Taylor. He attributed the weak links in his character to the Welsh in him, to an inherited "talent for decadence and corruption." But did he mean this remark any more than he meant the others? What was a put-on and what wasn't? After years of practice, did even Burton recognize the difference? Perhaps the most pertinent question is this: Was the real Richard Burton a passionate ham —and his manqué quality just another of the roles he liked to play—or was he a man with an unfulfilled passion for serious acting?

■   ■   ■

All myths, even the most glamorous, have to begin somewhere. The clues to the shape Richard Burton's life would take reside partly in his beginnings, in the bare Welsh landscape that bred him. Born in 1925 in the depressed mining valley of Pontryhydfen, South Wales, Richard Jenkins was the tenth of thirteen children. His mother died when he was two, and the family split up. Richard's fate might well have followed the humble pattern of boys from his and other impoverished villages had he not, at the age of eleven, received a scholarship. At the Port Talbot Secondary School, under the fiercely devoted tutelage of a young English teacher named Philip H. Burton (who would, as Richard's legal guardian, eventually provide him with his surname), Richard prepared for the stiff entrance exams to Oxford and Cambridge. An author of BBC radio scripts and lover of theater, Philip Burton first noticed the dramatic promise of his pockmarked protégé. He coaxed Richard's thick Welsh accent into a proper, precise, but un-plummy British and weeded out the brambles from a voice that he described as being "raspy and uncontrolled" and having "no range"; it became the richest of vocal instruments, referred to by the actor himself as "the Burton voice." Lest one deduce that the genius lay in the shaping rather than in the raw material, Philip Burton was quick to point out that his famous student had "a natural feeling for poetry from the word 'go.' I never gave him that."

Burton seems to have taken this appreciation of the music of words through his life with him. It embodied all that was positive—that was innocent—about his past, and it explains why he had a need to return to his Welsh roots, both emotionally and physically. Although fame and wealth would take him a great distance from the spare, orderly existence in which his siblings remained (and Burton was too realistic to imagine that he could return permanently), he continued to view the life he left behind with a degree of nostalgia. "This part of the world," he told a reporter who accompanied him on his pub-crawling one evening in South Wales, "is vulgar but honest. I couldn't settle down here, the life's too starved. But I was born here and I like to come back." It seems one of his most authentic and most heartfelt sentiments.

Audiences were always drawn to Burton's eyes: The palest of blue, they were wide set and, depending on his mood and the role, chilly or blazing. From the very first there was something about those eyes, some quality of almost feral awareness, that moved people to read excitement into the mere fact of Burton's presence onstage. "This young man," gushed a member of the Stratford company he joined in his early twenties, "brings on a cathedral in his eyes." Freshly down from university himself, Kenneth Tynan thought that the twenty-five-year-old Burton, playing Prince Hal in Shakespeare's *Henry IV*, could "make silence garrulous."

There were also a few who noticed that Burton's gaze was as impenetrable as it was penetrating—used to conceal aspects of himself as much as to reveal aspects of the character he portrayed. One director described Burton's face as "a magnificent mask"; another thought that he didn't really use himself in his roles. And Tynan, watching Burton's Othello *and* Iago in 1956, expressed doubts about the actor's willingness to extend himself emotionally: "Within this actor there is always something reserved, a secret upon which trespassers will be prosecuted, a rooted solitude which his Welsh blood tinges with mystery. Inside these limits he is a master. Beyond them he has much to learn."

None of these qualms detracted from an overall sense of excitement about Burton's future. The awareness of that "something reserved" may have added tantalizingly to the prospect of what he might do when he let go. The cognoscenti slated Burton for theatrical greatness—the heir presumptive to Laurence Olivier. But his real appeal was generated by a different undercurrent, as Anthony Quayle, the young Burton's director at Stratford, described it to Paul Ferris: "It's some peculiar quality which interests men and excites women, a latent power to disturb. You hardly have to open your mouth, if you have it."

By the time he was thirty-six, Burton had traveled—with slight and, in hindsight, quixotic deviation—the traditional route toward a classical dramatic career. He had spent years acting in productions of Shakespeare at Stratford and the Old Vic, England's most prestigious repertories. True, he had dabbled in a batch of mostly undistinguished movies for Hollywood (*My Cousin Rachel,* with Olivia de Havilland, was the exception, garnering respectful reviews). Burton also appeared in some domestic films, including the screen version of John Osborne's *Look Back in Anger.* His most recent role had been as King Arthur in the Lerner and Loewe musical *Camelot,* a hit on Broadway. The year was 1961, the season was spring. Burton, successor to a "throne" almost as sacred to the hearts of the British public as the monarchy itself, accepted after elaborate negotiations the part of Mark Antony in the trouble-plagued 20th Century-Fox production of *Cleopatra.*

From this point on, nothing would be the same. In the next two years Burton threw over many of the vestiges of his former life—most noticeably his marriage to Sybil, the Welsh native he had wed at twenty-four and with whom he had two children. With the dissolution of this union came not only the shadowing of his personal reputation as an inconstant but long-standing husband but also a tangible shift from his prior commitment to the stage. Once Burton married his violet-eyed Cleopatra in 1964, he began to focus his energies on movie projects, preferably those with parts for both of them. Then, too, by aligning himself with Taylor, a star since the age of twelve, Burton automatically became a star, a *celebrity,* in his own right. Now Burton had the visibility he had yearned for as a fledgling actor, when he had spoken to friends of wanting people to stand in line to see him—but on a scale he hadn't envisioned. "How did I know this woman was so fucking famous?" he once, somewhat disingenuously, exclaimed. "She knocks Khrushchev off the front page."

With his new celebrity and increasing film offers came ever more money. In fairness to Burton, it had never been clear that acting for him was an end in itself. He had never really aspired to be the sort of holy-oath actor that his old teacher had wanted him to be. He had always been open about his interest in amassing wealth. In the early days, well before this ambition seemed plausible, Burton anticipated it: In 1957 he became a Swiss resident to avoid paying English taxes.

Although the public construction he put on the misuse—or is it betrayal?—of his talent was vastly cynical, the motive behind it may well have been less of his making and more guilt-inspired than he allowed. If he were to escape the grimy fate meted out by the Depression to his father, siblings, and cronies, who knows but that the most acceptable excuse—to everyone, but mainly to himself—was that he did it for a concrete gain, "for the money in it," as he later would say. Movies, however trashy, paid; the stage, however classy, didn't.

Beyond this it is also possible that the man who said fame and money were "pernicious," while pursuing both, simply couldn't live up to his own dazzling endowment. There is an implicit burden in being so gifted: One is expected to deliver on the promise, to fill out the projected image with substantial achievement. Instead, Burton fell back on the glamour that his presence suggested and let it do his work for him. "In a sense," he told *The New York Times,* "I'm totally alienated from the craft that I employ so superficially and successfully." Eventually the role he played best was of himself as dissolute; an expense of passion in a waste of mind. Perhaps he needed an Elizabeth Taylor to feel out the limitless potential—and potential limits—of his primary desires.

His appeal, to both sexes, was enormous. He seems to have been possessed of a natural largesse, the sort that generates goodwill in others. Perhaps the depth of response he elicited, while withholding much of himself, had to do with the state of perpetual contradiction he suggested. Burton had an almost childlike habit of scanning the road not taken as though he just might travel it; he told a television interviewer in 1977 that he would have liked to be one of those "quiet, brilliant writers" who "notice, like Chekhov's Trigorin, that cloud is shaped something like a grand piano." To the rest of us, this seemed to propose the hope of impossible resolutions: that we could burn our bridges and then recross them, as the urge arose; that there is no right season in which to use our gifts, but that they are patiently waiting for us, ready to be reclaimed. By his lack of forthrightness—in love with the spot-light, he continued to profess that he most admired writers, the "absolute anonymity" of them—Burton enabled us to read the enigma of our own personalities, the impediments and incompletions, into his, and to be assuaged. His refusal to be pegged implied one of the most deeply ingrained and unrealizable of human wishes: that it is never too late and that nothing is ever lost.

Burton kept coming back to the idea of playing King Lear. In a career that seemed almost studiously insouciant, this was the one role that obsessed him. Here was Lear, who indulged himself in majestic mis-takes, in an imperious but infantile vision of love and splendor, and achieved a different kind of triumph in the end. Denuded of his former trappings, the king sees into the subtlety of things—the critical nuances that fame beclouds. Lear would have provided for all the selves within him, the flamboyant and lordly as well as the quiet and pensive. Burton had Lear's voracious will and his sustained capacity to revive himself. When his life ended, there seemed to be a little less energy, a bit less excitement in the night sky—as though a star had winked out.

The adjective used most often to describe him was *virile.* And there is no doubt that Burton suggested, in an age of increased sexual anxiety, an abiding male principle. But one sensed that he was more complicated than any one image. There was, in spite of his connection to others and particularly to women, a solitary essence at his core. Behind the poses of The Great Lover, The Great Boozer, The Great Lost Talent may have been dreams that no woman or drink could fill: a dream of coherence, perhaps, of a self well met. He called it up once when he referred to "a kind of longing for something, a kind of idiotic, marvelous, ridiculous longing."

This longing trailed him throughout his career, like a whiff of regret. It accounts, unmistakably, for the aspect of Richard Burton that was touching and admirable: his inclination, in a time of rampant soul-baring, to wrestle with the really bothersome inner demons offstage, in private.

1985

How Dreary to Be Nobody

Long ago, before the advent of Blaine Trump, before the concept of personal publicists had hit the world on its head and Howard Rubenstein had yet to set up shop, life was lived largely under the panoply of the private. It was considered unseemly—but how quaint a notion "seemliness" now appears, along with white gloves and straw boaters—for a woman to appear in print on more than the proverbial three occasions: birth, marriage, and death. As for men, they were allowed a bit more personal phosphorescence, given the right degree of civic-minded accomplishment or philanthropic virtue. (Ambition of the less righteous sort surely had its impact, but the rascally morals of the rich and famous were not yet overlooked with a wink and a smile.) For most of the people most of the time, it is safe to assume, the vision of fame remained just that—a vision, something embodied by the new stars of the silver screen and an occasional Rockefeller or Carnegie. To be *not famous* long ago was to be, simply, ordinary, a fate understood to be part of the natural order of things.

We breathe a different air now in the late eighties, the room-filling oxygen of incessant celebrity. Andy Warhol has come and gone the better to divide the world—with infinite adolescent cliquishness—into somebodies and nobodies. We are left, most of us who used to find private life sufficient, with the sense that we have been handed a fate worse than a glamorous death. No longer can we smile with bemused pleasure at the reclusive Emily Dickinson's couplet, learned in the innocence of childhood, extolling the wonders of anonymity: "How dreary to be somebody / How public like a frog. . . ." For we know better these days. The true dreariness is being a nobody.

> Everyone wants to feel like they're part of their time. In the past you got it from church and home: That was reality. Now you're not alive unless you see your picture in print. You're as young as your last flattering photo, as alive as your columns of print.
>
> —A young publicist

1

Le Cirque on Tuesday night toward the end of June quivers with an almost palpable aura of expectation. On the gleaming dessert cart near the entrance oval ramekins of crème brûlée sit in glazed perfection next to snowy mounds of floating island. It is minutes before the social season gives its last gasp and the season-conscious folk who frequent this restaurant on Sixty-fifth Street just off Park Avenue go away for the summer to their green places in the country—to the Hamptons, Connecticut, and the Cape. The women who occupy its crowded-together banquettes (the Frostian spirit of good fences making for good neighbors is obviously not the abiding one here) are dressed in expensive shades of blond hair and clothes shot through with persimmon and royal red. Flanking them are tanned men in crisp shirt cuffs, with here and there a prosperous double chin. Unveiled in the light of the figured wall sconces are any number of such couples, looking disconcertingly one like the other, dining in groups of four and six. There is a cover charge of five dollars per person at Le Cirque, and the reservations are still ego-gratifyingly hard to come by. But wait, hold it a second, *where's* the floor show? Andy Warhol would have a shit fit. *No one who is anyone is here tonight.* The room may be abuzz with the feeling of power, but the longer one attends to it, the more simulated it feels; the real wattage is clearly elsewhere.

Eleanor Lambert, who is the elderly but still-vigorous doyenne of upper-echelon publicists, and who "knows everybody and can make anything happen" according to *Town & Country,* explains the situation to me as I sample an appetizer of Le Cirque's famed and much-imitated pasta primavera: "Not one person who's social is here tonight—they go to people's houses this time of year. This is an entirely different crowd than lunch. They look like out-of-towners and Mafia, don't you think?"

To explain some more: At lunch Le Cirque is like a club, peopled with the nouvelle society—the faces one recognizes from *Women's Wear,* Liz Smith, Suzy, and the gaggle of gossip columnists who honk after them. Megabuckster Ronald Perelman holds his business lunches here, and a table is said to be reserved for him every day until twelve-thirty, complete with an elasticized cushion for his bad back. But at dinner tonight the blondes are not ashy enough and the tans are too beach-club brown: They are mere groundlings, to borrow Richard Schickel's term for the nonfamous, even I can see that.

There is a riddle-within-a sphinx quality to this thing called visibility. Not only are there specific seasons to show yourself, but specific meals. Then, too, there are the watering holes that have, due to imperceptible shifts in social reckoning, outworn their allure. What we seem to have stumbled upon here, apparently, is the tacit principle at work in the machinery of celebrity—a principle of exclusivity that tantalizes us with the idea of a charmed circle outside of which stand, Oliver Twist– like, the hungering multitudes. "Even if not everyone wants to be them," says a veteran of the circuit, "everyone wants to know what it's like to be there with them." Le Cirque, or so it seems on this evening in late June, has become well known for being well known (which is, of course, historian Daniel Boorstin's definition of celebrity) and in so being attracts less "society" and more of "the people nobody knows."

"Society," of course, no longer connotes the bounded, self-regarding world of the Four Hundred—that moniker coined for the number of lineaged, old-moneyed people who could comfortably fit into Mrs. Astor's ballroom circa 1880. What "social" now suggests is something infinitely more amorphous—"every guy with a million dollars, chic, and in black tie," to quote Warhol—and more compulsively intent on the limelight. There are no arrivistes in this set, no such thing as money too recently made or a background too déclassé. What there is instead is the craving for "exposure" and the magic wand of the personal publicist or well-placed socialite friend—a Marilyn Evins or John Scanlon or Patricia Patterson (the latter reputed to have "invented Anne Bass in New York")—helping to create a visible self for the charity circuit, for Alice Mason's coveted dinner parties, for the party pages of *Vanity Fair, Quest, Vogue, Town & Country* et al. The "social" are no longer content to "stay home and get massages," as they did in the days of Cholly Knickerbocker; they want a piece of the celebrity action. Blame it, among other things, on Truman Capote, and his fabled masked ball that's "never been topped." On November 28, 1966, at the Plaza Hotel, Capote gathered together the newly anointed—movie stars, writers, politicians, and power brokers of every stripe. His "social X-ray" friends, like Babe Paley and Gloria Guinness, were slyly thrown into the heap, and the portals of celebrity widened to include the rich, thin, mostly blond wives and tycoon husbands who dined at the power restaurant of that moment, La Côte Basque.

The ultimate restaurant of New York today, according to Eleanor Lambert, the restaurant to be seen having lunch and dinner at, is La Grenouille, of the justly famous flower arrangements. And the only place to be seated there, I am told, is the front room; the back room is "Siberia": "Anyone with any hope of belonging would be offended to be put there." The day I have lunch there—in the front room—the power seems to be coming off its lime silk-fabric-covered walls like a silent, energizing ether. Directly in front of me Diane Von Furstenberg, looking containedly leonine, is having lunch; at the table to my right is a debonair Oscar de la Renta and to my left is the publisher of a giveaway, advertising-heavy magazine devoted to covering subjects of particular interest to residents within the 10021 zip code. Not an out-of-towner or mafioso in sight . . .

2

What fuels the will to be visible? Why does it seem to have replaced other drives, or at the least matched them? How is it that the imagination of our culture—as reflected in the magazines that multiply like guppies, profiling (and, in the instance of *Spy,* parodying) the celebrated with rabid interest and equal lack of judgment—is so caught by the idea of fame? (There is even a magazine called, unrepentantly, *Fame,* whose publisher made his fortune hyping stock before he moved on to full-fledged hype.) When, in short, did private life lose its sheen?

An old-line shirt company not traditionally linked with anything more modish than good prices and fit has announced a new, perkier ad campaign: "In fall 1989, Arrow shirts will conduct a nationwide survey to find out which male celebrities most Americans think need to 'loosen their collar.'" Arrow shirts, like home-delivered bottles of milk, put me in mind of a time before designer labels, of a time when lives were not yet reconstituted as lifestyles and dinner was still something you ate at home. But nothing is safe these days from the pull of the lustrous association, least of all the humble accoutrements of private life. Even in the neutral world of objects, their immutable quality of being what they are and no more no longer applies. To speak of "the unalterable pathos of basin and pitcher," as the poet Theodore Roethke did, is to call up an era before Ralph Lauren printed his signature country-gentry look across a willing (or, at least, susceptible) nation. It seems that everything has become only as valuable as its refracted image of glamour—who it puts you in mind of to wear it, tell time with it, sleep on it, smell of it.

The process of self-validation has moved further and further away from an internalized, private axis—family, friends, community, religion —and increasingly closer to the realm of performance, of projection. What has happened is this: To be home alone in a room in the late twentieth century is to invite a Warholian state of panic, as though every night has become a kind of New Year's Eve, an imperative to be out and seen. "Well, it was a pretty starless New Year's Eve," goes one bedraggled entry in Warhol's diaries. "I feel left out. I think Calvin had a party and didn't invite me, and Bianca's in town and I didn't hear from her."

Indeed, our homes themselves have become less a haven than a proscenium in which to compel regard. Now we can buy basins and pitchers designed to bring excitement to our homes, to suggest that our ancestors came over on the *Mayflower* or that we travel in the higher realms of Italian chic, black matte all over with no pathos in sight. What do Calvin and Kelly Klein—who recently hired the French architect of the moment to give their East Hampton beach house a patina of age— know of Roethke's "dolor of pad and paperweight" anyway?

The concept of personal celebrity was not invented yesterday, although sometimes it appears that way. Even celebrity-by-association is not as lately born as one might think. Well before the image-savvy Kennedy administration produced its bevy of books by former nannies and personal assistants, there was Lord Byron, who, within twenty years of his death (as recounted in an essay from a recently published collection, *The Outermost Dream,* by William Maxwell), inspired memoir after memoir by real and feigned members of his entourage—including a countess who had known Byron for all of two months; a cousin of Shelley's who published his *Journals of the Conversations of Lord Byron Noted During a*

Residence With His Lordship at Pisa in the Years 1821 and 1822 in spite of the fact that "he at no time lived under the same roof as Byron"; a young ship's physician who had tried to convert Byron to Methodism; and a former fire master in the British navy. In his ambitious book *The Frenzy of Renown,* Leo Braudy tracks what he terms the "lust for recognition" down the corridors of time, beginning with Alexander the Great on through Caesar, Augustus, Jesus, Chaucer, and up to "the democratization of fame" in the eighteenth century when "a new kind of self-projected power" replaced the cult of saints and kings.

If this fixation on fame is not as contemporary as it might strike us as being, what does seem relatively recent is its overwhelming *prevalence*—its insidious presence in the collective background, like white noise. Whereas in the past certain prosaic categories of professional life seemed barred from entry into the portals of renown, now one can become famous for being a secretary (Fawn Hall) or a cook (Wolfgang Puck) or a hairdresser (Jose Eber, of whom it was recently noted: "Jose Eber will not touch *your* tresses unless you are famous, or at the very least, extremely important. Some of the richest socialites of the Valley can't get into his L.A. salon"). Through the ever more sophisticated instrument of the media—which eats fame for breakfast—it is possible to grab the spotlight on the slimmest of pretexts. So a murdered policeman's widow brings home their firstborn from the hospital to the accompaniment of cameras and microphones, and onlookers to street crime speak for the benefit of the evening news with easy candor, as though they've been preparing for this all their lives. One thinks, too, of the numerous waiters and waitresses who introduce themselves by name in chic eateries all over Manhattan, insisting on a spurious familiarity, on their right not to be anonymous. "People are strange when you're a stranger," the late Jim Morrison moaned in one of the Doors' biggest hits, "no one remembers your name." Sometimes it seems as if, deep down, everyone thinks they deserve to be famous, as if all it takes to get people to remember your name is the wish itself—the will to be known.

It could well be that the wish to be recognized and photographed and read about—the frenzied striving toward visibility—is no more than a newly vigilant, surreal effort to deny a certain axiomatic horror to life, which is that it is destined to end in death. Given enough distraction in the way of tinsel, in the way of *après-moi-le-déluge* spending habits, do we imagine that we can perhaps avoid what the essayist E. B. White called "the sadness of afternoons"? Celebrity, in its egotistic blaze, diminishes the ache of quotidian existence, suggests to us that there is a way to sidestep the natural rhythms of life, a way out of aging and encroaching mortality—that lonely exit at the end of the road. What the relentless documentation of the celebrated, in all their sealed-off grandeur, offers us has something in common with what the gay sensibility—or an aspect of that sensibility—offers: a questioning of the very notion of the normative, an ironic framing of it, and a worship of the heightened effect. *Vanity Fair* visits with Candy Spelling or Elizabeth Taylor or Phyllis McGuire, and what the reader comes away with is a profusion of diamonds. It is as though we have all become, almost without knowing it, connoisseurs of campiness, alert to the latest Gatsby-esque absurdity of gesture and style but helplessly addicted to the numbing rush this absurdity provides. "Oh, how do you escape this aging factor?" Warhol wails in another entry. The focus on fame is his—and our—answer, a refuge from consciousness, an infantile domain of larger-than-life figures whose aura of false juvenescence (abetted by the wonder of liposuction) colludes with us in our narcissism.

There are several tables at Le Cirque that are sacrosanct. Tonight, midway through my dinner, Ronald Perelman (chairman of Revlon) arrives with his wife, Claudia Cohen (late of the *New York Post*'s avidly read "Page Six" and now the celebrity maven for Channel 7's *Live with Regis & Kathie Lee*), to claim one of them. I wonder if they are disappointed—this paradigmatic power couple, this marital merger of money and gossip—that there is no one (no *somebody,* that is) to see them. It occurs to me that it is possible to crane toward the limelight only to discover that you are not who the limelight has in mind. (Of course, if you're famous enough—like Greta Garbo or Marlon Brando or Jackie Onassis—you can afford to be elusive, and the limelight will come trailing after you.) One senses, for instance, that in the nouvelle-society set too much passion—too much Jewishness, too much bosom, too much makeup, too much intellectual curiosity—is not only viewed as gauche but effectively puts you out of the running. Ditto being "too eager to belong." We are speaking here of a view of life usually propounded in ads for leisure clothing—"the casual route to success," as one copywriter for Macy's Men's Store described it, rather than the sort of furrowed-brow effort that calls attention to itself. "Anything that reeks of seriousness," says James La Force, a publicist who has helped out at the right parties, "is a downer."

One woman, who dabbles in beauty services based on the mysteriously beneficial effects of bee pollen, was described to me as being "too wrong in too many ways" and thus deemed inherently not acceptable—tolerated by but never to be one of the Nan Kempners and Mica Ertegüns. On closer interrogation it appeared that she is guilty of the entire list of inadvertent sins: She is buxom; she wears too much makeup; she has flaming red hair; she owns fake French furniture and bad paintings; and her husband sounds like a Jewish businessman straight out of *Goodbye, Columbus*. No wonder one guardian of the charmed circle, owner of one of its chosen bistros and generally conceded to be "the biggest snob there ever was," is loath to give this woman a good table! (Interestingly enough, although many of the same faux pas could be ascribed to Georgette Mosbacher—who has bought a cosmetics company of her own and whose cleavage and titian hair get significant media play—the slide rule on these social computations doesn't always work with equal precision: In Mosbacher's case, a powerful husband with direct ties to the presidential incumbent seems to have mitigated her flaws and rendered them merely colorful.)

The only excess that doesn't appear to be frowned upon—indeed is regarded with a kind of dazed wonder—is too much spending. (This in spite of the fact that one young and cynically inclined observer of the scene describes the women as "cheap" and always on the lookout for "freebies," and another of the initiate alludes to the "borrowing" of samples at the couture houses, where a certain amount of money is put aside to cover the clothes given to prominent people.) True, "the right people" are always described as extremely charitable, although another observer acidly points out that "they're more inclined to have parties for the arts —the library, the ballet—than for diseases or socially disadvantaged people. They came late to AIDS." Charity work, in fact, is the occupational hazard of the social rich: "There are no more 'idle rich,' as in Elsa Maxwell's day," muses Eleanor Lambert, whose grasp of this particular world stretches further back than most people's. "Socialites can't get away with loafing."

But, most important, the nouvelle society is, according to Lambert, "rich and attractive and knows how to give parties at home." One wishful parvenu couple, with enough journalistic credentials between them to float a summit conference at Ascot, is openly patronized because "they don't have enough money—they can't return invitations, can't send presents or do their part." Not so Susan Gutfreund—who is conspicuous even in this jaded group as an embarrassingly lavish gift-giver, a sender of huge bouquets and small items of jewelry. And if you, like she, have the good fortune to become friends with social lioness Jayne Wrightsman (whose incomparable collection of French antiques includes pieces from the Versailles repository) and to rent Blenheim Palace for your first party in England, more huzzahs to you.

3

As it happens, I grew up a virtual neighbor of Suzy, a.k.a. Aileen Mehle, then as now the undisputed (although Bill Norwich is giving her a run for her money) doyenne of the social gossip columns. She lived in the same building my family did, on a lower floor, and even as a child I recall the effect her presence in the small, wood-paneled elevator created. I knew who Suzy was, although a full grasp of the filaments of the social web she helped spin was beyond my ten-year-old ken. For one thing, she was one of the few women I had ever seen whose actual person was preceded by the persona of her hair—puffed-up, taffy-colored, "big" hair. She was usually accompanied by a good-looking young man (a "walker," if I had only known the term), and the smell of her perfume was heady. From my corner of the elevator, unnoticed, I would watch her and her attentive companions; although Suzy and I never exchanged a word on these occasions, I felt a slight but definite tingle of importance, a glazed sense of certification. She was always dressed to dazzle for the evening ahead, in full maquillage, while I was in my schoolgirlish pleated skirts or corduroy jumpers. She was the chronicler of the rich and famous and I was an introspective, largely unhappy child. But for a moment or so it was as if I, too, were caught in the rays of her reflected power—*made visible,* not just myself anymore but an extruded version of the self that went on its lonely way inside of me, My Self bound up in silver ribbon for the world to take note of.

I would find the first, and best, articulation of this sense of borrowed glory some years later during college when I read Walker Percy's 1961 novel *The Moviegoer.* Binx, the laconic narrator and ardent moviegoer of the title, is caught up in what he calls "the search"—the search for as "plenary an existence" as that which seems to be offered by the movies, by the "resplendent reality" of movie stars. On his way to lunch with his aunt, Binx spots the actor William Holden in the French Quarter (the novel is set in New Orleans) and, strolling along behind him, notes his effect on a young "not really happy" honeymooning couple:

> Holden slaps his pockets for a match. . . . By now the couple
> have caught up with him. The boy holds out a light, nods
> briefly to Holden's thanks. . . . Holden walks along between
> them for a second; he and the boy talk briefly, look up at the

sky, shake their heads. Holden gives them a pat on the shoulder
and moves on ahead.

The boy has done it! He has won title to his own existence. . . . He is a citizen like Holden; two men of the world
they are. All at once the world is open to him. . . . His girl is
open to him too. He puts his arm around her neck, noodles her
head. She feels the difference too. She had not known what was
wrong nor how it was righted but she knows now that all is
well. . . .

Holden has turned down Toulouse shedding light as he
goes. An aura of heightened reality moves with him and all who
fall within it feel it.

There you have it, the malaise of ordinariness spelled out in lyrical prose
more than a decade before *People*—that self-described "sourcebook on the
stars"—burst on the scene to inject us with our weekly serum of heightened reality. One wonders what Binx would have made of *People,* he of
the fanzine frame of mind. Perhaps his "search" would have ended then
and there with the first issue, with this manual given up not to hortatory anecdotes but to the simple lessons of adulation and identification:
everything done with mirrors.

Who's to say where admiration lets off and envy—of a sometimes
lethal variety—begins? (The urge to be famous takes root, I suspect, in
the unhappier of souls, and there is a touch of vengefulness in it.) I used
to keep a mental list of people whose fame I took personally, whose
celebrity I judged to be a matter of circumstance or luck, easily dupli-
cated by me. These included a mannered and idiosyncratically dressed
actress whose very appearance onscreen set my teeth gnashing. When a
profile of this same actress (whose visibility also had a lot to do with her
being the on- and offscreen love interest of the funnyman of the age)
appeared some years ago in *The New Yorker,* I read of her preference for
white-on-white, her love of photography, her eccentric flair for socks and

hats, with incredulity: *This* made for celebrity? One might as well draw attention to one's feeling for texture, one's appreciation of fine linen, and hope it makes one Coco Chanel.

Is there anyone who can resist fame, who can look beyond the hot spotlight of the moment to the long, lambent light of history? (Even the snobbish Virginia Woolf succumbed, remarking: "This celebrity business is quite chronic.") Sometimes it seems as if History itself is an old and infirm actor who has been shuffled offstage, leaving us only with the puckish and insolent Now, with the hawking of personality and the rehabilitated persona. In truth, we live in increasingly ahistorical times, where "hotness" is all: "Amnesia," suggested one aggrieved letter writer in a recent issue of the Sunday *Times Magazine,* "has reached a new high. . . . Is there abroad some kind of memory-destroying virus?" Ours is an age of moral lassitude, and value judgments are an anachronism. Where once there was notoriety and public censure, there is now only celebrity and public attentiveness. (In the fifties the still-married Ingrid Bergman was made to suffer for her dalliance with director Roberto Rossellini in a way that, a mere decade later, the still-married Elizabeth Taylor, aflame with Richard Burton on the set of *Cleopatra,* was not.) Increasingly, the line between the famous and infamous grows ever more faint. A taint of the right kind of scandal can do a lot for a career: Witness the Mayflower Madam, Sydney Biddle Barrows, and the Hip Hotelier, Steve Rubell. Still, Eleanor Lambert, who calls publicity the "essential fluff of life," notes, ruminatively, that "like insider trading, it is morally wrong in many ways."

On a Wednesday in mid-June, on the corner of Seventy-fifth Street and Lexington (within a block of two buildings whose co-op boards won't accept Jewish applicants), a late-twentieth-century version of the French royal court is going at full throttle. It is lunchtime at Mortimer's, and the Ladies Who Lunch allay their status anxiety with retro-nanny food —meat loaf, chicken hash, spaghetti with tomato sauce, and sugary desserts. Glenn Birnbaum, owner of Mortimer's, sits at one of the desirable window tables, glasses fussily low on his nose, and at a table across from ours Anne Bass chats animatedly with another slim, blond woman. Further into the room Carolyne Roehm and Henry Kravis are hosting a lunch for one of Kravis's children, and beyond them is a large table of people who have been mysteriously supplied with individual copies of the latest issue of *Vanity Fair.* In the back room some Spence students are being treated to an end-of-the-school-year celebration: The worshipers at the shrine of Mortimer's get their training early; the younger generation that pop in and out today seem as well dressed—as primed for visibility—as their elders.

To sit in Mortimer's as an all-but-invisible observer is to realize how public the cornerstones of private life have become, how children's birthday parties are no longer homey, "hip hip hooray" affairs but are now part of the dominant, exhibitionist impulse to *compel regard,* whether of the media or of the spectator. What I also realize, sitting crushed up against the bar as I am, outside the charmed circle, is how ruthless a spectacle the spectacle of being seen is. For what those who rotate within the circle's merciless orbit have to contend with, of course, is the inherent fickleness of regard. "If you let yourself drop out—if you're not in the columns," comments James La Force, "you're forgotten." Personal loyalty seems to be in short supply in the world of somebodies, which makes me wonder where you go if you're a somebody in need, say, of solace. Do you end up like Andy Warhol, in the dark about your own growing isolation, resorting to high-school stratagems to win companionship: "And Sam's still mad at me, so to teach him a lesson and make him feel he was missing out on so much glamour by being mad, when I got to the office I had Wilfredo write in my date book for every night this week: John Travolta . . . Diana Ross . . . Warren Beatty . . . Sam always checks my book, and when he sees I'm doing something glamorous that night he plays it goody-goody all day so I'll invite him."

"Terrible that old life of decency / without unseemly intimacy or quarrels," Robert Lowell once wrote. Equally terrible, I would argue, is the unseemly familiarity of the new life, where we study photos of parties we are not invited to and are more conversant with the wardrobe and preferences of celebrities—those "intimate strangers," as Richard Schickel calls them—than we are with those of our nobody friends and family. In a time when the primary analytic impulse is not, I think, to discover the truth but to uncover falsehood, celebrity is the perfect deconstructionist icon, one of the least-pure products our culture has to offer, the ultimate put-on.

Where this leaves us is with a heightened sense of unease about our own place in the cosmos. Celebrity—the projected image of self—is a perfidious seepage into the pores of our collective skin. After the advent of Blaine Trump—who is best known for being a sister-in-law of someone whose publicist is Howard Rubenstein, someone so self-bedazzled as to be trying to prevent a card company from using as its trademark a term (*trump card*) that has been around since the sixteenth century—private life just doesn't hack it. The question you have to ask yourself before you go to sleep at night is this: *Am I visible?*

1989

Clean Streets:
Martin Scorsese Among the Gentry

It's taken a little over a decade for the discreet object of Newland Archer's desire to burrow into Martin Scorsese's imagination, finally emerging this fall as cinematic flesh and blood. The situation—a late-nineteenth-century love affair manqué—has burned at the back of his mind since 1980, to be exact, when Scorsese's friend and dramaturge, Jay Cocks, gave him *The Age of Innocence,* Edith Wharton's deeply knowing novel about the ways and means of old New York, telling the director, somewhat patronizingly, that he'd "grow into it."

On a sultry day in New York City, in August of '92, Scorsese and I are sitting in his not-yet-fully-moved-into offices at Fifty-seventh and Park Avenue. As I discover when I arrive for my appointment with the director, you can't just stumble, willy-nilly, upon Cappa Productions: The man at the solitary front desk seems to have no clue that Scorsese & Company have set up shop beyond him, and the door to the premises is conspicuously unmarked. (It remains so when I return ten months later.) Once you pass "Go," however, you enter a warren of gleaming woodwork, highly polished brass handles, muted lighting, and spank-

ing, emerald-green carpeting. Cappa Productions will eventually be fitted with all the requisite trimmings of the industry: a screening room
and a video library with lots of television monitors, as well as framed,
oversize old-movie posters—from *La Dolce Vita* and Rossellini's *Paīsa*
("It was the first foreign film I ever saw," says Scorsese) to *Nightmare
Alley*—arrayed along the hallways. Right now, though, it would be
hard to determine the actual business being conducted in this atmosphere of muffled elegance.

Scorsese is speaking wistfully, almost elegiacally, about this seemingly improbable project—this Edwardian psychodrama set at a far
remove from the world of pool sharks, psychopaths, and wise guys that
is his more customary turf. Edith Wharton's fictional almost-adulterers
—the principled, newly betrothed Newland Archer and his wife's
cousin, the unconventional, newly separated Ellen Olenska—glimpse a
perfect love, only to let it go in favor of more temperate and less self-
fulfilling impulses: "Part of what she loves about him," the director
explains, "is his decency. He can't act any other way, especially by the
time his wife tells him she's pregnant. That's what I found so moving
about the book. He may not have Ellen, and Ellen may not have him,
but he has the memory of Ellen. The memory of that incredible passion,
that beautiful love." Scorsese pauses, his hands clasped, staring into his
own thoughts: "Ultimately there's a part of me that thinks memory
might be better than actuality. . . ."

It is a steamy afternoon at the end of June almost a year later, and
Daniel Day-Lewis, fresh from completing his role as a man falsely
accused of being an IRA terrorist in Jim Sheridan's *In the Name of the
Father,* has rushed in late for our interview, apologizing for having over-
slept. We are sitting in his agent's office at William Morris, and Day-
Lewis's legs seem too long for his chair. The actor (who plays Newland
Archer) is wearing jeans, a rust-colored work shirt, and expensive,
Italian-looking suede shoes that pick up exactly on the color of his

shirt. Even in this contemporary globe-trotter's outfit, there is something craggy and inward about the actor that makes me think someone should remake *Wuthering Heights* for him, if only because he is such an obvious Heathcliff.

Day-Lewis speaks with great thoughtfulness—even stiffness—and is clearly wary of the glib publicity-making machinery that is such an integral part of his profession. I have been warned not to ask him anything too personal. The gangly actor talks about Wharton's "extraordinary ability to reveal the trickery of the mind—the moment-to-moment subtle changes and endless deceit." He goes on to discuss, with great acuity, the psychological climate of the novel on which the movie is based: that the outcome of Newland and Ellen's grand passion is predicated on "a degree of sacrifice removed from contemporary life," and that the groundwork for the author's vision is laid early on by Wharton's incisive detailing of her protagonist's sensibility—in particular, his "attitude toward emancipation." In other words, says Day-Lewis, Archer is someone who *needs* to comply with the terms of his society. Then he adds, obliquely and profoundly, "The fulfillment of fantasies is a terrible responsibility." For a moment I wonder if he is referring to his character's life or his own.

"Martin and I talked a good deal before we started," Day-Lewis says, "and very little when we were working, which is ideal." (He's the only person I've encountered on the film who refers to Scorsese, formally, as Martin; everyone else calls him Marty.) Working with the director is, for Day-Lewis, in the nature of a miracle: "It never occurred to me for a moment that I'd work with him—and yet it was a dream above all others." Before they actually began shooting, he explains, sounding a little like a creation of Lewis Carroll, he'd *dream* about making the film. "'Today we're going to work with Martin Scorsese,'" Day-Lewis cites. "It gives you a sense of great privilege. But because of the way he is, you forget the privilege."

The actor is in New York to do some looping in the studio, and I ask him if he's seen the movie yet. "Tomorrow," he replies, and then flashes a beguiling, unglib smile. "In an empty room with a large ashtray."

The Age of Innocence is, in its way, a page-turner; one wants to know "Do they or don't they?" with the kind of disinterested human curiosity that never goes out of style. In an exquisitely nuanced narrative, which casts a clear, cold light on the social mores and emotional confinements of her time, Wharton builds to a crescendo of renunciation. Scorsese, who grew up on the mean streets of Little Italy in a household without books, discusses the rarefied dilemma of Wharton's characters with great fluency. When I ask him if there's any physical intimacy in the movie—even so much as kissing—he shows me a silver-framed photo of the fully costumed Day-Lewis and Michelle Pfeiffer (who plays Ellen Olenska) in answer. The two are close but not touching, as though they were permanently stuck in separate frames of the same picture; there are miles of longing between Pfeiffer's jutting shoulder bone and Day-Lewis's well-defined chin. Scorsese proffers this photo of corseted and waistcoated sexual confinement as if it were a family heirloom—relatives of his from some gilded and quiescent past. (He has actually hired an etiquette specialist—one Lily Lodge, great-granddaughter of the first Henry Cabot Lodge—to advise on white gloves and oyster forks.)

Although it would be too easy to dismiss the director's latest undertaking as a case of wishful thinking—in which a connoisseur of the gutter takes on high culture and hopes some of the polish will rub off—one can't help but note that this particular matchup of film auteur and literary subject is ripe for the snickering. Wharton's ode to bygone form and eclipsed decorum is definitely not the sort of project one associates with this particular director. What the shrinks call impulse control would hardly seem to be his strong suit: Scorsese has made his name and built up a fanatical following for wearing his tangled passions on his sleeve, both professionally and personally. It is difficult to think of another filmmaker who has so persuasively suggested, without resorting to the distancing devices of irony and camp (*Cape Fear* being an arguable exception on both counts), that the more twisted crevices of the psyche are worth looking into: Travis Bickle staring down all our superegos in the rearview mirror of his taxicab, or Jake La Motta venting his anger and self-doubt with his fists.

It would be harder still to think of another director who has sufficiently identified with the excesses of the rock 'n' roll culture to live it as well as film it: In the late seventies, after he finished making *The Last Waltz,* Scorsese's documentary on the Band, guitarist Robbie Robertson took up residence in the director's Los Angeles home for what seems to have been a lost weekend that lasted several months. Scorsese eventually landed in the hospital, critically ill with internal bleeding. He returned to make *Raging Bull,* a picture whose stark expositions and atmosphere of internally driven darkness might have been taken as an accurate reflection of the filmmaker's own angst. But Scorsese's private demons were apparently still outrunning Jake La Motta's back in 1980: "I hadn't reached the kind of serenity I projected for Jake. I was trying to be like the guy at the end," he says, "looking in the mirror and talking very quietly, but I wasn't there at all. It took me another ten years to get there." Later, with a wry chuckle, he comes back to the subject, refining it in his characteristic rapid patter: "I was still pretty much spinning in a whirlwind of activity and anger and rage."

Those whirlwind days—the wild and crazy times of hanging out with his buddies, checking out the rough stuff—are now way behind him. His vaguely menacing over-the-ears hairdo and beard are long gone. (Scorsese tells me that when he was living in L.A., he was stopped one night by the police, who mistook him for the Hillside Strangler.) On the four or five occasions I see him, he is dressed nattily, in an ongoing variation of a casual, monotoned Armani theme: a collarless shirt and pants and a belt that looks to be of prepossessing financial heft. His clothes, somehow, match the sense I have of Scorsese as a relaxed titan, concealing his powers to make the commoners feel more at ease. There is a cultivated air of diffidence about him that's very engaging; he doesn't act like a great director, but then again he doesn't have to, given the retinue of assistants and secretaries and publicists that scurries around him both on and off the set.

June '92: On a soundstage at Astoria Studios, eighty-four extras are dressed for a rehearsal of the all-important ballroom scene in which Archer's—and therefore the movie's—point of view is established. There are carefully placed fronds and a chandelier built from scratch (for $25,000); paste jewelry and boned waists abound. Amid an orgy of ruffles and flounces, Winona Ryder (who plays May Welland, Archer's fiancée) comes onto the set, a vision in cream, screeching "Ahhh! . . ." Scorsese sits enthroned in his director's chair emblazoned with the name of his beloved bichon frise, Zoë (she's credited with a tiny onscreen role), in front of his monitor, which has snapshots of Frank Sinatra, Nat King Cole, and Tony Bennett glued to it. A *haimish* elderly couple— the man looking Floridian in a tropical shirt and a gold chain, the woman looking like anyone's unhip mother—sit a few yards behind Scorsese: They are his parents, occasional but honored visitors. Thelma Schoonmaker Powell, Scorsese's longtime editor and widow of the British director Michael Powell (whose infamous *Peeping Tom* is one of Scorsese's lodestars), want to know: "Am I going to say 'Pan' softly to you or yell it?"

Ryder grimaces on the monitor, waiting to reshoot the scene in which she preens with her girlfriends over her just-received engagement ring from Archer. There is an astonishing amount of dead time on movie sets, of the Lower Orders—the crew and extras and lesser stars— being kept waiting while the Higher Orders decide when and where to proceed. I wonder what Wharton would have made of the intricate hierarchy, the mixture of casual intimacy and slightly ludicrous distinctions between one job title and the next. Amy Marshall, a set decorator, explains to me the difference between her role and that of a set *dresser:* "If I were a set dresser I'd have to lift much more furniture."

Although there are moments of levity, most of the time the atmosphere is charged with self-regard, as though the collected ensemble were rebuilding the Sistine Chapel.

Scorsese confers often with Michael Ballhaus, his German director of photography. Ballhaus is given to wearing odd sartorial combinations—red suspenders, for instance, together with sandals and socks—which make him look like a cross between a mountain climber and a circus barker. Although he seems affable enough, Ballhaus strikes me as very much the Teutonic technocrat, fiddling with some perfectly framed image in his head. He and Scorsese huddle between takes, talking esoterically about camera inserts and a shot being "off high-speed." They are like two kids with great big expensive toys.

Finally they are ready for another go-around. "Action!" someone calls.

"Cut in tight," Scorsese yells. "Faster, faster, faster . . ."

All eyes are on Scorsese, and Scorsese's eyes take in everything. He notices a male extra lurking behind the plants. "Is he stalking someone?" the director wants to know. "He's supposed to be a footman."

Earlier, in the commissary, where a fairly tasteless lunch can be had for $1.84, etiquette coach Lily Lodge has explained to me that the implicit message of Wharton's novel is that "everyone meets on a level of passion." It sounds poetic, but the less poetic reality of Wharton's novel-into-film is that everyone meets on the level of Scorsese's tension. "You can never relax on a shoot," he remarks. Someone else recalls that on the set of *GoodFellas* he played with Zoë's fur like worry beads. Of course, when he is happy, everyone's happy, and sometimes the director almost swoons with pleasure: "This is good here. Oh my God . . ." Of another tableau that meets with his approval, he jests: "I liked it so much, I'll do it again. I can't stop shooting this scene." But when Marty is irritated and hot, everyone looks worried. Jay Cocks banters with him, and eventually more drastic measures are taken—a personal air-conditioning system (an amazing snakelike contraption) is hauled in to cool the director down.

"We got one," Scorsese says to Day-Lewis, who registers astonishment.
"What?"

"A shot," the director replies. It is the eighth take.

The ninth take. "Print that one also," Scorsese says.

It is late May of '93. While I wait for Scorsese to arrive at his office, a young publicist chats with me about belle epoque New York—discoursing on old patterns of silver and Federal-style homes. Everyone on *The Age of Innocence* seems to be imbued with a curiously proprietary attitude toward Wharton and her world—as though the sober, self-denying ethos it espoused has suddenly become a hip, Hollywoodish way to be. There is a way, of course, in which all artists—and Scorsese is at least as much an artist as a creature of commerce—can be said to be one step ahead of the Zeitgeist. If he was once a detonating free spirit, now he is bringing it all back home. It is the nineties, after all, and "family values" are back in style.

Although the original release date of *The Age of Innocence* was five months ago, the director has taken his own sweet time about getting the movie in. His father's been in the hospital several times, which has eaten into his schedule, but the real problem seems to be that Scorsese finds official, studio-dictated calendars blatantly unrealistic. He points out that *GoodFellas,* which he finished shooting in August '89, was released in September '90. When I ask him what he does in these extended editing periods, he gives one of his hearty, embracing laughs. "I don't know . . . look at the thing all day in a little room with Thelma and get on each other's nerves." Then he grows serious as he comes to the heart of the matter, his professional raison d'être: "We work scene by scene. I go through a full first cut. I can't have someone—even if it's Thelma—put the film together while I'm shooting it. . . ."

Indeed, his articulate, white-haired coconspirator calls him "an *editing* director—like Kurosawa." Thelma Schoonmaker Powell met Scorsese around 1963, when she was taking a summer course at New York

University, and has been with him since the days of his ten-minute student effort, *It's Not Just You, Murray.* She becomes passionate on the subject of Scorsese's "unique eye" and how it helps him get the most subtle portrayals out of actors. "He's very strict about what he calls 'television acting'—the raised-eyebrow stuff." ("My performance was very minimalist," Winona Ryder concurs. "He kept saying, 'Less.' I thought I was a Stepford wife.") Paradoxically, Schoonmaker Powell explains, although he prefers underplayed performances, Scorsese doesn't like underplayed "Hollywood-style editing," in which everything slides by seamlessly. "Marty likes the awkward moment that other editors take out. He mostly likes to make editing obvious."

Scorsese is a perfectionist through and through, compelled to understand whereof he directs. There is much of the anthropologist in him, studying the tribal habits of one group after another—from the lower depths of the mafiosi to the upper realms of a striated, vanished society. Many of the elegant rituals that are a background for Wharton's book—how women blotted their lips between sips of wine, for example, or the custom men had of dropping a white glove on the table along with their cards each time they changed dancing partners—seem to have become occasions for cinematic deconstruction. "The way he shot tight on the cigar clipping," Schoonmaker Powell says, "it becomes savage."

Scorsese and I sit in Cappa Productions' spacious screening room and, while his beloved Zoë keeps vigilant watch, Scorsese describes with anecdotal relish how all the best planning can go briefly, tragically wrong: "This *Age of Innocence*—you get on the set . . . I had it planned out for two and a half years in the script. *Two and a half years.* You get there, it's working. One very funny thing happened one morning. Okay, there's going to be a close-up of the oysters. It's supposed to be a very special dinner, oysters, right? I look at it, lined up the shot—I said, '*What's that?*'—there's the oysters, there's the dish, but there was too much ice in the oysters, or *something was wrong.* I said, 'This looks like an ad for Lenny's Clam House!'" He chuckles. "I said, 'This could be any-place!'" He chuckles louder. "All the prop guys were looking at each other, and we move them around and we finally got it to look . . . and then, of course, it was the wrong angle. I was shooting it in the front, this way, tilting it up to the person. I had to go *this* way."

Robin Standefer is a ponytailed former art-history graduate stu-dent to whom Scorsese gave the credit "visual research consultant." She spent two and a half years researching background for the movie and eventually accumulated at least twenty-five large reference books, which she refers to as "bibles." Her work led her from the Frick Col-lection and the New-York Historical Society to the Library of Con-gress, Christie's, and various Wharton and art-history scholars such as R. W. B. Lewis and Linda Nochlin. It covered everything from the daily habits of upper-class life in the last decades of the nineteenth century—china, flower arrangements, number of dinner courses (thir-teen), and the specifics of keeping fresh oysters cold in a prerefriger-ated era (they used specially made ices in flower and fruit shapes)—to the more arcane aspects of that culture, like an obscure school of Ital-ian pre-Impressionists (the Macchiaioli) whose paintings were sensu-ous, almost Oriental in nature, and were likely to have graced the drawing room walls of Ellen Olenska. "Marty's really meticulous about detail," Standefer observes, musing that "maybe, in a way, he does it for himself." But if indeed there is something fussbudgety about Scor-sese, in the end practical considerations seem to reign. "There's always further you can go," she says. "The decision was how to fit the details into the budget."

Barbara De Fina, the movie's producer (and, until their recent sepa-ration, Scorsese's fifth wife), agrees that much of the budget "went below the line into sets and costumes." De Fina is a slight, youthful-looking woman who seems swallowed up by the large desk in her office at Cappa Productions. On her wall hangs a promotional clock from *Cape Fear,* and the ever-present Zoë growls protectively whenever I lean forward. De Fina tells me Columbia doesn't want her to discuss the budget and in the same breath assures me that they came in close to it; she notes that there were many "trade-offs" and that they actually built very little in the way of sets. (Three sets were built, including the main hall of the Metropolitan Museum, circa 1880.)

Depending on which estimate you believe, *The Age of Innocence* cost $30 million or nearly $40 million. Scorsese says a bit defensively that the average film costs between $25 million and $27 million. (*GoodFellas,* for instance, was $26 million.) He admits that the disparity between this and his current film's budget went into capturing the all-important details of an alien world: "Where that extra three or four million went was for the structure and the anthropology of the scenes. In other words, the look of the dishes has to be a certain way, and that's what I thought would give it the extra love and care. And maybe the audience can feel that, get a sense of sumptuousness. . . ." Scorsese goes on to ask, somewhat plaintively, "Is that inordinate, to have costumes and horses and carriages? Is that an inordinate amount extra?" He believes the kind of attention he gives his pictures pays off on second and third viewings. It is, you could say, a mathematics of obsession, a pursuit of a certain coherence at a certain calculated cost in the hope of capturing a solitary, no-holds-barred vision. "When I really feel a certain way about a project, I throw everything I have into it and know that nobody may see it, and that might give me a problem in making pictures for the next five or six years," Scorsese explains in one long run-on summation of the method behind his madness. "That's what I used to call kamikaze filmmaking: Just jump into it, put it all there, and leave the country. . . ."

Lauded artist, even solid citizen though he may now be—when I ask him if he sees *The Age of Innocence* as a love story, Scorsese replies, sounding several centuries away from his former acting-out self, that it's about "the conflict between love and obligation to other people"—he seems to be imperceptibly trailed by a sense of having suffered one too many casu-

alties. Before the sideshow with Robertson, there were the rumors of
drug use and general sensory overdrive around the time of *New York,
New York;* later came the financial flop of *The King of Comedy* and then
the brouhaha and perceived antivision of *The Last Temptation of Christ.*

So far, an Oscar has eluded Scorsese, although everyone keeps mur-
muring about Academy Awards in connection with *Innocence.* And perhaps hearth and home will carry the day where hit men didn't. Still, it
looks as if it's once a sinner, always a sinner: In the eyes of the critical
establishment, at least, Martin Scorsese at fifty is doomed to be viewed,
each time around, as the comeback kid—on the verge of a glorious
redemption. "What am I coming back *from?*" he asks me, half angrily,
half in jest. "What's their problem? Where did I *go?*" And then he continues, in the very next sentence, to feed this perception of himself as
perpetual penitent—to speak of "proving himself," of being "vindi-
cated," of "coming back" with *GoodFellas.*

Maybe it's the Catholic background, the narrow escape from becoming a priest, the professed obsession with religion. Or maybe the
cineasts' prevailing attitude bespeaks something more complex—both
more adulating and more cynical, something to do with his convincing
aura of uncompromised youthful genius. "Will This Be Scorsese's Comeuppance?" he remembers the cover of one film magazine screamed when
Raging Bull came out. Certainly it helps that Scorsese gives good talk—
both on and off the subject of his films—in a way that many of his con-
temporaries don't. He speaks in great staccato gusts, evincing intense
curiosity about whatever subject he's on. He conveys, too, a genuine
sense of artistic aspiration that is rare in mainstream American film
directors and is no doubt one of the reasons actors revere him so. He
talks about "sharpening up again and going back into training" after *The
Last Temptation.* "Everything you do, you're learning," he says, sounding
disarmingly like a novice after two decades behind the cameras. "Every
damn picture you do." Listening to him, one feels the heat of his focus,
as though he were walking uphill toward some moment of cinematic
revelation that only he can see.

∎ ∎ ∎

He has strange powers, this Scorsese fellow. Winona Ryder, whom I observed briefly on the set, looking very young and self-possessed, is currently working on a new movie called *Reality Bites*. When I ask her about *Innocence,* she sounds as if she's been through a conversion experience: "I learned more than I've ever learned," she tells me, her voice breathless over the phone. And then of its director: "He has incredible energy. It's not just that he talks fast; he's incredibly soothing. He made me feel not only that I was proud of my work and made sense; he made me feel great. I actually looked forward to showing up at six A.M. I think he affected my life in a deep way that doesn't even have to do with movies."

Daniel Day-Lewis, who is given to a less rhapsodic style, is nonetheless similarly enthusiastic about Scorsese as the guiding angel of the set: "Martin works in tremendous detail," he recalls in his quiet yet commanding voice, "and knows beforehand what he wants technically and emotionally. Yet he manages to create huge amounts of freedom for performers: Within boundaries, you can ask for anything." And then, as if to explain the delicate, almost therapeutic chemistry between actor and director, he adds, "You can go quite insane during the period of shooting. A moderating influence has to be there."

It's almost eight o'clock on a summer night, and on the set of *The Age of Innocence* they're making like jingle bells. A horse in harness stands patiently before a coach with old-fashioned globe lights, on which is seated a uniformed and top-hatted coachman. The "snow" on the ground is bleached wood pulp, and more snowflakes—shredded polyethylene dispensed by fans—are falling. It is a glowing winter night—lighting courtesy of smoke machines, and silk panels suspended from the ceiling. The dirt on the snow is real, and when Joseph Reidy, the associate producer, calls for rehearsals to begin, a black-eyed mutt named Spanky scampers behind the coach, its tail wagging. "Smoke it up, please,"

Reidy says, and an air-conditioning pipe is used to disseminate steam. "Let it snow. Roll. Action." Spanky barks, not on cue. Someone from the prepping crew layers on additional snow through a large strainer. And the director hasn't even arrived yet. . . .

It occurs to me that the last outpost of artistic obsession is a Martin Scorsese film.

Scorsese has put in a lot of fast work these last years. There was the tightly budgeted *After Hours,* and then to prove his mettle, to prove he could bring in a *movie* movie—the generic article, the kind his father likes, with a strong story line and not too many moody personal touches —there was the shining commercial bauble *The Color of Money.* Following that success came *Last Temptation,* a lauded segment of *New York Stories,* and the much heralded *GoodFellas.* Based on Nicholas Pileggi's book *Wiseguy, GoodFellas* was a return to the world of mobsters and meatballs, a world Scorsese imbibed along with the catechism and fierce family ties of his upbringing. Most recently came the intentional lowballing of *Cape Fear:* He was seeing if he could make a classic thriller even edgier.

So here's the $30 million question: How has this child of grungy, gritty Gotham reached a place where he is concerned with the archaeology of calling cards, boutonnieres, and formal dinner services? Is it too much of a stretch? What do Martin Scorsese and a Merchant-Ivory-ish *period piece* (brought in almost a year late and for at least $22 million more than *Howards End*) have in common, anyway?

Scorsese seems prepared for the inevitable nit-picking, for the possibility that he will be seen as a costly and hopelessly nouveau aspirant to old-guard material. He is the first to point out that the Merchant-Ivory team has a "very different sensibility" from his own, and he goes on to compare their way of working to the "old studio system, where there's a body of work built up." Although he gives these longtime practitioners their due, it is clear that Scorsese believes he has something different to offer the period genre. Perhaps he's been preparing for this debut longer

than we know: He admits to a hitherto unsuspected weakness for costume pictures made in England—"I adore James Mason," he says, by the
by—and explains that watching a Victorian crime story called, pic-
turesquely, *Pink String and Sealing Wax* freed his mind to do certain shots
in *The Age of Innocence* that were giving him trouble.

All along, I keep thinking there's some subliminal link—some con-
nective tissue—between these very different ventures, *Raging Bull* and
The Age of Innocence. I mention this to Scorsese and he nods. "I feel it," he
says, "but I can't articulate it." When I watch *Raging Bull* again, I am
struck by the lyricism that hovers, from the very first, behind its brutality—by the elegiac slow-motion dancing of the hooded boxer as the title
shots roll, the civilized impulses going up against the instinctual. . . .

Maybe it's not such a stretch, after all: Jake La Motta loses out
because he *can't* help himself; Newland Archer loses out because he *can.*
Either way, reality—what you are left with when you grow up—packs
a pretty hard punch. Maybe Daniel Day-Lewis wasn't being so opaque:
"The fulfillment of fantasies is a terrible responsibility." It's something
Jake La Motta learns too late and Newland Archer knows all along,
knowledge bred into his bones.

If you listen to Martin Scorsese, what he longs to do most these days is
read. He buys books, stacks and stacks of them, history, biography,
books. He seems deeply interested in people—how they behave and the
emotions that drive them—but from a remove. He says his life is more
solitary these days, and he likes being alone. "If he could only make
movies and show them to his friends in the living room," De Fina says,
"he would be a happy man." Withal, Scorsese is a fairly cerebral guy,
and it would not be too sentimental to suggest that there remains in
him much of the small, sickly boy he once was—lost in his head, sitting in his room, drawing pictures, "making my own little movies,"
curious about the brawling life around him but from a safe distance. In
a loud and peopled business, the isolated activity of film editing

remains the part of moviemaking that Scorsese likes best: "I guess when I'm editing," he says, "I feel like I'm there in that little room, by myself. And that's what I really enjoy. Maybe it's a way to get back to that feeling. . . ."

As Scorsese moves from one seemingly disconnected movie project to another, his films begin to take on a pattern, establishing an unconscious blueprint for what his life holds in store for him a decade or so down the road. Perhaps the scenario of *The Age of Innocence* appeals to him because it is where he'd like, someday, to be living: in an ordered universe where tradition and duty reign more firmly than impulse. These days, Scorsese is, to all appearances, very much the respectable gent, ensconced in a Whartonian town house in the East Sixties, where he says he can hear the clatter of horse-and-buggies late at night— much as Newland Archer might have—as they make their way down Fifth Avenue. These days, he says, he prefers the memory of love to the thing itself.

1993

Mailer at Sea: The Writer as Director

It's a long trek out to Provincetown—from wherever you begin—and the trip seems even longer on a gray day in early December. There's nothing more desolate than a summer haunt off-season, with the sea gulls cawing and the waves pounding and the people all gone, but members of the press have been thronging to "the very tip of the little finger of Massachusetts" (as one of the characters in *Tough Guys Don't Dance* calls it) undeterred since the fall. Norman Mailer—than whom there is no better copy—is in town, filming his screenplay of his novel. The publicity Mailer generates has always been enormous, even when he is only writing another book. But Mailer on a movie set is like doubling your money: It's a made-for-media occasion, and although there's been a lot of coyness about "closed" sets and strictly limited interviews (I've been promised a dazzling half hour—twenty minutes over the usual), it's clear that those with access to a column of type have found themselves on the Boston-Provincetown flight, winging their way to the lunatic doings that were first the book's, and are now faithfully the movie's, inspiration.

■ ■ ■

"They could call this film *Come to Provincetown and Die,*" jokes Ira Lewis, a playwright friend of Mailer's, spotting what appears to be a rarity around here this time of year: an open restaurant. I am sharing a ride with him to the Holiday Inn, where I will be staying, and where a ground-floor room has been converted into editing facilities. Among the many people milling around the writer turned director—referred to, with ostentatious familiarity by one and all, as "Norman"—Lewis alone seems not to be caught up in what he himself, in an unguarded moment, describes as an atmosphere of "unbalanced reverence and awe."

There are six interior sets and fifty-nine locales scheduled for *Tough Guys.* Many of the interior scenes are being shot in Mailer's own house in "P-town" (as it is affectionately dubbed), which has been redone to reflect the expensive but untutored tastes of its cinematic inhabitants, the ruthlessly ambitious hillbilly Patty Lareine (Debra Sandlund) and her husband, Tim Madden (Ryan O'Neal). I imagine that Mailer's house was previously a casual, homey retreat suited to the writer's sprawling family life. It has fallen to Armin Ganz, fresh from wrapping *Angel Heart,* to design the production, subject to the exigencies of budgeting and the vagaries of Mailer's vision. In order to better understand that vision, Ganz has lived in the house with the director for three weeks and talked with him about his characters. "The longer you're there," Ganz explains, "the more you realize Patty Lareine's perversity." (And the longer you hang around Mailer, the more you seem to sound like him.)

With a relatively small budget ($5 million), a crew of ninety-seven, and a lot of "cover sets" in case of bad weather, Ganz has his work cut out for him. "There's a reason," he remarks ruefully, "people don't shoot movies in Cape Cod in winter, a reason they shoot in Jamaica." An open-faced, bearded man who doesn't look as if he ruffles easily, Ganz discusses the "fine line" of Patty Lareine's aesthetic sensibilities—how he has "pushed to the threshold of being gaudy, then pulled in the reins quickly."

In order to give "an immediate impression of wealth and refinement," the interior of the house has been provided with bleached floors, white couches, a brass chandelier with amber glass shades, lots of *objets* and California-style, pastel-toned art. There are Busby Berkeley touches in the living room: a mink-white piano, equine statuary, sherbet-colored Persian rugs. The coffee table, a circular slab of glass, sports a giant half-opened clam containing a giant pearl. The house suggests to my eye nothing more than the wishful accoutrements of taste, a kind of monied tackiness: It's hard for me to believe that anyone would mistake the high gloss of cheesiness that marks these rooms for an elegant environment, but then again I probably don't understand Mailer's and Ganz's understanding of Patty Lareine.

What really fascinates me, in any case, is the painstaking effort that has gone into the creation of the kitchen set. It is an elaborate, Brueghelian mess: a drainboard full of dishes; cartons of Stop & Shop milk, Mueller's twists, and a bottle of 409 stand around on various counters; there is a half onion on the cutting board next to a bag of carrots and an opened package of Pepperidge Farm white bread. Bowls and plates of congealed food. A box of Domino Dots. An oddly old-fashioned toaster. Someone has thought long and hard about the state of Tim Madden's kitchen on the twenty-fifth day after his wife has left him. I keep thinking that if I study the contents of the kitchen long and hard enough, I will figure out some incongruous truth lurking beneath the chaotic surface of Mailer's cinematic venture.

Drew Kunin, the mixer—he's worked on three movies in P-town, which must be a record of sorts—dryly compares the mechanics of filming this modest-seeming production to "forming Ford Motor Company to make one car."

"Rolling."

"Quiet in the house, please."

"No flushing."

"No *flashing,*" another male voice amends.

"Cut."

A sign posted in the back entrance of Mailer's house, near the bathroom, where anyone not immediately required on the set hangs out: NO NUDITY, HILARITY, FREEBASING. Another sign upstairs near the grips and electricians' lounge reads, NO EATING, SMOKING, DRINKING, DANCING, OR SODOMY. The crew—a uniformly bearded and scraggly haired bunch— reminds me of sixties rock musicians backstage. They sprawl among the film equipment, reading newspapers, attended by doting and blue- jeaned girlfriends. A page of script from the current day's shooting is posted right outside the lounge and someone has crossed out portions of the script and written in changes, viz:

> *100A INT. MADDEN'S*
> *BEDROOM—DAY*
>> *Tim finishes cleaning the ~~shaving cream~~*
>> *body fluids off the mirror.*

Such is my readiness to believe in the macho ribaldry of Mailer's screen- play—I am still recuperating, after all, from yesterday evening's shoot- ing of a fellatio scene with Ryan O'Neal—that it takes me several minutes to realize the scurrilous editing has been penned in by humor- ous crew members. (Nancy, an assistant director who dresses in early Madonna clothing, eyes me suspiciously when I read the sheet, and when I come back to look for it a while later, it's been taken down.)

Norman Mailer, dressed like a college sophomore in chinos and a crew- neck sweater, always seems to say, "Action," a bit lamely, as if after the fact. One might ask *who* is directing this movie, since in both this and an earlier shooting I have witnessed, Mailer's presence seems more meditative than active. He regales the set with stories from the Actors Studio—he has belonged since 1958—and imparts nuggets of armchair wisdom gleaned from years of moviegoing, such as, "Movie logic is when things are spooky, they move." He is assuredly good at soothing potentially explosive situations—"I'm not taking your fucking abuse," Lawrence Tierney, who plays Madden's father, tells an equally irate O'Neal, after a ten-minute debate about how to pour a drink ("I was a bartender," O'Neal insists, "I should know how to do this")—and at conferring quietly with perplexed actors: "Don't speed through it," he suggests to a defensive O'Neal about a tiny but charged patch of dialogue. "Ryan," Ira Lewis concedes, "is a little confused himself how to play his character."

I stand in Patty Lareine's living room and watch takes and retakes of O'Neal speaking Mailer's dialogue from where he sits on one of the white sofas: "I feel demented tonight. I could fuck your woman right in front of you." I think about the degree to which Mailer has been empowered, by virtue of his gifts and his brashness, to act out Everyman's fantasy—a fantasy as powerful as it is primitive. What would it be like to have someone else's woman suck you off in front of him in your own home? Could it be that the very excessiveness of the notion, its rabid, narcissistic intent, blinds the rest of us to all judgment? That what we are left with, finally, is a form of shock that is indistinguishable from awe? Perhaps one of the clues to the continuing fascination he exerts is that Mailer speaks to the omnipotent infant in each of us, the untamed renegade that lives alongside our more socialized, adult selves. After five or six takes of what Mailer has referred to as "a sensitive scene," the writer-cum-director finally says, "Cut, cut, cut." "You're a sick man," O'Neal says.

"Ryan hit me," Norman Mailer says impishly, explaining the origin of his cracked front tooth the moment he meets me with all the intact vanity of a still-handsome man. (He's actually broken it eating an apple.) I catch up to him as he crosses the street, dressed in running shoes, a blue parka, and a black watch cap. Mailer may affect the amiable uniform of a Cape Cod native, but from the back he has a pasha's walk, and it takes only a second to realize that you are in the presence of a professional charmer. This impression is strengthened during my official interview with Mailer, which takes place in O'Neal's—i.e., Mailer's—upstairs study.

"One reason to have a movie made in your house," Mailer announces, tilting back in his desk chair, "is to get the windows clean." His Sinatra-blue eyes twinkle. This is Mailer's ironic, beguilingly abashed side speaking, the same Mailer who avers that, "at the very least," he wants *Tough Guys* to be known for "how good a picture you can make for $5 million in forty-two days." Whereas novel writing "is like having a difficult second wife," making a movie is "elegant work."

Sitting there, I begin to realize how persuasive Mailer's self-image is —that he has, in fact, come to be perceived by the world at large as he perceives himself: a sixty-four-year-old boy wonder, someone whose artistic abilities recognize no bounds. Mailer likens being a director to being an "impresario," adding that boxing has given him "an abstract sense of confrontation" that's useful for dramatic scenes. He prefers single to master shots because the latter "tend to disappear." At some point in our conversation, a prearranged signal to bring the interview to an end is acknowledged and then ignored by Mailer. He goes on talking, an astonishingly smooth hoofer on the verbal floor. "Film," he opines, "is not unreligious in its character. It's for devotees, churchlike, incanta-tory." And: "The interface is more interesting than the centrality of any event." Bring him down to the particular interface at hand and he hints, almost shyly, that the movie he has in mind as a model is *Chinatown*. But then, in an instant, even that becoming glimpse of tentativeness is gone. "I'm looking for perfection," Norman Mailer confesses.

■ ■ ■

Ryan O'Neal is startlingly good-looking, his features less blurry than I had expected, his thick hair dappled with gold, his soft mouth still wearing the pained expression I remember from his Rodney Harrington days on *Peyton Place*. There is a lot of vibrancy in his face, especially around the eyes, and he keeps the set loosened up with his flippant wit. O'Neal and Mailer are boxing partners at a gym in New York, and he sounds remarkably Maileresque when he comments on the "kind of homosexual thing—the fight and embrace" that boxing embodies. Given O'Neal's energy, it's puzzling that when the camera rolls he seems to project a certain slackness—at least from my angle.

Debra Sandlund, who plays Patty Lareine, is slated for starletdom. O'Neal calls her a "comer." "She can do anything," he says, "sing—do splits." Sandlund is a wide-eyed, smooth-skinned, long-haired platinum blonde with a show-stopping body that is poured, Marilyn Monroe–style, into the sort of clothes that inevitably send your eyes to her stronger points. A voice major in college, from a devoutly Christian family, Sandlund refers to herself in the third person. She has competed in the TV show *Dream Girl U.S.A.* and won twice—"a car and piano." She seems to identify with Patty Lareine, who, she says, "makes the men melt," and she feels "together" with Mailer. "Norman writes such vivid characters," she pronounces breathlessly.

The really interesting newcomer to me is Frances Fisher, a sapphire-eyed, bleached blonde whose lot it is to play the ever-ready Jessica Pond. Fisher tells me a joke illuminating the five stages of an actor's career: (1) *Who is Frances Fisher?* (2) *Get me Frances Fisher.* (3) *Get me a Frances Fisher type.* (4) *Get me a young Frances Fisher.* (5) *Who is Frances Fisher?* She laughs heartily, seated before a mirror, smoking a cigarette as her hair is being set by "Hollywood," the stylist.

It is Hollywood, the hairstylist, strangely enough, who solves the conundrum of *Tough Guys* for me. "I was prepared," she says of Mailer, "to hate this man's guts." She has found him, however, to be "as kind to the upper rung as to the lower." Hollywood, a self-described "card-carrying feminist," informs me without a trace of irony that the troubles besetting the characters in this movie are caused by "bad manners." Just in case I don't get the point, she adds: "These are people you don't want to be friends with." *Bad manners?* It has seemed to me that if *Tough Guys* is about anything tangible—anything, that is, beyond its inflammatory presentations of Mailer's usual Big Themes: Sex, Money, Masculinity, Faggots, Cunts, Divorce, Alimony, Death, etc.—it's about the power of drugs. "This movie is about sick people," Don, the makeup artist, has confided diffidently. "The women are as sick as everybody else; they're too busy doing cocaine and killing each other to fix their lipstick."

But the official line on the movie is clearly much more high-minded. Michael Kaplan, the costume designer, parrots Hollywood's view of *Tough Guys'* morally instructive intentions as though the movie were a cautionary tale for the late eighties. "If these people had better manners," he affirms, "none of this would've happened."

"The ego wars are over," Mailer has told me in his study. I have noticed that he talks about himself with a certain grand remove—as though he were an institution rather than a person. He is, clearly, a man used to watching himself in a reflected light, to keeping constant track of his effect on others, and it is hard to say whether his current benign aspect is a role he's trying on for size or attests to a genuine change. Still, if I have trouble warming to Mailer in the Grand-Nanny persona he has created for himself on this set, few of the people around him are aware of his unruly past (including his unmannerly stabbing of a former wife) and seem inclined to accept him at his own evaluation.

Right before I leave, I have lunch with Mailer at Tulips; a section of the restaurant's tables have been cordoned off for the crew and cast.

Although Mailer has declared Provincetown to be "the last democratic town left in America," the star system holds sway even here. Mailer may eat with the rest of the team, but O'Neal, Sandlund, and Isabella Rossellini, who plays O'Neal's ex-girlfriend, eat in their trailers. Mailer is talking about the perspective the last six months has brought him. He admits he thought his film *Maidstone* would be a "hit," and that he thought he'd win the election for mayor of New York City. "I'm either a success or a failure," he says, shrugging his shoulders.

Everyone keeps a respectful distance from our table except Tierney, who comes over to register a complaint about Mailer's directing skills. "You're supposed to ask the actor if he's ready," Tierney protests. "I will," Mailer says, equably. Then the bald, bellicose old actor goes on, as if it were a perfectly reasonable segue, to complain about transvestites. "Six-foot men with broad shoulders dressing up in women's clothes," Tierney scoffs incredulously. "What could they possibly want?" "To get back to infancy," Mailer shoots back, without missing a beat.

I sit there, watching the two aging tough guys spar, and I am suddenly struck by the force behind Mailer's power—the force that informs his pasha's walk and enables him to take up movie directing on a lark, the way someone else might take up fly-fishing. It has something to do with the elasticity of his mind, with the connections he alone dares to make; something to do, as well, with those penetrating blue eyes. But it has most to do, I think, with a quality of personality—a belief in himself that is nothing short of magnetic, pulling in male and female admirers, as well as producers with money to spare. It doesn't seem to matter much that Mailer is proving inept as a director, or that the antics on his set resemble expensive bedlam more than they do "elegant work." What matters is that he is never at a loss for confidence—or for glistening words with which to spin fabulous theories, and thereby reflect back to us an image of ourselves that is taller and more imposing than we might otherwise have dreamed, here at the tip of New England on a bleak December afternoon.

1987

In Search of Adam Duritz

This is a story about the promise of rock 'n' roll, my own lost youth, and a band that disappeared on the way to fame.

It began more than two years ago, on a long plane ride, when I was thumbing through a magazine and came upon a negative review of this new group I'd been hearing a lot about that went by the oddly memorable name of Counting Crows. It seemed that the sales of their debut album, *August and Everything After,* had been phenomenal, and that the music on it caused jaded, aging rock enthusiasts to weep tears of joy for the first time since the early seventies. Those who loved the group, composed of five musicians and one lead singer out of the Bay Area, claimed to find in them nothing short of a miracle—a tribute to rock's eternal recrudescence. After years of rap, heavy metal, hip-hop, grunge, and various subsets like "house," "techno," and "Gothic," the Crows were proof that rock 'n' roll in its original, pristine form hadn't died but had merely been hibernating. What piqued my curiosity, however, was that the review in question waxed full of scorn for the derivative nature of the band's "classic" sound, accusing the Crows of appropriating enough musical influences—Dylan, Tom Petty, Springsteen, Van Morrison, R.E.M., Pearl Jam—to fill half of Tower Records. So a day or two after I got home, before a fresh wave of cultural stimuli drowned my interest, I went out and bought the tape of *August and Everything After.* (CDs have come too late in my personal discographic history for me to treat them with the consumerist abandon I reserve for cassettes.) The last thing I remember is tearing open the cellophane wrapper and putting the tape in my Walkman—and then the phone must have rung or a kettle whistled or my daughter needed help tying her sneakers: Life intervened in its prosaic but imperious way, and I forgot about it for a while.

How do you explain the lure of good 'ole bass-driven, guitar-riffing rock 'n' roll? The way it hits somewhere inside your brain, like a painkiller, making everything all right?

"Rock music has one appeal only," thundered Allan Bloom in his best-selling jeremiad *The Closing of the American Mind,* "—a barbaric appeal to sexual desire—not love, not eros, but sexual desire undeveloped and untutored." David Frum, a smart thirtysomething conservative, quotes Bloom's indictment in his own book, *Dead Right,* before going on to add his fulminations against rock and "the twenty-four-hour at-home lubricity of MTV: pulsating sexual beats, gyrating near-naked bodies, and gleefully Dionysiac lyrics." Aside from the fact that Frum seems awfully young to be writing off the pleasures of lubricity, he doesn't seem to have bothered to listen to the music he's so quick to caricature as "hymns to the joys of onanism or the killing of parents." Such damning generalizations notwithstanding, one must note for the sake of accuracy that the contemporary music scene and its electronic concert stages, MTV and VH1, are varied enough to include the subtle likes of Freedy Johnston and Liz Phair as well as the come-ons of Bon Jovi or gangsta rap.

Rock 'n' roll is partly, of course, about riotous hormones as well as the natural dissension—even anarchism—of youth. But it is also about something that springs eternal, no matter what temporal age one has arrived at, and that is the primal and wholly unbelligerent urge to connect. It seems misguided to assert that the message of rock music is one of unregenerate lust for no other reason than that in order for the magic of a particular group or singer to work, there's got to be more than sexual chemistry. The power of rock is purer, actually—closer to the power of falling in love just when you thought you couldn't fall in love anymore, and the world fades out like the background in a movie, leaving just the music and you, gone breathless around the ribs. The impulses the music speaks to derive from adolescence, when one characteristically teeters between hope and malaise and is free to probe existential aches of all sorts—especially those of loneliness and romantic longing. But adulthood doesn't so much bring an end to these tensions as tamp them down. Leonard Cohen, that gray-haired and cracked-voiced chanteur whose deadpan vision of desire both sacred and profane was embraced by college students of my generation and is being rediscovered some twenty years later, touches on the durability of these yearnings in almost everything he writes. The women in his songs are always addressed with great Weltschmerzian relish (rather than Mick Jaggeresque disdain) as "baby"; the world is always about to be renounced; and love is a faint glimmer in the eye of a desperate man.

Perhaps the thrill of discovery is best when it happens this way, inadvertently, sort of like what must have happened when whoever it was who spotted Lana Turner at that mythic Hollywood soda counter knew he'd found a star. It was a sunny day in March when I finally got around to the Crows. Here I was on the cusp of forty—wave good-bye forever to green youth—and I'm walking along Lexington Avenue, plugged into my Walkman, and I'm *dumbstruck* by the music and voice and lyrics coming over the headset. A guy with a haunting voice was singing literate, angst-filled lyrics to me, taking me back down the vista of years to my teenaged days when I couldn't stop playing the Beatles or Buffalo Springfield or Jackson Browne or Neil Young or whoever it was who seemed to have a grip on all the important feelings that got left unsaid. Suddenly the city seemed new and shining, and I wanted to stop at the next pay phone and call everyone I knew and make them listen to Adam Duritz of the Crows, whose voice sounds like it was born to sing of the wistfulness that attaches itself, willy-nilly, to the subject of romantic love.

Is there anyone who enters the portals of adulthood without great apprehension—without suppressing the thought that nothing good can possibly lie ahead? The promise of rock is that you can duck back out, if only temporarily, and become who you were meant to be before the sheer passage of years took over. Perhaps it's as simple as the fact that from time to time we all need a reprieve from reality, and that rock—the rhythm and the volume and the very non-nine-to-fiveism of it—provides the least costly form of escape. In my case, it might have been the *sturm und drang* of going through a divorce, or the specter of middle age staring me down, etching lines around my eyes. What I know is that the Counting Crows took me back to the first time I heard *Layla* in someone's darkened dorm room, reminded me of the way I had once seen myself, slim-hipped and blue-jeaned, ready to run into the arms of a guy who called me "baby."

I couldn't stop playing the Crows, or talking about them. I dragged an older friend to a coffee shop one night, made her don my earphones, and then played her samples from different songs in a veritable disc-jockey frenzy as a bewildered look slowly crossed her face. Long-deferred groupie tendencies came alarmingly to the fore; the closest I had come to actually acting on these inclinations was to indulge in groupie-voyeurism, which included ordering a book called *Body Count* from Jann Wenner's short-lived Straight Arrow Press—mostly because I was fascinated that its writer, a Jewish groupie, had gotten within whispering distance of Paul McCartney before Linda Eastman nabbed him. I found myself lying in bed waiting for the eleven o'clock news to be over so I could guiltlessly zap my remote to MTV or VH1, there to watch the video of the Crows' hit single, "Mr. Jones," and gaze upon Adam Duritz as he loped around in front of the microphone with his dreadlocks flying and those peculiar half-balletic, half-klutzy movements of his.

Shortly thereafter, another video was released; this one was more ambitiously produced, with overtones of a Jim Jarmusch–like narrative, and it featured the lead Crow out on a limb of his own. The song, an intense and somewhat dreary meditation on a suicidal young woman named Maria, attested to Duritz's way with articulate, word-happy choruses and also to his ability to hold the camera, dressed in cutoff shorts, a sweatshirt, and army boots, making like Marcel Marceau. I decided I preferred him without the mustache and Van Dykish goatee he had recently sprouted, and wondered whether the character of Maria was based on a former girlfriend. I was lost in adolescent daydreams, but to those who knew me as a creature of presumed substance, I presented my newfound enthusiasm as an intellectually based fascination, sure evidence of my wide-ranging tastes and *au courant* sensibilities.

Even though I felt that I'd discovered the Counting Crows, while other people in my age group were busy discovering new wines or better workout regimens, more than 5 million people were discovering them along with me. The band went in less than a year from struggling contenderhood to virtual anointment as the princelings of nineties rock. Robbie Robertson of the Band was an early enthusiast, and it was at his suggestion that the Crows were asked to play at the 1993 Rock and Roll Hall of Fame's ceremony before they had even finished cutting their first album. (*August and Everything After* was recorded after the band had performed in concert together a mere nine times.) Somewhere between the band's setting off to perform in small towns across America and their appearance on *Saturday Night Live* half a year later, the Counting Crows happened—generating the kind of attention that is probably acquired through some mysterious confluence of luck and talent. When the band showed up on *Alternative Nation,* the droll deejay, Kennedy, remarked, "You have to almost plug your ears if you don't want to hear something about Counting Crows."

The momentum showed no sign of slackening: The Crows were selected to open for the Rolling Stones on the first eight dates of their summer '94 tour, and they appeared on the cover of *Rolling Stone* billed as "The Biggest New Band in America." I read the article and discovered that Adam Duritz was the son of two Jewish doctors, that his Rastafarian-styled dreadlocks were hair extensions, that he had majored in English literature at Berkeley, and that he liked the paintings of Mark Rothko. Then, for my fortieth birthday, I was given a present of a pair of tickets to a Crows concert—one of four sold-out performances in New York. On a sultry July evening, armed with a younger male friend, I found myself standing in the airless, smoky lobby of the Beacon Theater on Seventy-fourth Street and Broadway, surrounded by a sea of ripped jeans and flat, tanned midriffs.

Rock bands aren't rock bands unless they go on hours after their scheduled performance time, and that night was no different. While we waited, the unmistakably acrid perfume of marijuana wafted through the faux-Grecian splendor of the Beacon, and bets were being placed on what song the Crows would open with. (It turned out to be "Omaha," a Springsteenian-inspired, dirgelike tune with a self-mocking refrain that is the closest the rather earnest Duritz, who writes all of the Crows' lyrics, gets to outright humor.) The crowd was filled with lots of shiny-haired girls who looked like they'd be returning to Ivy League campuses come fall, and boyfriends in ponytails; near us there were several rows of Beavis and Buttheady–looking guys sitting five or six across. There was a scattering of old fogies like me as well, and a few couples with small children.

Counting Crows must be the least menacing bass-driven band ever to have gone triple platinum—which partially explains why they have been embraced by a variety of improbable, rock-averse types, ranging from David Letterman to Ed Koch. There is little about them of the

Rolling Stones' truculent hauteur (it's impossible to envision them treating stretch limos as bedrooms or trashing elegant hotel suites), or of the leave-me-alone-to-pluck-my-guitar cultivated disinterest of the late Kurt Cobain. Although the whole notion of appropriation is inherently postmodernist—and Duritz is not only comfortable with but open about his musical influences—there is, interestingly enough, nothing postmodernist about the spirit of the Crows, nothing remotely campy or even ironic about their style. The group's music appeals to those old enough to have been at Woodstock (in its original version) as well as those young enough to have mythologized it. What this would seem to suggest is that young listeners have tired not only of grunge and its postmortem perspective, but of defining themselves in opposition to the generation that preceded them. Then again, I've been told that really hip twenty-year-olds don't rate the Crows highly, and this, too, makes sense to me. There is something distinctly grounded and accessible—even familiar—about the melancholy vision offered up in the Crows' songs, a way in which their message of anomie-ever-on-the-lookout-for-glimpses-of-meaning is a throwback to the discourse of rock as it emerged from the sixties and seventies rather than a reflection of more recent developments, in which an over-riding sense of alienation emerges out of nowhere and the very urge to communicate is declared suspect.

The band—a quintet of musically meticulous if slightly robotic young men and the charismatic Duritz—retained a makeshift attitude in performance that was less arrogant than nerdy. In between songs they quaffed yuppie drinks—Gatorade and spring water. But from the moment the slightly chunky, baby-faced singer slouched over to center stage, gotten up in a version of his usual uniform—T-shirt, army boots, and baggy cutoff sweats—he commanded attention. Duritz hugged himself, pointed fingers at his own head as if to demonstrate a state of turmoil, and in general acted as though he were conducting an interior dialogue with the songs. In his less expressive moments he chewed on a fingernail, turned his back on the audience to explain something to the band, ambled briefly offstage with sagging shoulders, played air-guitar, and generally acted like everyone's younger brother who ever wanted to be a rock star. Except for this: Adam Duritz has a great voice, a tender yet burly instrument with traces of Celtic bluesiness, of yes, Van Morrison, Springsteen, Joe Cocker, and other impassioned rock 'n' rollers. And this: When he stands onstage, the lead singer of the Counting Crows grabs the spotlight so effortlessly he makes it look like your younger brother has suddenly, overnight, become mesmerizing to behold.

After the show, Duritz—who'd changed into a promotional T-shirt for the movie *Spanking the Monkey*—was surrounded by female admirers. (In a lull during the concert three girls had run up to kiss him, which elicited his wry comment, "This isn't a fucking love-in.") One fetching young woman demanded to know whether he was Israeli— "No, Russian," he replied—and another comely fan came over to congratulate him on his lyrics. As I watched him, it occurred to me that he exuded the sort of casual doe-eyed magnetism that would have made him the object of female adulation even if he had never written the anthemic "Mr. Jones."

"It hurts me to do interviews," Duritz announced when he finally sat down to talk with me in an empty section of the theater. Away from the posse of friends and fans, he shifted from graciously accepting tributes to musing upon the disconcerting phenomenon of sudden fame. "It's getting bigger and bigger," he said, "and I'm scared." There is a curious air to him, unself-assuming yet pious, as though he'd decided the best way not to be hurtled out of the recognizable firmament is to keep delineating how *un*recognizable it's become. Then, his tone of wounded artistic integrity slipping over into something more angry and put-upon, he added: "MTV made all these changes in my life." Duritz was at pains to point out—almost as though there were a referee inside his head keeping track of any possible compromises in the name of success he might be charged with—that the endlessly aired video of "Mr. Jones" came out three months after *August and Everything After* appeared. (Music videos are more typically timed to come out in con-junction with an album's release.) There'd been dancing in the aisles when he broke into "Mr. Jones" tonight, although Duritz resisted the song's hit-single seduction by giving it a more jagged treatment than it received on the album or video. "I don't understand it," he contin-ued. "My whole life is changing so much. At best it's okay if you're in a good mood."

Duritz told me that he was currently reading Paul Auster and that he read science fiction whenever he felt depressed; his literary idol, how-ever, is Saul Bellow (the song "Rain King" was inspired by Bellow's novel *Henderson the Rain King*). When I inquired whether he'd ever con-sidered becoming a writer, he asserted with a trace of irritation that he *was* a writer, and that the kind of writer I meant limited his audience, since who reads anymore? What Duritz is most impassioned about, however, more serious than he is about books or the price of fame, is rock music. His knowledge of rock history is nothing short of encyclopedic, and he makes rapid-fire references to obscure, vanished groups and little-known recordings of songs that later became hits. (It is undoubt-edly this grasp of musical antecedents that has led to the charge that his songs and singing style are derivative, as well as to the gets-under-your-skin appeal of the group's melodies.) He admitted to a fondness for the early Rod Stewart of Faces and said that he began listening to "all kinds of music—show records, the Beatles, the Fifth Dimension"—when he was four years old. It seems that even as a toddler Duritz had eclectic tastes; two favorites from those years were "Wild Irish Rose" and the Kingston Trio's version of "Sloop John B." When I asked him why the Crows have agreed to open for the Stones, which seems like an odd move for a band as self-consciously unatmospheric as this one, he answered, simply, "I want to meet Mick and Keith."

Outside the Beacon an elderly homeless man wandered around ask-ing "Who's the Crow?" There was a bunch of girls waiting to catch sight of the band, and for a moment I found myself wondering what Adam Duritz, so acutely aware of how fickle the whole fame gig is, would feel about returning to being just another ordinary guy, an unknown singer trying to get his music heard.

Two days after the Beacon concert Adam Duritz returned the message I'd left for him at his hotel and called me at home. I was sitting at my desk when the phone rang and someone asked for me and it turned out to be *him:* For a moment, my pulse racing, I was fourteen again. (Would Adam Duritz have wanted to sleep with me if I were years younger and pounds lighter? Was this the real source of my fascination—an elaborately disguised game of "what if," in which I hoped to achieve a retrospective righting of history, with myself in the role of the Rock Star's Girlfriend?) Our conversation was brief: He wanted me to know that he thought I was "cool, too" and that he would agree to meet for another interview when he was back in New York for the Stones tour in spite of the fact that he didn't want to be "fodder for the press."

Had I known I'd never get to speak with Adam Duritz again, I could have saved myself the schlepp out to the Meadowlands to catch the Crows' opening act for Mick and Keith. I'd never been a bona fide Stones fan, never warmed fully to Mick's pouting swagger or to Keith Richards's been-to-hell-and-back persona. The truth is, I'd felt too old for stadium rock—for the likes of Pink Floyd, Arrowsmith, and U2—even when I was of the age to enthuse. So the notion of voluntarily putting myself in the middle of a Roman mob of true Stones believers just to catch the Crows doing their restrained, intimate thing didn't exactly appeal to me. But I was still faithfully doing my tagging-at-their-heels journalist's thing; besides which, I was *worried* about the boys. I couldn't imagine how their brand of up-close music—the way the band focused on the song rather than on solos or being guitar gods, and the way Adam kind of huddled around his own vocals, intent on keeping his world small— would translate when placed in the context of a bigger arena.

The answer is that it didn't.

The Crows seemed lost at the Meadowlands, amplified out of their natural state into something they weren't cut out to be. They're essentially a club band, and even at the relatively cozy Beacon they weren't as good as they were in the privacy of my home (which explains, too, why R.E.M. tours so little, electing to let their music speak for itself). Duritz's careful lyrics seemed lost in the vast spaces, filled with an impatient, party-hearty crowd; the band itself sounded cobbled together, like a bunch of guys who'd been practicing in a garage and yanked prematurely into the big time.

When they were done, the Crows put down their instruments and walked off, no introduction and no postscript, either. After a suitable wait, the Stones burst on—and you could see in a flash what the whole stadium thing was about, the unabashed spectacle of it, replete with fireworks, giant floats, and catwalks. Jagger's energy was unflagging; he strutted and growled and projected all over the place. Maybe we'd grown too old and encumbered, but my friends and I left before the Stones were done: Baby-sitters were waiting, tomorrow was a workday.

Later that same night—it was one in the morning, actually—the phone woke me up. It was Bryn Bridenthal, head of publicity at Geffen Records, calling apologetically from Los Angeles to cancel my interview with the Crows, which had been scheduled, after much back-and-forthing, for the next day. I couldn't quite figure out why she couldn't have waited until the next morning.

Shortly after that, they disappeared. The Crows canceled tour date after tour date—seventeen concerts in all.

I was supposed to catch up with them in L.A. at the end of September—Bridenthal assured me it would happen, if only because "the nice thing about Adam is he's a Jewish son, subject to guilt"—but that possibility turned hazier and more indefinite the closer it got. Rumors began to percolate that the Crows had stopped performing because of bad notices, and that Duritz was having a hard time. Eventually, after September had turned into the second week of October, I was faxed two press releases by Geffen. The first one was dated August 15, and gave "exhaustion" as the reason for the canceled shows, with an oblique quote from Duritz: "I guess the main thing is that the shows were starting to suffer. In the end, you don't do this to sell records, you do it because you love to play music and you need to play music. So when the music started to suffer, we figured it was time to take a break. . . ." The second one was dated September 26 and explained that the Crows had been forced to reschedule the second two of three sold-out shows at the Greek Theater in L.A. for less esoteric reasons—because of Duritz's throat problems: "Upon examining Duritz this morning a Los Angeles throat specialist found soft nodules on his vocal cords and forbade him to sing again this week. . . ."

Ah, but was it not ever thus? Aren't most love objects worthy of the name inclined to be elusive? I persisted, scouring for clues, and came upon one tucked away in an article about R.E.M.'s new album, *Monster*. There was a reference to Michael Stipe's difficulties in handling his first bout of fame, back in 1985—"I had kind of a nervous breakdown, I guess"—and then mention was made of the fact that "Adam Duritz . . . is trying to deal with it right now."

So *there* he was, the skittish creature, buffeted by the winds of the hype machine. I remembered something he'd said on the phone. "This is my whole life," he said. "It matters to me." It's easy to make fun of people who become famous and then have second thoughts—they wanted it, didn't they?—but Duritz seems to have been anxious about stepping into the ring, about the hollowness at its center, even before he became a star. I faxed him a letter, which his publicist promised to forward, trying one last time to coax him to talk with me, explaining that I understood the pressures he was under, the difficulties of being an artist in a material world. (If it was too late for me to be his groupie, perhaps I could still be his therapist.) I never got an answer.

■ ■ ■

I continued to ask around about the Crows, until I happened to mention the group to a friend out on the West Coast who suggested I call T-Bone Burnett. The forty-six-year-old Burnett is a songwriter and highly regarded free-lance record producer; he has produced the music of Elvis Costello, Roy Orbison, Los Lobos, Sam Phillips (to whom he is married), Peter Case ("He's obscure," Burnett says, "but I always mention him"), and Counting Crows. Burnett, who talks like someone who's managed to age gracefully beyond the confines of coolness, explained that he was given a demo tape of the Crows by a mutual friend and was immediately struck by the number of good songs: "It's very seldom that you hear more than one or two songs you like, but on this tape there were ten or twelve." Even more significantly, he was taken by the sound of Adam Duritz's voice. "Electric guitars are electric guitars," he says. "What distinguishes one band from another is the sound of the singer. Adam Duritz has a very distinctive voice—a voice that carries emotion."

When I asked him about the persistent accusations of musical plagiarism, Burnett said, with a dismissive flourish, "Everyone's derivative." As for the claims that the Crows were backed to an unusual degree by Gary Gersh, their A&R man at Geffen (Gersh has since left to head Capitol Records), Burnett countered that "Geffen never knew, in fact, exactly what to do with the record, because it didn't fit into their format. They put the record out and gave them tour support, but the Crows weren't treated like hothouse flowers. They went out, nine guys in a van, and worked hard for six months." And then I asked him the question that had been rubbing at me ever since I saw the band perform at the Beacon: Why weren't they better in live performance? Burnett's answer surprised me, because it came slowly, without a trace of irony, as though in order to formulate it he'd reached down beyond industry blather to a place not yet eroded by cynicism: "Most performers get bits—sort of like set pieces—that happen; they throw them up like cannons that go off every time. I think the kind of thing Adam goes for—the spontaneity, the emotion in the moment—is very hit-and-miss. They don't have a polished show that works. The Crows don't have a *shtick*."

■ ■ ■

Had Adam Duritz faltered under the burden of ceaseless promotion and exposure that's involved in becoming a music superstar? Had the pressure done strange things to his head? (The Crows were nominated for three Grammys the next year—recognition worth genuflecting about, one would have thought—yet they didn't even show up at the ceremonies.)

Of course, such questions may in themselves be beside the point in a culture that believes that celebrity and talent come down to one and the same, and that any artist who insists on maintaining a private space —on trying, in other words, to keep the hype and the art apart—is no more than an oversensitive weirdo. And in truth, most performers who cozy up to the spotlight seem to relish it, to willingly go along with the demands on their time and the marketing of their talent in exchange for fame and glory. (Even so low-key a group as Hootie & the Blowfish are hocking their names on golf balls, key chains, and sweatshirts—all featured in the merchandising insert that accompanies *Fairweather Johnson,* their latest release.) But in both his songs and his person, Adam Duritz has seemed intent on preserving a certain mystery, a protective cocoon from which he can spin his musical visions.

I suppose you could say the story ends there. More than two years have passed since I first happened upon the Crows, and I've returned to reality—to paying the bills, helping my daughter with her homework, living my life in due chronological order. I still go into HMV to browse the new releases (where, for a while, *August and Everything After* held remarkably strong on the charts). I continue to have a weak spot for female singers who focus on their interior lives at least as much as on the opposite sex—Dar Williams, Aimee Mann, Iris DeMent, Nanci Griffith, and Shawn Colvin—and for hoarse male crooners like Bryan Adams, who've just lost the girl or the band or their high-school hopes. But no one's managed to make the city seem new and shining like it did that day when I first heard the Crows; no one's spoken directly to my adolescent heart like Adam Duritz. I suppose you could say I've given up searching for him, although that wouldn't be quite true. I still stop and listen whenever a cut from the Crows' one and only album is played on the radio; I still put on "Mr. Jones" when I feel like I need a jolt of its peculiarly mournful energy, its nostalgic but inspired sound. That long-ago vision of myself as a groupie may be receding further and further into the misty past, but I know one of these days Adam Duritz will be back, dreadlocks flying, singing of love and its consequences.

1995

POSTSCRIPT

Well, three long years after the Crows first topped the charts, Adam Duritz finally came back. It was the fall of 1996, to be exact, and the much-anticipated follow-up to their multiplatinum debut album was titled, with an oblique allusion to inspiration lost and reclaimed, *Recovering the Satellites.* The album came out to reviews that ranged from respectful to dismissive; there was more than a whiff of that no-second-act-in-American-lives gloating, that *why have you failed to surpass your masterpiece* insinuating undertone. Early on, before the critics weighed in, the Sunday *Times Magazine* (which had originally commissioned my article on the nature of my obsession with rock 'n' roll in general and Adam Duritz in particular, but finally axed it after much hedging) thought they'd be interested once again, with the inclusion of an updated interview with Duritz. I promptly got in touch with the Crows' manager, Martin Kirkup, who seemed very eager to facilitate things and suggested that I fax my piece to the singer's hotel room in Sweden, where the band was touring. Duritz must have been faxed that piece at least four times, twice from me and twice from my own agent—just to make sure he'd get it, what with front desks and it being Sweden and faxes being easily smudged, and so on.

I never heard from Duritz, and after several days of unreturned calls to Kirkup in Los Angeles, I gave up. I must say if anything surprised me about the whole venture it was my perseverance in the face of repeated rejection, which I suppose I was able to manage under cover of journalism. In real life I was far too thin-skinned to go chasing after elusive romantic heroes. And there was another thing about real life: In the interval between the Crows' first and second albums, it had bumped me along to another stage. I still kept an ear out for the occasional rock album—The Lemonheads' *car button cloth,* say, or Elvis Costello's *All This Useless Beauty,* but I was listening more and more to Schubert and Mahler and Brahms. None of which is to say I don't stop and watch Adam Duritz when I catch him on VH1 singing "Long December," a cut from the new album. Still, I can't help but notice that his hairline has receded and his dreadlocks, as if to compensate, have gotten longer. He's traded in his T-shirt for a slightly more buttoned-down look, and the video features Courtney Cox from *Friends,* who was reputed to have been his love interest for a while. I've never watched *Friends,* and maybe all of the above is nothing more than the sniping of unrequited love. But God, does he have a beautiful voice.

1997

Acting the Victim:
Claire Bloom vs. Philip Roth

Philip Roth's lavishly misogynistic imagination has long been a scourge of the banner-bearing feminist, so it's hardly surprising that his ex-wife's new revenge memoir, *Leaving a Doll's House,* is being heralded as an inspirational text, a strategic sortie against patriarchal malevolence. It is, we have been assured, an especially apt form of comeuppance. Hasn't Roth habitually pillaged his most intimate relationships in the service of his scabrous, cruelly funny novels? Isn't turnabout fair play? In short order, the delicate-featured memoirist has become a source of lurid fascination—a sort of upscale Lorena Bobbitt for the kaffeeklatsch set.

Dante himself could not have imagined a more blistering inferno than the one that's been unleashed by the dissolution of a relationship which, on the face of it, seemed almost picture-perfect. Claire Bloom was the actress whose melting, dark-eyed beauty caught the attention of Charlie Chaplin and led to her starring in *Limelight* at the age of twenty; and Philip Roth was the novelist of lanky build and brooding, Heathcliffian visage (a writerly version of "tall, dark, handsome Tyrone Power," whose cinematic presence the actress had been smitten with as a young girl). There they were, living in disciplined but creative splendor in Connecticut and New York and London, sharing a high-minded interest in "books, and theater, and music," and there they were again, in a television documentary made on the occasion of Roth's sixtieth birthday, celebrating with friends at an elegant restaurant, laughter and good feelings all around.

How little we knew! It turns out, as she writes, that he thought "I behaved oddly in restaurants, looking at my watch and humming to myself," when he wasn't playing footsie under the table with other women, or sinking into deep depressions, or carping about money. Turns out that he was always something of a monster ("feral, unflinching, hostile, accusative"), and she was always intent on being long-suffering: "From the beginning, the scrutiny I was under was considerable, making me feel as though there was a trial under way and I was the defendant." But she continued to cling to him for the next eighteen years, in spite of the malevolent aspect he had revealed early on, because he was so damned brilliant and she was so damned vulnerable: "My fear of abandonment . . . has never left me." Then, one day in the summer of 1993, he threw her out of the "still, beautiful, and austere" clapboard house that she had shown no signs of leaving on her own, however bad things got. At which point the English Rose, as the British press once dubbed her, decided to show her thorns. If our image of this fine couple has been bloodied, at least the record's been set straight. Or so *Leaving a Doll's House* would have us believe.

Some of the trouble with Ms. Bloom's book can be blamed on the lackluster quality of her prose, which is evident from the very first pages. She gravitates toward shopworn couplings—"hopeless gambler" (page 8), "considerable anxiety" (page 9), "greatest joy" (page 9)—as well as strangely inverted locutions—"In my child's eye I sensed that the quarrel had been about money, and saw Mother upset terribly" (page 8). She has, too, a somewhat dreary, even banal, way of describing the impact of events on her psyche. Commenting on the arrival of her younger brother, John, Ms. Bloom sounds like a walking compendium of everything we have been told an Older Sibling is supposed to feel about the birth of a Younger Sibling: "Apart from his birth, which immediately filled me with fierce jealousy—alongside a secret desire to have him quietly disappear—I remember little of that early period before moving to Bristol."

But the truth is no one really expects famous people's accounts of their lives to win any prizes in the writing department. Although a greater skill with words might have enabled us to form a better understanding of the forces that drove the actress—presuming she herself understands them—it is not her failings in this area that make *Leaving a Doll's House* strangely uncompelling. (Its ostensible dishyness notwithstanding, I defy anyone to read this book cover to cover.) More troubling is the oddly secondhand, almost canned quality of the emotions Bloom records. After she ended her steamy six-year-old adulterous affair with Richard Burton, she tells us, as if reading off cue cards, "I was left with a profound sense of loss, of panic, and humiliation." And here is her explanation of her precipitous and passionless decision to marry Rod Steiger a year later, at age twenty-eight: "I was searching for the paternal masculine support of the kind I had been deprived of when I was a child." Even when she writes of abruptly leaving Steiger for Hillard Elkins, a flashy theater producer with baroque tastes in everything from interior decoration to sex, Ms. Bloom eschews the hazards of self-reflection in favor of cultural theory à la Margaret Mead: "Women of my time and upbringing were offered very few opportunities for sexual exploration or expression. . . . Between the Judaic abjuration of sexual pleasure and the Victorian stricture against anything sexual whatsoever, my generation of Jewish women were thus doubly trapped."

At age forty-three, having lost her manager/husband Elkins (who, when he isn't initiating his wife into something I take to be S&M but which she demurely describes as "games stretching the boundaries of physical experience," handily produces *A Doll's House* and *Hedda Gabler* for her) to another woman, Claire Bloom finds herself at a personal and professional standstill. Enter Philip Roth, who bumps into her on Madison Avenue as he is on his way to his shrink and she to her yoga teacher.

Bloom has told us that she has been drawn to saturnine, "emotionally unavailable" men and Roth does not disappoint. When he's not snarling at her or having nightmares that lead to "high-pitched cries . . . in the night," he is balking at her sensible plan to buy "a small, inexpensive holiday retreat" in Umbria. Roth even asks her to kick her eighteen-year-old-daughter, Anna, out of their London apartment, a request to which the ever-accommodating Bloom agrees.

Don't get me wrong: Roth appears to have been a difficult and sometimes hair-raising partner—although not enough to have stopped Ms. Bloom from desperately pushing to formalize their fifteen years of non-connubial nonbliss, in spite of some rather striking indications that Roth was anxious to the point of phobic about committing himself to marriage. The latter included his taking three weeks to consider her proposal and finally accepting upon the condition that she sign a prenuptial agreement, which her lawyer would later describe as "'unconscionable,' the most brutal document of its kind he had ever encountered." (One assumes that this indignant fellow was a different attorney than the one she had consulted with before signing.) But what Ms. Bloom declines any credit for throughout this saga is the exertion of her own dazzling and truly formidable will. It was, after all, that steely instrument that propelled her out of a financially uncertain and peripatetic childhood onto the London stage, and then gave her the resolve to dump one husband (Steiger proved too melancholy, especially around Christmas) and use the second, Elkins, for his connections, even as she shuddered at his arriviste ways. One can discern, through the pious gloss Bloom puts on the events of her life, the shrewd maneuverings of a stage brat. Many of her passing amours find her work, and later the blackguard novelist is also pressed into service: He helps her restructure her career around a successful series of one-woman performances and recitals —beginning with Shakespeare and moving on to interpretations of Henry James and Anna Akhmatova. Undoubtedly, Roth's cultural authority was part of his allure, although to hear Claire Bloom tell it, you'd think she married him out of some sort of abstract sense of literary appreciation—almost as though she were the flesh-and-blood embodiment of one of his own worshipful female creations. ("I could be his Muse, if only he'd let me," one such character says in the epigraph to Roth's *My Life as a Man*.)

A friend of mine, after skimming the galleys of Bloom's book at my dinner table, impatiently demanded to know where the "bad" parts were; clearly, she wasn't satisfied with the misdeeds that *were* documented. I understood how she felt: Notwithstanding the narrator's breathlessly ominous tone, no one is actually slapped around in her book. The marital torments recounted in *Leaving a Doll's House* are of a subtler order, often resembling the standard dissensions that occur in any long-standing relationship. The account of her years with Roth actually involves little sense of physical intimacy, violent or otherwise. More than that, it is curiously without erotic charge. (Underneath its veneer of high and tragic drama, the Roth-Bloom alliance sounds as monotonous in its derailment as any next-door neighbors' squabbling about whose turn it is to throw out the garbage.)

Equally absent is any sense of moral accountability. There is always something out there—marijuana, her Absent Father, and handiest of all, her unconscious—that forces the hapless narrator to do things that are less than exemplary. The price that Bloom's heady ambitions and desires exacted—the things she was willing to sacrifice or jettison "in pursuit of the perfect role and the purely imaginary lover"—is never acknowledged except as evidence of her being in thrall to forces stronger than herself. "The truth is that I was unable to oppose him," she writes, and it is upon this convenient fiction—this self-deception, rather—that her story is precariously perched. In her recollection of history, the adult Claire Bloom still sounds much like the "undeniably self-centered . . . willful and high-strung little girl" she recollects having once been, playing "potted versions of Shakespeare plays": "My chosen heroines were rarely, if ever, heroic; instead they were tormented by hateful stepparents, imprisoned by wicked witches." The grown-up femme fatale of whom Anthony Quinn said, "You look at me with those big brown eyes, and all the time your little mental computer is noting everything I say," remains forever in her own mind a fatherless little girl searching for a safe place to land, a supine creature drawn to men who issue demonic commands she has no choice but to obey.

The real problem with Bloom's book is that it asks the reader to do more than feel sympathy and outrage on behalf of its put-upon heroine: Beginning with the portentous echoing of its title, it asks us to take her plight as paradigmatic of something larger than her own misbegotten amorous choices. She presents her book as a classic drama of captivity and release, tracking her emergence from swanky Connecticut bondage into the lonely freedom of her own apartment on the Upper East Side. Indeed, this glamorous and resourceful woman—with her numerous lovers, her three husbands, and her career as an acclaimed stage and screen actress—would like her audience to see her as just another emotionally battered wife with a horrific tale to tell. She is not convincing in the role.

I suppose that for a female reader to reject Bloom's he-made-me-do-it perspective is to risk sounding unsisterly or simply hard-hearted. Truth to tell, it's not easy to say which of this pair comes off worse, Bloom the willful masochist or Roth the tormenting narcissist. In many respects, though, they seem an uncannily perfect match—a symbiotic couple if ever there was one. Each is talented, Jewish, good-looking, supremely manipulative, tight-fisted (there is much high dudgeon over Bulgari rings, stereo equipment, and dinner tabs); each ardently looks out for the other, until real life—with its dying mothers, ailing fathers, demanding daughters, and nervous breakdowns—intrudes, in its ungainly way. One of the abiding mysteries of their relationship, as gleaned from this version of it, is how a man with such a keenly developed sense of irony ended up with a woman who sounds so prissy and humorless. What emerges to particularly comic effect is the sacral atmosphere that surrounded Roth's vocation—so vastly different from the approach taken by Isaac Babel to *his* work, as recounted in a recently published memoir by his wife, A. N. Pirozhkova. (In *At His Side: The*

Last Years of Isaac Babel, Pirozhkova explains that she came to understand "how much Babel disliked talking about literature, which he would do almost anything to avoid," recounting that when someone once tried to interview Babel about his literary plans for the coming year, he answered, "Well, I am seriously thinking about buying a goat.")

Leaving a Doll's House is written in the blinding light of determined unknowingness by a woman who smiles sweetly (not for naught is she an actress) as she scatters poisoned morsels. The book is less persuasive as a feminist fable than as a vehicle of vengeance; where it undeniably succeeds is in being a shrewdly conceived salvo aimed at the man who dared to scorn Claire Bloom. ("Hell has no fury like a woman scorned": That phrase—a variant of the original Congreve—has been invoked thousands of times to explain the tendency of women to react in vitriolic, Medea-like fashion to the end of a love affair. Still, I don't think the significance of the remark has ever found its full literary application until now.) Its triumphant existence is made possible by a culture awash in simplifications and elasticized terms, increasingly inured to the distinctions between parody, spectacle, and tragedy. Thus sexual harassment is reduced to a second-grade boy kissing a classmate on the cheek, and the author of *Leaving a Doll's House* is the victim of a man whose sexual fury she expertly analyzes when it appears in his work but finds inexplicable when directed at her own person.

Claire Bloom is finally not interested in exploring the complex reciprocations and moral ambiguities of actual human relationships. For all her demure flutterings, she is a scorpion posing as a butterfly—a classically female approach to aggression. And yet to read this book is to realize that, even in our age of unfettered autobiography, certain sorts of confessions remain unseemly—producing less of a salacious thrill or an energizing jolt of *Schadenfreude* than a sense of discomfort at having glimpsed more than one wants to know or than the writer is aware of having revealed. Stanley Elkin once wrote that "at its most daring, and maybe even at its best, all autobiography is 'authorized,' a striptease with the pasties or G-string that covers the mind left on. Left on, too, is some final, ultimate, impenetrable eighth veil, the nasty hoard in the secret cellar." Which is to say that it's easy to forget just how much artistry is required to shape candor into something other than the yelps and shrieks of *Look at me! Watch me run, smile, get hurt, cry!* Too much discretion may result in a tasteless literary broth, but too much revelation —or, more accurately, too much revelation without an accompanying level of self-awareness—is curdling.

The one service Philip Roth's ex-wife has unwittingly rendered him is to remind us that a writer's voice—"something that begins at around the back of the knees," as he once described it—is everything; and that even so self-plundering a novelist as Roth is not performing an act of mimesis, not simply slapping his interior existence onto the page and adding a few well-chosen bits of dialogue. Despite nearly two decades in his company, Bloom has somehow failed to learn from his greatest strength, which is an intensity of scrutiny that spares himself least of all. If the unexamined life isn't worth living, surely the unreflective memoir is not worth reading.

1996

The Self,
New and Improved

These Unhappy Breasts

I never thought I'd end up—a girl who once worried she'd wear an undershirt all her life—posing for a mug shot of my breasts. But there I was, stripped to the waist, facing too-bright lights, my usually protuberant nipples shrunken shyly into themselves, as a studiously neutral photographer clicked her camera. My breasts were being shot every which way, to the left and to the right, from above and below. If it wasn't for its being the Don Allen Studios, which specializes in photos for cosmetic surgery, you would have thought I was trying out for a spread in some downscale girlie magazine.

Big boobs: The very phrase has an overheated quality. Think Mae West and Jayne Mansfield. Marilyn Monroe and her dark-haired rival Jane Russell (the recipient of a special brassiere designed by engineers who worked for Howard Hughes, a breast man if ever there was one). Dolly Parton and Loni Anderson. Give up forever on the vision of Audrey Hepburn, whose boyish chest allowed her to flit through the movies wearing Givenchy's achingly chic creations even when she played a hooker dreaming of breakfast at Tiffany's. Think, again, of the chest preceding the rest of the woman like a pair of headlights. *Vroom, vroom,* warm up the sensual engine. Men—American men, in particular—are supposed to love them; women everywhere, to envy them.

Why, then, would anyone endowed with hefty breasts think of cutting them down to a more manageable size? How, in other words, is it possible for there to be too much of a good thing? It flies in the face of the myths we carry around with us—all those antiquated Barbie-doll myths that have no bearing on current reality or on the complicated ways we form images of ourselves. Marilyn Monroe has undoubtedly made way for Kate Moss, and streamlined bodies have replaced hourglass figures, but 1994 might as well be 1954 in this one respect: Try telling another woman that you want smaller-sized breasts and she'll either laugh incredulously or ask you to give her some of yours. Since I first started seriously entertaining the thought of having my breasts reduced, I've encountered few exceptions to this rule, and two of them were masseuses. (Massage and other fitness professionals must be in a unique position to render up dispassionate assessments about a given human shape.) "Men want women to be big," says one small-breasted friend with great certainty, seconds after I've disclosed that I've had my own big breasts reduced. "It's every man's fantasy."

Breasts are quintessentially female, as bound up with our ideas about women as the color pink or the concept of maternal nurturance. When Bob Dylan wailed, "Once I had mountains in the palm of my hand," no one who listened to the song had trouble figuring out that he was bemoaning the loss of a girlfriend; they understood that the part stood in for the whole, even if they had never heard of the literary term *metonymy*. Breasts are soft and cushiony; they can, magically, feed a newborn child for months on end, and they're a major reason women have never clamored en masse to play touch football. All of which makes breast reduction a tender business, a subject around which we grow uneasy, women at least as much as men. In an age when we profess to understand the most wayward and blatantly narcissistic of desires, the wish to be less bosomy remains the desire that dares not speak its name, meeting up with little comprehension and even less empathy.

And small wonder: We're dealing with a touchstone of female identity here, even if it's become a parody of said identity. (When I checked in *The Describer's Dictionary*, there were three lines under "[of a woman] having large breasts"—including the oddly dated-sounding *stacked*—as opposed to a single entry for "[of a woman] having a flat chest.") Although breast augmentations have merited an enormous amount of coverage, both serious and sensational, breast reductions aren't much talked about, except for the occasional teenage starlet's confession in *People* magazine—in which case it gets a cover. (Hard to image Punky Brewster's nose job getting a cover, isn't it?) Although reputed to be the most psychologically successful of all elective operations, reducing mammaplasty—as it's clinically called—remains the untold story of cosmetic surgery.

As for the operation itself, plan on leaving your vanity at the door. Perhaps the worst moment for me was right on the operating table, when I was propped up in the first woozy but still sentient stages of sedation, to be marked with a purple felt-tip pen (a Wiscot surgical skin marker, actually) like a chicken being readied for slaughter. Arrows pointed to where my nipples would be relocated, and demarcation lines were drawn. *Bigger,* the surgeon wrote on my poor asymmetrical left breast, in front of what seemed to me to be a milling surgical team of thousands. *Bigger!* I lay back down, happy to be knocked out and spared further indignities. . . . But let me begin at the beginning, as all good tales of self-transformation, physical or otherwise, are supposed to.

I was, as I mentioned, a girl who worried she'd wear an undershirt forever—a late developer. I was sixteen before puberty put in a full-fledged appearance, but when it finally decided to do so, I went from wearing training bras to filling out a white turtleneck quite persuasively. Throughout my twenties I remember being self-conscious about my chest: It seemed to herald the rest of me in a fashion I wasn't prepared for. Perhaps it was the fact that I wore a 36C in a decade when everyone else I knew was getting ready to go braless and had remained an indeterminate 34B the better to be able to do so. Or the fact that I strove to define myself via my intellect rather than my heterosexual assets. Or, let's face it, perhaps it was the fact that I was preternaturally uncomfortable around boys, in spite of the fact that I had grown up with three brothers. What could a guy want from a girl with "big tits" (that's how I'd begun thinking of them) but something to do with sex?

So began the Great Cover-up Period, extending from my college years into my thirties. I took to wearing shirts in the stiffest, most obscuring cotton; T-shirts in extra-extra large; and dresses that were cut with due vagueness around the upper half of my torso. One man who was in a writing class I took at the New School during my twenties referred to me as "the Jewish Sophia Loren"—a flattering description, to be sure, but one that I connected more to my vaguely guessed-at bosomy charms than to anything else. When I went to be photographed for the book jacket of the novel I published at the age of thirty-one, nothing seemed sufficiently disguising among the array of shapeless tops I had brought along, so I borrowed a man-tailored shirt from the photographer's own closet. All of these stratagems worked well enough—until, that is, the hot weather rolled around.

Every summer since my nephews and nieces have been old enough to notice, I have dreaded going into the water. (It's not only old men who ogle; children—little boys, especially—do, too.) Oceans and lakes and swimming pools require bathing suits, and bathing suits disclose cleavage and fleshy cliffs beyond. "Why do you have such fat boobies?" one of my more vocal nephews wanted to know. Actually, I can't say I blamed his wide-eyed interest. My breasts seemed to take on a life of their own in the water, bobbing around like beach balls. Come the warm weather, I realized more and more what an encumbrance large breasts could be. They got in the way of so many things, running and swimming and sleeping on my stomach. I had also begun to notice that no matter how acceptably thin the rest of me might be at any given time, my chest weighed me down, giving me a somewhat matronly appearance.

My breasts took up a disproportionate amount of space, no doubt about it, and every summer for the past eight or nine years, I'd lie in the sun envisioning myself less top-heavy. So why, you may be wondering, did it take almost a decade for the plan to go from conception to execution? A major reason had to do with my own indecisive, profoundly ambivalent nature; I had trouble picking which movie to see, much less making larger decisions. Another had to do with what I consider to be a strength of mine when it isn't hindering me, and that is my considerable psychological-mindedness; the latter trait made me cautious of an operation that revolved around so crucial a piece of my body. There was always the possibility that I was playing out internal conflicts, blaming the size of my breasts for things unrelated to them. Was I denying my femininity? Expressing hostility toward men? Rejecting the softer parts of my own personality?

And then there was this: Right around the time I had finished my novel, I treated myself to a weeklong visit to a spa. That visit was probably responsible for scaring me off a breast reduction for the next few years. In the atmosphere of physical intimacy that such places induce, a woman proudly showed me her own operated-upon chest, and I was shocked by the two stumps she boasted instead of breasts. She seemed entirely pleased with the effect, but I was horrified: I could see wanting to be smaller, but I wasn't looking to be castrated. I also heard a bit about what the operation entailed, and wondered whether I was prepared for the discomfort and pain. Then there was the man I had been seeing on and off, who composed odes to my breasts when he wasn't being critical of the rest of me. I decided to live with what I had.

The years passed, I married (a different man, also enamored of my breasts) and had a child. Pregnancy blew my breasts up to, first, a DD and then, with nursing, to a staggering E. After weaning my daughter (which I did more quickly than I might have if I had felt less self-conscious about the size of my chest), my breasts settled down to an unwieldy 38D. Large to begin with, my breasts were now positively pendulous. They had also begun to—how shall I put this delicately?—sag. I started rethinking my situation.

Four and a half years ago I made my first appointment with a plastic surgeon. I will admit here and now that I've panicked and canceled a dazzling array of scheduled appointments over the last two years and that I've consulted, all told, with enough surgeons to fill a good-size cocktail party—ranging from a sculptor-cum-surgeon whose aesthetic instincts dictated that I become an alarmingly undersized A (why not chop it *all* off while he was at it?) to a society doctor whose town house doubled as a hospital to a contemptuous, sexually ambiguous physician who seemed bored with the whole notion of women and their bodies. I finally went with a surgeon—Stephen Colen—on the basis of a chance recommendation I'd got at the last minute from a saleswoman who'd helped me with some bathing suits.

How does one decide such things? Intuition and—this is more important than you would think—the atmosphere of the doctor's office. Plastic surgery thrusts you on the kindness of strangers, even though you're paying a mint for it, and aftercare involves at least as much interaction with nurses and secretaries as it does with the doctor. I liked Dr. Colen's nurse and office manager, Marijane, from the first moment I aired my anxieties on her. She indulged my stalling and changes of heart and accusing questions (Is he really good? Shouldn't he be seeing me once more before the operation?) with the greatest good humor and patience. I also liked everyone else on the doctor's staff: from Justine, at the busy front desk, to Aida, the surgical nurse, whose touch when I came in to have my stitches removed or bandages changed was consistently gentle.

I finally kept my appointment with destiny—my cosmetic destiny, that is—this past fall. On November 29, at an ungodly hour in the morning (Marijane scheduled me first because, as she later confided, she wasn't sure I'd show up if I was third or fourth and had the presence of mind to reconsider), I was wheeled down the halls of New York University Medical Center and into a bustling operating room. Dr. Colen—a vision of medical competence if ever there was one—was there to greet me. I noted that he managed to look handsome even in his shower cap and green surgical scrubs; I noted, too, that he looked genuinely surprised to see me. (It was, after all, only a year and four canceled appointments since my original surgery date.) I looked up at the anesthesiologist and asked him if it was possible that I would be awake during the operation and no one would realize it, like a living nightmare. He assured me that it was not. Then I was lifted up for Dr. Colen to draw those chicken markings I mentioned earlier, and at last I was out, zapped into lovely unconsciousness.

There are moments I'd prefer not to remember, having mostly to do with the immediate month or two postsurgery. For one thing, I felt quite blue, which I wasn't prepared for. I was helped in this regard by a passing comment made by Dr. Colen's wife, Helen, a prominent plastic surgeon working out of the same office. "For women of a certain age," she told me, "it's like a postpartum depression." And, indeed, it made an odd sort of sense when looked at in that light. I was in my late thirties, not a teenager; I had grown accustomed to my breasts, cumbersome as they were, and now they were gone. Not only were they gone, but what had been sculpted in their place was swollen and bruised, and for a long while I couldn't quite make out whether I liked them or not. I felt as if I was carrying a secret, and I'd never been comfortable with secrets. Would people notice? Would they *not* notice? I couldn't make up my mind if it mattered either way—I had done this for me, hadn't I? Meanwhile, I continued to dress the way I always had.

Now that my breasts have settled into their new shape, I'm beginning to appreciate the revised landscape of my body. I'm not slouching anymore, and it's nice to look down and see a modest slope where a large promontory used to obscure the view. If I haven't yet moved on to a wardrobe of clingy clothes, I have cautiously invested in one or two of the sort of brassieres that weren't carried in my old size. You know the kind of lingerie I mean—exquisite and costly as only a fantasy of women's undergarments can be, hand-stitched by some underpaid factory worker in a country where they know about such things. A mysterious and delicate architecture of silk and lace, it's the sort of bra that makes me feel a long, kittenish way from 38D—almost an imposter. But that I can live with.

1994

The Pursuit of Thin

It is a few minutes before one in the morning when, my face flushed with excitement, I exit a town house in Manhattan's East Sixties. Outside on the tree-lined block all is dark and silent. As I raise my hand for the lone cab edging its way up Madison Avenue, I feel buoyed by the possibilities so recently envisioned. While the rest of the city sleeps, I have been wakened to radiant new vistas. The man I have just left, who has closed his apartment door gently behind me, is . . . no, no, he's not my lover. He's my diet doctor.

Oh, the agony of being fat, or neo-fat, or almost fat, or just Not Thin Enough; the ecstasy of having no pudge between you and a pair of calipers! Call it nutritionally enlightened or mentally deranged, the issue of weight and weight loss is the obsession of our age—a subject about which we wax suicidal or blissful, depending on what the scale says. "'Soft flesh,'" observes sociologist Stuart Ewen in his book *All Consuming Images*, "once a standard phrase in the American erotic lexicon, is now . . . a sign of failure and sloth."

My own slimming campaigns have been waged off and on for about a decade now, ever since it became clear to me that I couldn't accommodate my gustatory passions the way I once had. Throughout my teens and most of my twenties, I successfully dealt with an appetite that was partly unreconstructed borscht belt (I salivated to anything oniony, herring-y, or fatty) and partly a more delicate yen for things sweet and buttery. Somehow, I managed to retain a fairly slender body. Then I approached my thirtieth birthday and was given my first expense account. I dined on a constant parade of hefty, first-rate meals (all followed by dessert, of course) and my body began to rebel. Still the gods remained kind—remarkably so. The extra pounds I accumulated here or there I took off with relative ease. I had never aspired to model-spareness after all; I was just looking to be passably thin.

During the next few years, the battle intensified as I continued to eat like Oliver Twist just sprung from the orphanage. I was eclectic in the strategies I chose to countermand these tendencies: I walked in and out of a variety of diets, ranging from Weight Watchers (too much jargon, too much cheerleading) to Nutri/System (I objected to the jail-like look of their offices), to a regimen that touted the wonders of eating a potato for breakfast. Let's face it: If I was never committed, it was because I wasn't desperate enough. I relied on my limbs—my thinnish arms and very thin legs—to carry me through, and turned increasingly to elasticized waistlines to disguise my widening middle.

All this subterfuge came to an abrupt end, however, when I became pregnant in my mid-thirties and gained fifty pounds. Since then, the struggle to rid myself of twenty-five lingering pounds has turned ugly. Lest you miss my point, my daughter turned four in October, and I am still excusing my size twelve-ish shape to saleswomen with the blithe lie that I have recently arisen from the delivery table. I've sought out spas, diet doctors, nutritionists, powdered supplements, and the latest non-amphetamine, prescription-only pills. I actually found a nutritionist who made house calls, but she was fooled by my ubiquitous leggings and big sweaters and couldn't see what the problem was. When I insisted that there was one, she pondered for a moment and then told me to avoid all *shiny* foods.

And so this unhappy state of affairs has brought me out tonight, at a time I would normally be settling into a book or some late-night chat show, to consult with Stephen Gullo, Ph.D., he of the late-night appointments. After being buzzed in via closed-circuit TV, I seat myself on a couch in the waiting room and—forewarned by Gullo's crisply efficient Austrian assistant, Norbert—prepare to wait. Leafing restlessly through outdated magazines, I feel the sort of anxiety you experience when you decide to give up on a gratifying but hopeless love affair. I don't want to say good-bye to my crème brûlée, although I know I must.

About twenty minutes past my scheduled appointment, Gullo emerges from his inner sanctum. He apologizes for running late, offers me peach tea, and hands me a questionnaire to fill out, before he disappears again. In my brief glimpse of Gullo, I notice that he is (a) thin and (b) appears to be wearing face bronzer—neither of which should count against him. But I realize that the potential for fantasy is not that much different from the psychic brouhaha that attends the selection of a shrink: The situation is rife with idealization and projection and all of that transference business.

After I answer a bunch of questions about family history and weight, my anxiety level borders on acute dread. It is at this moment that I notice a copy of Kitty Kelley's biography of Nancy Reagan sitting on a side table. The former first lady, wearing one of her size-two, social X-ray, bright-red outfits, stares out from the book jacket with that preternaturally wide-eyed gaze of hers. I begin to wonder whether she is or once was a patient, and suddenly Gullo's office seems to close in around me. I've never liked myself in red, and I'm not sure I want to get as skinny as all that, anyway.

Every era has its hot diet gurus, those two or three stars who shine brightly in the crowded and lucrative firmament of appetite control. Whereas the field was once limited to experts flashing their credentials

(Tarnower, Pritikin, Atkins, Berger) and movie stars touting their fanatically worked-on silhouettes (Jane Fonda and her clones), there are now infinite variations on these two prototypes. Nongorgeous, formerly flabby semicelebrities (like the perennially bubbly Richard Simmons, or Tommy Lasorda, the baseball manager who doubles as a Slim•Fast promoter) have gotten into the act. One particularly potent combination pairs an Expert on Calories (Robert Haas) with a Great-Looking Celeb (Cher) in a regimen called, optimistically, "Forever Fit."

Stephen Gullo is the diet world's Marianne Williamson, a New Age personal trainer/messiah whose idiosyncratic method has been honed over twenty years. He has earned the allegiance of a die-hard clientele, ranging from a financially pinched woman who travels in from the outermost reaches of New Jersey (he charges her a token forty dollars, the first instance I have come across of pro bono diet work) to people who can afford to *buy* New Jersey. Although Gullo's lifestyle includes a weekend house in Westchester and appearances at the charity dinners of glitzy clients, one can detect traces of his less exalted origins in his strong "Noo Yawk" accent. With a communicative style somewhere between a knowing hairdresser's and an impassioned rabbi's, he has navigated his way to diet-doctor celebrity.

For an initial consultation fee of $475, Gullo (a psychologist, not an M.D.) will meet with you—his packed schedule permitting (his wait list stretches for four and a half years). Although I was originally under the impression that Gullo was part of a research team that combined various medical, psychological, and nutritional specialists (a perception that is helped along by the fact that one makes out a check to something called the Institute for Health and Weight Sciences, not to mention that Gullo's business card lists three associates), it quickly emerges that this is pretty much a one-man operation.

If you decide to work with him, you are asked to step on his scale— the true, old-fashioned doctor's kind, the one with the sliding gizmo on top. Then, seated on opposite sides of an antique French desk, the two of you get down to the nitty-gritty. As he listens attentively to your par ticular case of adipose blues, Gullo scribbles notes on a yellow pad. Based on his assessment of what makes you tick foodwise, he will go on in the next session ($175) to make you an individualized ten-to-fifteen-minute tape that will exhort, cajole, and challenge you to overcome your base desire for putting things into your mouth (i.e., "You're much too intelligent to take orders from a piece of food").

The doctor speaks into a recording device, after first disconcertingly replaying the gluttonous details of my eating life. There is hope yet for what Gullo calls "foodies," it seems, although the task is huge and the temptations unceasing. Gullo invokes the Bible ("Love thy neighbor as thyself") and points out how the diet undertaking is "part of the privilege of loving yourself." He pauses for a bit of visualization ("See yourself slender and graceful," he says solemnly), then moves on to several seconds' worth of deep-breathing exercises before focusing on my food plan. To me, the menu seems like a dreary landscape of steamed vegetables, diet bread, tiny portions of pristinely cooked chicken and fish (Gullo, in a gesture to my hopelessly ethnic tastes, allows me gefilte fish), nonfat yogurt, and Weight Watchers' dressing. But Gullo holds out nothing less than the hope of a conversion experience after all the renunciation and deprivation.

When did it start, this madness whereby women feel endangered by five —or ten or fifteen—extra pounds? To be sure, Frances Cornford, at the beginning of this century, wrote an ode in which she commiserated with "the fat white woman whom nobody loves"—but she probably had in mind genuine obesity rather than the softly rounded Edwardian silhouette that today would be regarded as laughably out of shape. Anyone who has ever looked at old photos knows that famous beauties of yore were downright hefty compared to our contemporary ideal. Sarah Bernhardt, the great nineteenth-century French tragedienne, was an exception to the rule—and was viewed as sickly in her skinnyness.

Somewhere between Marilyn Monroe—who looks positively meaty

by today's measures—and Kate Moss, the tide turned irrevocably against the voluptuous female form in favor of the toned and tightened. As the image of the perfect female body paraded before us in the media grows ever more sculpted, the standards we set for ourselves become ever more stringent. Between the glimmers of salvation offered by passing dietary fads (remember set point theory, with its vaguely thermostatic view of the body as human machine, its excited talk of "resetting" and "unsticking" the hypothalamus?) there is scant relief from that essential female wisdom, attributed to the Duchess of Windsor and embroidered on a pillow my mother gave me, which admonishes: YOU CAN NEVER BE TOO RICH OR TOO THIN.

The perils of being fanatic about the number that shows up on your scale include, of course, potentially fatal eating disorders like anorexia and bulimia. But there is a lesser spectrum of damage, observable among women everywhere. The grimly humorous reality is that we are all enslaved: Inside every thin woman, it seems, is a fat woman struggling wildly to get out. (I suppose it's comical, this battle of the bulge—if you can see the joke for the pathos.) Some of us display our desperate compulsions to strangers—like the woman in Geneen Roth's account *Breaking Free from Compulsive Eating,* who tells of driving back to eat the soggy cookies in a rained-upon, almost empty bag that she had thrown out her car window the night before.

Some of us keep our anxieties to ourselves, the only clue to our fascination lying in the keen interest we show when others discuss their dieting strategies. Then there are the women who expound lovingly upon varieties of mustard and sing the praises of lemon juice and balsamic vinegar. These are the true zealots—women who have bought the obsession whole. They have managed to convince themselves that there is nothing warped about standing guard over one's net daily intake, about vigilant attention to sugar and fat content and fractions of inches on their waistlines.

"I trade off every minute," proclaims one such proponent. "If I'm going to have dinner at a good restaurant, I'll do juices and water or club soda and maybe one yogurt all day. One day a week, I do liquids till nighttime. It's very cleansing."

Ah, yes, somewhere out there for the starving is our ideal body image, an achingly slender splendor. To get closer to that impossibly tiny-waisted dream—which, even for those of us blessed with racing metabolism or gaunt genes, sails farther out of reach as we move away from girlhood—many of us resort to dire deeds. Consider, for instance, the human-balloon trick that one friend tells me is her tried-and-true gambit: drinking a packet of Knox gelatin dissolved in juice or water. There's nothing like it, apparently, for filling you up and making you feel as though you've eaten.

But perhaps the most twisted strategy of all is the one practiced by those women caught between exhortations to be healthy on the one hand and the social imperatives of image on the other. They end up embracing a fit-for-life approach even as they inhale toxic puffs from a cigarette: to wit, my friend who confesses to a regimen of "running, smoking, and starving" in order to keep her weight unnaturally low.

"Daphne," Gullo's smooth voice intones, "you don't want to eat Italian, you want to *wear* Italian." Yes, but . . . As the reams of literature on the psychology of eating point out, the oral gratification of gobbling down, say, fettuccine Alfredo has everything to do with bigger cravings, for love and safety and creature comfort. Next to sex and money, food is the most powerful of metaphors—and calling someone a "fatty" is the most powerful of pejoratives. "Fat as a fool" went the coinage as far back as the Renaissance. Today, however, fat implies something more shameful than mere folly. To exhibit visible evidence of having lost control of one's appetite is to invite a damning, if not pitying, response. Indeed, it sometimes seems as if all is forgiven these days except incest and corpulence.

So there you have it, the *danse macabre* we do around the diet maypole. Watch us as we flutter, young and old, like virgins dressed in white, to the beatific vision of ourselves carrying ten or twenty or thirty —or even five—fewer pounds. The thing to remember is this: It doesn't seem to matter how little or how much over your dream weight you are. "When I'm thin," remarks another woman, "I feel more romantic about myself." This friend, whose idea of a full meal is an unbuttered bagel, goes on to recount that after a recent celebratory dinner, at which she ate approximately five ounces of steak, she canceled an annual physical scheduled for the next day—for fear she'd weigh too much and would be embarrassed in front of the doctor.

I wish I could point to myself as living proof of Gullo's persuasive powers. But repeatedly listening to tapes that inveighed against the "poison" of foods like cheese and brisket and Nova (foods I love) and promoted the wonders of such ersatz confections as diet soda and frozen-fruit sticks and Tasti D-lite made me feel as if I had joined a privileged cult, a Jonestown of chubbies. (One of Gullo's patients has tried to order a ten-thousand-dollar Tasti D-lite machine of her very own.) "THIN TASTES BETTER," goes the slogan inscribed on the gold-tone key chain Gullo bestows on his patients, along with this prompting: "I don't begin. I don't have any problem. It's just a piece of food!" Just try convincing yourself that the spun air of Tasti D-lite tastes anywhere near as good as Häagen-Dazs.

There are those for whom Gullo's mantras have worked. But considering that I dropped out of his program after four or five visits, I guess I wanted to eat Italian more than I wanted to wear it. Sure, I had taken off a few measly pounds, but I was hungry—not to mention irritable— all the time and still hadn't figured out how practicing such monkish self-denial would help me see the light. What can I say? I went back to my old, bad "foodie" habits—and to my leggings.

I hear there's a Russian nutritionist-acupuncturist living in Brooklyn who puts silver balls behind your ears to suppress your appetite. My sister-in-law knows someone who went to him, dropped fifty pounds, and swears by the guy. . . . Help! Somewhere along the way, we've lost the pleasure of satiety, the sense of completion that begins in the stomach and proceeds from there to the brain. When will they stop, these trendy and bizarre panaceas for the growling hunger pangs in our heads? And where will it ever end? If eating is being part of the circle of human warmth, then perhaps too many of us have banished ourselves to a lifetime out in the cold.

1993

Donna Karan's World

Donna Karan, whose ad campaign suggests an image of aesthetically organized disarray—the messy but high-powered late-twentieth-century female, a child in one hand, a Filofax in the other—is lost in the labyrinth of the Puck Building; the penthouse studio where she is due for a photo shoot is not where it's supposed to be. Dressed in one of her beloved anoraks—this version is in white silk—and showing lots of black leg, she bounds into a small office along the back stairway to ask for directions.

In person, she is prettier than in her photos: She has good skin, her eyes are a clear blue, and her nose is interestingly unfixed. She has recently shorn her brown "baby hair" (as she calls it) into a becoming gamine length. And it's impossible not to notice that the woman who is famous for being a self-confessed "hippie" size twelve has gotten skinny. Well, *skinnier.* She has dropped fifteen pounds on Medifast, and with the ministrations of not one but two trainers sports a trimmer, firmer figure than she used to. (When I ask about her weight loss, Karan, like most women, seems reluctant to admit that the issue is a burning one. She shrugs off my question, remarking opaquely, "Conceptually I've lost a few pounds.")

Donna Karan, in toto, could be any one of many attractive, chic—but not intimidatingly so—New York City women, so it's hardly surprising that no one recognizes her. Still, her vice-president of advertising and publicity, Patti Cohen, a vibrant strawberry blonde, is getting nervous. "Relax, Patti!" says Karan in her full-bodied voice; within minutes she is exclaiming from up ahead, "How fabulous . . . Hi, darling . . . Look at this *light*!" And to the two assistants who've brought up the clothes and the props, including stacks of big suede pillows from Karan's own couch, she crows, "You are the fastest people I have ever seen!"

Karan speaks in a mixture of hyperbole and the occasional, endearing malapropism. She *loves* rather than merely likes cashmere and "clothes that feel good"; she promises an *ex-pu-lo-sion* of color for her upcoming resort line; and on the phone with designer Carolyne Roehm, her enthusiasm is unwavering: "I think it's wonderful. I absolutely adore it. I prefer it." As to the linguistic fumblings, they seem like further proof of her high-spiritedness—emanations from the boundless fountain of energy that is hers, energy that can't be contained by the dictums of spoken language. So in describing the evolution of DKNY, her immensely successful lower-priced line, she refers to white shirts, a khaki raincoat, and a navy jacket as "quinssential" fashion items. And I am told there was one season the designer kept telling editors that a certain item was the "peer de resistance."

Behind the blizzard of words and ideas that Karan throws out is a singularly calm and concentrated eye. The atmosphere in her Seventh Avenue offices is electric but strangely unfrenzied. "Don't ever try to talk within four hundred yards of her," says Cohen, "and think she's not going to hear you." Karan is, by her own admission, a perfectionist. "My job," she says, sipping on a mug she keeps filled with hot water and lemon, "is to constantly make it better. . . . I don't rest on my laurels."

"I'm always asking, 'What's wrong with this picture?' You're only as good as your last collection." Hers is a coherent fashion philosophy; its tenets are comfort, luxury, and sensuality. Her clothes are "about construction." The fabrics—or "fabrications," as Karan calls them—are where she begins and what she keeps coming back to, making her wool more weightless from year to year, putting in form-flattering stretch wherever she can, adding Lycra to merino wool, to cashmere. "Once your hand turns sophisticated," she explains, "once you've touched something, it's hard to go back." From there, her main working premise seems to be a higher form of mix-and-match, the fluid interchanging of pieces, daytime to evening with the addition of a lacquer-sequined sweater or scarf. "You want to make sure things coordinate, look right, and have many ways to go."

To talk with Donna Karan about what she does and why she does it is to get an immediate sense of her bold, no-nonsense appeal: "I don't like fashion," she declares while nibbling popcorn in her custom-stretch Lincoln Town Car. "To me, it's the woman, the body. The fact that she's wearing clothes is incidental." Eyebrow-raising assertions for someone who, as she says, "grew up on Seventh Avenue," and whose exceedingly well-remunerated job it is to create closetfuls of tempting new clothes eight times a year. It seems to me that Karan is deliberately distancing herself from the sort of designer who presents clothes as a covert challenge (are you refined or sexy enough to wear this?). What she is out to do is to project her clothes in a demystifying light, as a natural extension of her own understanding as a woman: *I* can wear these, so *you* can, too.

Then there is the way she transforms the daunting issues of style and appearance into graspable, tangible principles. "Silver illuminates the face fantastically well," she remarks, flinging a sequined scarf across her shoulder. Or: "Once you start with the foundation, you can go any which way." For someone rumored to be hard to follow in conversation, Karan opines succinctly: "Hosiery is part of the body"—which must be why she designs her own, and why she has provided heathery shadings to go with the rich grays, beiges, and browns of her fall collection. She gives an almost mathematically satisfying explanation of her fondness for draping: "It takes the most amount of fabric and brings it to an apex." She adds in a singsong: "Accent the positive, delete the negative."

Accent the positive, delete the negative: I have heard this anthem of female renovation from Patti Cohen, and I will hear it at least twice more from Karan herself, always with the same show-biz reading. It is the equivalent of a team cheer, part of the designer's spiel—her half-ironic, half-earnest take on herself and all the women who look to her the better to be themselves. Cohen speaks of her boss's "power," of her ability to "bring something out in me, to make me go one more step." Kal Ruttenstein, fashion director of Bloomingdale's, waxes even more rhapsodic. "I have seen women," he proclaims, "transform themselves when they put on her clothes. They make you look sexy and strong, a rare combination."

There is, indeed, something of the professional coach about Donna Karan. In my own meetings with her, she almost has me persuaded to take up a stringent exercise routine and convinced that I can satisfy my craving for sweets—"cookies are my nemesis," she claims—with a sixty-calorie bran cookie she has discovered. Of course, it can be argued that what American women need most in their corner when they get dressed in the morning is someone inspirational, someone who can help them work with what they've got. In the midst of the projected ideals of glamour and beauty with which the fashion industry seduces and cajoles its audience, Karan's own carefully marketed image seems to suggest a greater congruence with reality. Dawn Mello, former president of Bergdorf Goodman and currently creative director of Gucci, has been a friend of Karan's for years (Karan refers to her as a "mentor"): "Donna is aware of both the good and the bad points of the average woman. Few are built to perfection, and she never loses sight of that fact." And Robert Lee Morris, the jewelry designer who's worked with Karan since 1983, points out, "Her clothes are designed to hug and hide. They're about looking svelte and hidden at the same time."

It's ten-thirty on a Monday morning in June, and the woman who designs for the Modern Woman—that sleek, professional, and confident being with "a long cool stare" whom Billy Joel has serenaded in a song of that name—is having a manicure at her desk. Donna Karan has nice, capable-looking hands, and her shortish nails are being painted an oyster pink. Her face is bare of makeup, and she is dressed in a loose, boxy black sweater and the ubiquitous anorak—this one in white cotton poplin from DKNY. She wears a quietly dazzling array of jewelry: a square-faced gold Cartier watch, several Barry Kieselstein-Cord rings, some antique-looking earrings, and two necklaces by Morris. Under a short, stretchy black skirt, she crosses long legs clad in Donna Karan hose. Although she swears her hosiery is indestructible, she is also quick to point out that this pair happens to have a run.

Karan's office is much like her clothes—subtly conceived, pared down to the essentials, with a lyrical touch or two thrown in. It is black, white, and gray, right down to the black, white, and gray mugs that are stacked on a bookshelf. One wall is empty—save for an army of push-pins, strategically arrayed. A framed diploma from Parsons School of Design—Karan received a belated B.F.A. in 1987—hangs near her desk, and there are photos of Donna with her husband, Stephan Weiss; in one, they straddle the back of a motorbike, looking every inch like an advertisement for their own lives. Other photos and an invitation to dinner at the White House from President and Mrs. Reagan are all in simple silver frames. In this coolly efficient setting, a vase of Rubrem lilies and two rhinestone tiaras (gifts on the occasions, respectively, of Karan being crowned by the press "Queen of New York" and "Empress in the Making") come as surprising, romantic flourishes.

Donna Karan's much-repeated explanation for the success of her clothes is that she designs for herself, for the gaps in her own wardrobe. DKNY, the alternative to her more costly Collection—where you can find a skirt for three hundred dollars, but a more typical outlay for an outfit would be between two and three thousand dollars—came about because "I needed a pair of jeans." More interesting than the fact that she designs for herself—and, with the advent of DKNY, for her teenage daughter—and that she tries out her clothes on her less-than-rail-thin body is the fact that "herself" is, as Ruttenstein put it, "a collection of various women across America whose essence she's boiled down." Karan describes the look of her clothes as "casual executive," and there can be no doubt that she has almost single-handedly revolutionized female power-dressing, taking it well beyond the dress-for-success ethos with its rigid, male-imitative rules. Where once stalked pin-striped suits and coyly collared blouses, Karan has introduced cashmere bodysuits, silk body blouses, alpaca-jersey rompers, sweatery chenille jackets, uncon-structed flannel blazers, and wool-jersey unitards.

Stephan Weiss, Karan's husband of seven years and business partner, describes his wife with bemused admiration: "She reminds me of the Human Torch," he says. "She flames on in the morning and off at night." He adds that "containing her gift" has been the biggest problem; with the opening of shops in London and Tokyo, and with licenses for the Donna Karan label including hosiery (Hanes), furs (Birger Christensen), eyewear (Bausch & Lomb), patterns (Vogue), and shoes (Pupi D'Angieri), it might seem that the forty-one-year-old Karan has already extended her grasp as far as it can possibly go.

Fat chance. In the brief time I watch Karan at work, she moves like a maelstrom, asking, reflecting, honing in on a vision only she can see. While the conception is deceptively easy, the execution of her collection comes about through slavish, workaholic attention to nuance, to the look of the feel and the feel of the look. "This is killer stuff," she says of some organza, woven with gold threads, that one of her staff has brought into her office for her to see. "This pattern is a killer. I'd love to see how far we could take the whole process." Then it is back to fitting the fall line with her production manager, Larry, and his female assistant, who offers her opinions in rapid-fire Italian. Within minutes Karan has shim-mied into a pair of stirrup pants and is sitting on the floor, limberly, knees crossed, legs behind her. After much wiggling and stretching and bending, she remains dissatisfied with some imperceptible aspect of the fit. She requests last year's sample, and this time she squats on her knees like a chimpanzee, testing for pull in the crotch. "Now I don't feel that thing, that strain, I was talking about before," she says with satisfaction. Another design Rubicon has been crossed.

It is late in the day, and Donna Karan is still going strong. I leave her sitting at her desk, playing with a pile of Wacoal bras (her husband is delighted she wants to do a line of bras, if only so she'll start wearing one), happy as a child in a sandbox. She makes it look like fun, which must be partly why she inspires such devotional fervor in her staff. But only partly, for there are people in this world with incalculable appeal, whose draw on others is such that it's a talent all its own. Undoubtedly there is something of the marketing genius in Karan, but there's also the genius of her personality. In spite of—or because of—her down-to-earth quality, she herself has achieved celebrity status. The designer "who understands real people," as the customer who wore one of her olive jackets grouse-hunting on the Scottish moors described her in one of the many worshipful fan letters Karan receives, has become someone who is stopped for her autograph at airports. It is, in its way, a "quinssentially" American story, one where image and reality have somehow, magically, conjoined: In those hyperkinetic ads where Rosemary, the model who is a more beautiful variation on the designer, lives the life of the Modern Woman, Donna Karan has succeeded in becoming who she says she is. As for her clothes, they are nothing less than what they promise you you will be if you wear them— effortlessly real, with a touch of celebrity around the collar.

1990

Am I Tan Enough?

Some of my happiest moments have been spent in the sun. In fact, there is something magical to me about the very puttering that precedes sunbathing (it's my more indolent equivalent of gardening, I guess): the careful positioning of my chair or towel for the best angle; the gathering of requisite accessories—books and magazines, along with an arsenal of tried-and-true tanning preparations; and the selection of some music (classical being less conducive, to my way of thinking; rock or blues, more so) to filter through my ears. Finally, following the application of my favorite lotion, gel, or spray comes the blissful moment itself, when I have nothing left to do but lie back, close my eyes, and soak up the warm rays.

Alas and alack, this luxuriant idyll of mine has been all but ruined. As anyone who has not been living in a cave for the past fifteen years has to know by now, there is no such thing as a free tan. It has become virtually impossible for me to conjure up this golden-hued reverie without its being interrupted by other, less pleasant images—running on a spectrum from the narcissistic apprehension of developing the kind of wrinkled, reptilian skin that would make me look old before my time ("the women in Florida whose skin looks like luggage," as one friend describes them) to the bottom-line fear of dying of melanoma. While I am humming along with the music, anticipating my skin's turning an enhanced peachy-brown shade of its regular color (and looking particularly becoming with my favorite white sweater), I am, most certainly, inflicting damage. This damage can range in its effect from, at one end, *erythema* (the surface epidermal reddening we know as sunburn) to the overexposed, liver-spotted skin dermatologists call "photoaged" to, at the far end, skin cancer.

Surely, one would think that with all the dire warnings and cautionary tales of the last decade, vacation spots in the Caribbean or other points south would be faring dismally, and summertime would find everyone indoors. But this is undeniably not the case. Suntanning, especially to "heliolaters," otherwise known as tanaholics (a breed unto themselves, who share some of the traits common to other addictions), continues to hold an invincible allure, like any pleasure, forbidden or not. If Alexander Woollcott, one of the Algonquin Round Table punsters, had enjoyed the sun, his famous quip—"All the things I really like to do are either immoral, illegal, or fattening"—would now have to be revised to include "dangerous." But just how dangerous is the sun? And why do we continue to lie in it when our health may be at stake?

In his new book *The Pursuit of Pleasure,* anthropologist Lionel Tiger divides the experience of pleasure into four different categories, noting that the *physiopleasures* (pleasures of the body) "include the sensory experiences involving the sexual organs." He lists "lying in the sun" as a physiopleasure along with "massages, exercise, plunging into hot or cold water . . . stretching, and the like." And surely its sensuous aspect—the way, quite simply, tanning makes one *feel*—has much to do with its enduring appeal. For many people, basking in the sun has a languid physicality; they feel cosseted by the warmth and light, almost as though they were being touched. One man I talked with, who describes himself as "tanned in perpetuity," declares: "I cannot overemphasize the sexual nature of lying in the sun, the heat of it." Another explains that he is "after the purity of the experience, which is just to lie there and let your mind frolic in the sands of time. Mostly, I think about sex when I'm lying there. . . ." Women seem drawn to the erotic component as well. "There's something very sensual about a tan," says a female investment banker. "It makes me feel like a young Indian princess, because I get very dark. Whenever the spring comes, I think of being in high school and lying with a reflector in the backyard, naked. . . ." And another woman asks plaintively, "How could something that feels so good be so bad for you? I tried using that self-tanning gook," she goes on to confide, "but it's not the same at all. It actually feels good to tan."

Not the least of the seductions of tanning has to do with the siren call of vanity—with the seemingly unassailable conviction that the results will make you look better. "I looked wonderful tanned," says a friend who has since stopped. "I'll never look as good untanned. I had all sorts of elaborate systems: I used baby oil mixed with iodine—it stains you while it tans you . . . it doesn't filter out the sun at all. Then, when you come in you rub your entire body with tea bags, which contain tannic acid and enhance your tan even more." She adds that, in her case, "it wasn't about the pleasures of lying in the sun, it was about looking Polynesian." Yet another ardent sun worshiper stoutly maintains that "for washed-out people with brownish hair, it's associated with being beautiful."

Of course, it is not only the hoi polloi who turn to the sun for cosmetic improvement. George Hamilton's rigorously maintained shade of mahogany has become the stuff of bemused legend (taking the entrepreneurial approach to obsession, Hamilton has started his own line of products), and Brigitte Bardot has been relentless in her pursuit of a deep-brown glaze ever since she burst onto the international scene as the *ne plus ultra* of sex kittens. As for less extreme examples, Aristotle Onassis was reputedly of the opinion that "you should always be a little tan," and Jackie—who was caught sunbathing on Skorpios in the near-buff on more than one occasion by paparazzi armed with telescopic lenses—seems to have agreed with him. Elizabeth Taylor appears to sport a darker complexion with each passing year, and Cary Grant's constant but moderate tan (modeled, rumor had it, after the perennially tanned Douglas Fairbanks, Jr.) always seemed an extension of his natural animal grace.

Then there are the larger-than-life images of sun-gilded beauty held up to our admiring gaze on the silver screen: Who can forget the ferociously tanned Ali MacGraw darting through the water at the opening of *Goodbye, Columbus,* the emblem of everything unattainable? Or the tawny Cybill Shepherd of *The Heartbreak Kid,* against whom the piteously burnt Jeannie Berlin, peeling like a hard-boiled egg, didn't stand a chance? Or the final, torpid shot of Kathleen Turner in *Body Heat,* insouciantly lounging on a beach chaise in sunglasses and a perfect tan? More recently, we have been treated to the vision of Bugsy Siegel, as played by Warren Beatty, obsessively roasting himself in front of sunlamps with a slice of cucumber over each eye for protection. The gangster is so enamored of his slavishly bronzed mien that his most pressing concern after an arrest is that the news photos may not have done justice to his tan. "I look like a fucking marshmallow," he barks at a crony. "I don't look the least tan, yet!"

Paradoxical as it may seem, given its undeniable dangers, a tan is associated in many people's minds not only with beauty but with health and fitness. Bodybuilders, both male and female, like a tan for the definition it gives their muscles (the Amazonian appeal of the early Raquel Welch probably had as much to do with her amber-toned skin as with her shape). A friend who claims, only half-facetiously, that one of the reasons she left Los Angeles "was to be relieved of the pressure to be tan," puts it this way: "After a day in the sun you have this sense of pseudohealth, as though you've been working outdoors." And one man explains his love of tanning with a perverse yet gripping logic: "As I grow older, I insanely feel that all my worst habits, like smoking and drinking, can be hidden behind a facade of 'good living,' embodied in the cliché of a tan."

For true aficionados, however, the draw seems to go much deeper. "If there's sun in the area, I have to go get myself some," a devotee admitted. "For years I sat on roofs, terraces, and street corners. I've been spotted turning my face up to the sun, just standing there. . . ." Those who feel compelled to hunt down the sun's rays do so, I would speculate, because they find the experience of tanning self-corrective; for them, the activity represents a means of transforming or numbing consciousness not dissimilar to that of more radical agents, such as drugs and alcohol. "I don't read in the sun," comments one adherent, "because that would require me to open my eyes and digest the external world. Suntanning is the cultivation of my inner life."

"A tan," suggests Marshall Blonsky, a semiotician, "is a mask. It covers over specificity. It is a superb makeup that removes all the asperities of the face. It removes sadness." For the "tanaholic," then, the psychological appeal of lying in the sun has an almost primordial component, bringing him or her back to a timeless, preverbal sense of unencumbered self. The process of tanning appears to offer the embrace of anonymity, even of oblivion—what the writer John Berger has termed "the skin without a biography." Interestingly enough, two gifted poets—both of whose lives ended in suicide—seemed to have been tanaholics, according to recent biographies. In *Rough Magic,* the latest in the unremitting flow of accounts of Sylvia Plath's life, the author paraphrases Plath's own description of herself to a young male correspondent during the summer of 1950, when she was seventeen: ". . . five feet eight, slim, her hair streaked blond by the sun, she was so deeply tanned that women stopped her on the beach to ask what suntan oil she used. . . ." But the real fanatic, apparently, was Anne Sexton. Her biographer, Diane Wood Middlebrook, recounts that Sexton often worked on her poetry outdoors during the summer, and would hold impromptu workshops by the pool when friends stopped by. She loved the sun so much that she sought out beach resorts even when she had to sit under an umbrella because of the Thorazine she was taking. In "Angel of Beach Houses and Picnics," Sexton extols the sense of power —of completion—basking in the sun gave her: "Once I was a couple. I was my own king and queen / with cheese and bread and rosé on the rocks of Rockport. / Once I sunbathed in the buff, all brown and lean, / watching the toy sloops go by, holding court. . . ." And in another poem she invokes the sun's force—". . . O yellow eye, / let me be sick with your heat"—as if the energy contained in this "burning magnifying glass" were capable of warding off death itself. In her graphically candid fashion, Sexton summed up a lifelong romance: "Somehow, letting the sun wash over you, letting its heat adore you, was like having intercourse with God."

The history of suntanning is an intriguing one, reflecting the changing concepts of class and stature around the middle of this century, when the old world order of lineage and breeding gave way to the new, more mobile (and presumably more egalitarian) order of money and leisure. In a seismic social shift, pallor and high color traded places as badges of, respectively, privilege and working-class origins. The inception of the tan as a symbol of exoticness rather than of manual labor has been dated by some to the end of the Industrial Revolution, when workers moved indoors from the fields to the factories; whatever its generative moment, it is undebatable that the suntan came fully into its own in the period right after the Second World War. With democracy triumphant came glamour for all, and one of the first signs of glamour to hold popular sway was a suntan. (Some credit Coco Chanel with starting the rage, when she returned from a trip with a deep tan.)

Coppertone introduced its first suntan cream in 1944, developed by a Miami Beach pharmacist who, the story goes, cooked up cocoa butter on his wife's stove and then tested it on his own bald head. Where once upper-class women shielded themselves with parasols, they now could be found recumbent on deck chairs, oiled and daringly bared. Democracy, to be sure, had its own preferred mode of separating the haves from the have-nots, and there was no quicker way of conveying one's access to a life of affluence and freedom than by the conspicuously leisurely acquisition of a tropical tan, certified proof of having been to St. Maarten or Barbados. (Noël Coward, that witty connoisseur of class distinctions, once wrote: "Sunburn is very becoming—but only when it is even—one must be careful not to look like a mixed grill.")

Today we swim in a glut of sun-protection products—a marketing sea of ever-higher SPF factors and ever more ingenious ways of getting a tanned look without the damage. What we now understand is that the tanning process is essentially a *defensive* one; melanin, the brown pigment that gives the skin its tanned appearance, is nature's way of protecting—and thickening—the skin against further exposure. The accumulated findings of the past twenty years led to an unmistakable consensus: You should stay out of the sun, whether for health or cosmetic reasons.

Hard as it is to believe from our current vigilant perspective, a generation ago sunscreens were almost unheard of. But the deep, dark tan of the fifties, sixties, and seventies has ceded to the burning question: How to protect skin from photodamage and skin cancer? One of the first and most effective sunscreens was PABA (para-aminobenzoic acid), but since a small percentage of users were found to be allergic, PABA-free sunscreens were developed. Although there are only two basic methods of protection—either to absorb the light energy or physically block it— the consumer market has responded by sending forth a parade of products containing a daisy chain of incomprehensible chemical additives and accompanied by a dizzying barrage of claims. Coppertone began placing the now-ubiquitous acronym SPF ("sun protection factor") on its products in 1977.

■ ■ ■

Our feelings about the sun—whether to imbibe it like a restorative or
flee it like the plague—remain divided, and it is no surprise that new
theories and strategies crop up all the time to accommodate the
dichotomy. Thus, one and the same company is offering everything
from a "dry oil/dark tanning spray" (SPF 2) for worshipers, to a sunblock called Shade (SPF 44) for those who eschew the sun. There is a
glitter-flecked suntan oil as well as neon-colored nose-coats; a cherry-
flavored sunblock lip balm for children and a brand-new, transparent
alternative to zinc oxide (the pasty white cream lifeguards smear on
their noses) that promises optimal protection without the aesthetic
drawbacks. For those who find a tan irresistible but have been scared off
the real thing, there is a new generation of "sunless" products that are
not dyes or bronzers, but contain a chemical that reacts gradually with
the skin's own amino acids and proteins to produce a more natural, if
counterfeit, tan color. (The first of the self-tanning products—the mysteriously named QT, which produced a very visible orangey glow—was
introduced in 1960.) There are even companies that allow you to have
your sun and beat it, too, so to speak—by wearing one of their self-
tanning-in-the-sun products. Then there are the so-called tanning
accelerators. Introduced to a groundswell of promotional acclaim in the
mid-eighties, they feature tyrosine—which is supposed to stimulate
the production of your own melanin and encourage a quicker tan—as
their chief ingredient.

We have gone, in the span of less than forty years, from exalting to
demonizing the sun. Half a century ago wisdom had it that the more
sunshine the better, for everything from one's disposition to one's complexion. But with all the opprobrium being cast on what was once an
innocent pastime (smoking and tanning seem to bring out a peculiar
righteousness in others that drinking doesn't), the phalanx of dedicated
sun worshipers grows smaller and more guarded. "There is an embarrassment about admitting to it," remarks a rueful sun worshiper. "No
one wants to go on the record anymore. If you say to someone, 'Oh, you

have a tan,' they'll jump to deny it with, 'Oh, no, no, I've just been working in the garden,' or something like that. . . ." She goes on to muse wistfully: "There's a hysteria about the warnings, don't you think? I wonder if it's going to turn out to be like cholesterol—if it's going to turn out to be not so awful, after all. . . ."

It would be nice, indeed, to lie back and give oneself up to the sun again without a flicker of anxiety, but the chances of a dramatic scientific reversal in favor of tanning are unlikely. Still, it's curious that all the preaching seems to be falling on the ears of the converted: A recent Gallup survey found that the highest incidence of awareness of the link between tanning and melanoma (skin cancer) is among thirty-five- to forty-nine-year-olds and decreases significantly among younger women. In other words, when you're eighteen you can't envision being thirty, much less fifty.

Finally, there is this to consider: How can anything that alleviated John Updike's psoriasis and is being studied by scientists for its beneficial effect on depression be all bad? The high winter suicide rate in sunless northern countries like Sweden is thought to be a result of the undernourished pineal gland, which shrinks without sufficient sunlight. And light therapy—which makes use of fluorescent bulbs to mimic outdoor light—is being successfully administered for the extreme form of the winter doldrums known as seasonal affective disorder (SAD). There are even one or two hopeful glimmers on the scientific horizon: Recent research indicates that regular application of potent sunscreens not only prevents further damage but may enable sun-damaged skin to repair itself; Retin-A is being used successfully in the treatment of "liver spots," those telltale signs of too much sun; and a professor of dermatology at UCLA has posited the heterodox theory that while intermittent periods of sun increase the risk of melanoma, chronic year-round exposure may actually have a protective effect.

In the end, the decision whether or not to tan may be more of an informed, risky choice than the absolutist, do-it-and-die proposition that it's been made out to be. You can take the approach of my ex-tanaholic friend, forswear the sun completely and "try to espouse the ethic of whiteness." Or you can load up on sunscreens, hit those rays sometime before ten in the morning or after three in the afternoon (thus avoiding the peak burning hours), and hope the fates—genetic and otherwise—will prove kind.

1992

The Shoplifter's High

On a hot weekend afternoon I am browsing with a friend in one of those Upper East Side shops dedicated to the selling of beautiful, largely unnecessary objects. It is the kind of store whose enticingly arrayed goods seem expressly put into the world to elicit desire in its most abstract form, rather than to satisfy any conceivable human need.

So my friend and I—both of us relatively upstanding people, wives and mothers, imbibers of high culture—are cruising by a sparkling display when I say to her, sotto voce: "If you weren't here, I'd take one of those." Take without paying, I meant. We are standing in front of a bowl filled with fake hard candies, ingeniously designed to look like the real edible thing, only prettier. Imported from Italy, these small glass bonbons are luxuriously tagged at ten dollars apiece. I think how good they would look in my living room, and how no one in the store would be any wiser if I were to pocket one or two. Indeed, I reason to myself with an impassioned lack of logic, I would be righting the scales of mercantile justice on behalf of all my fellow consumers, since the candies are so prohibitively overpriced to begin with. . . . But somehow, on this particular day, I've decided to articulate the impulse instead of harboring it (or, as has happened on more than one occasion, acting on it). In doing so, I discover, to my surprise, that the urge is shared: "Oh, you shoplift, too?" my friend asks, with a discernible note of excitement. You would have thought that we had just discovered that we shared a blood tie—instead of an embarrassing penchant for small-time thievery.

As the saying has it, "There's a little larceny in everyone." And, indeed, the impulse to take things on the sly among those who can afford to pay is a hardy one; it withstands the dictates of morality as well as the opprobrium of one's peers. Everyone knows it's wrong—and, of course, it is. (I know it's wrong enough to want to distance myself from being implicated even as I choose to write about it.) Yet the temptation to filch an item or two is apparently irresistible to a surprising number of upscale shoppers, people who otherwise instinctively resist the seduction of the criminal act. Removed from an ethical context, the act of shoplifting arouses responses other than simple condemnation: It is a puzzling, even fascinating, pathology that continues to elude theorists of human nature and to frustrate the legal system.

One could make a riddle out of it, a timely conundrum for trivia buffs: What do Bess Myerson and two teenaged daughters of Mia Farrow have in common? Their dirty secret has crept into the headlines, but for most women who do it, shoplifting remains the crime that dares not speak its name. Typically conducted clandestinely (except in adolescence, when it is often undertaken as part of a communally induced sense of daring) and thought to be more characteristic of women than men, shoplifting remains what criminologists call a "dark number." The majority of incidents are not prosecuted, largely because so much shoplifting activity goes undetected, and even when offenders are apprehended, they are often let off with a cautionary warning.

Still, the financial losses incurred from shoplifting pose enough of a problem to merchants and department stores that thirty-two states—including, most recently, New York—have enacted civil recovery laws to deal with it. These allow retailers to bypass the courts and extract payments directly from those they catch in the act once the shoplifter signs an admission of guilt.

Although shoplifting costs the big department stores a hefty chunk of their profits, the stores' spokesmen are reluctant to discuss it on the record for fear of harming customer relations. The very fact that this offense is committed by well-heeled shoppers with charge accounts at some of the tonier emporiums poses a dilemma: how to approach a suspected customer without disturbing the velvety, buyer-friendly mood for the rest of the clientele. A security guard for one such store revealed that the staff is instructed to take a gingerly approach to the whole issue. It seems that the management is willing to lose a certain number of items rather than risk offending (i.e., losing) a good customer by questioning the wrong one. "We must be absolutely positive," this guard comments. "If someone is walking out the door and the alarm goes off, we have to ask if we can search the customer's bag, and if the customer says no, then we can't." According to the New York district attorney's office, there are no official figures compiled for the activity, per se; as if to ensure its continued marginal existence in the annals of crime, shoplifting is not identifiable as an offense in its own right, but is always subsumed under the general heading of larceny. (Larceny itself is categorized as petty—under one hundred dollars—or grand, with the latter further divided into five classes.) The maximum penalty associated with shoplifting is one year in prison, although this sentence is hardly ever levied. The more usual punitive scenario in cases where charges are pressed is the payment of a fine and the promise of reformed behavior.

Elusive as it may appear to be, shoplifting is nonetheless a very specific form of deviant behavior, clinically speaking. It falls into a clear diagnostic category—"disorders of impulse control"—but is not to be confused with kleptomania (which, strictly defined, is the larger aberrance and includes the lifting of goods in private settings as well as commercial venues) or robbery (which involves violence or intimidation). Such subtle distinctions between one kind of pilfering and another tend, however, to get blurred in the courtroom. In a much-publicized incident last summer, two of Mia Farrow's adopted daughters tried to make off with a shopping bag full of fancy underwear from a Connecticut department store; this offense officially translated into the very criminal-sounding "fifth-degree larceny." Still, most of us aren't fooled by fancy legal semantics and can distinguish between an amateurish case of shoplifting and full-blown robbery. When an aging actress like Hedy Lamarr is accused by a Florida drugstore of "failing to pay" for twenty dollars' worth of merchandise or French actress Beatrice Dalle (*Betty Blue*) is caught walking out of Paris's Bardou jewelers with five thousand dollars' worth of trinkets allegedly tucked into her thigh-high boots, you can be sure gossip columns will dutifully allude to the technical charges, only to bypass them swiftly with the term *shoplifting,* plain and simple. (Just as you can be sure that the highly visible perpetrators of such acts, if arrested, are usually acquitted with the help of their lawyers.)

The kind of upper-middle-class stealing I'm talking about is, needless to say, a far cry from theft that is spurred by raw life circumstances —the loaf of bread, say, grabbed by one of the starving underclass in *Les Misérables*. It has next to nothing to do with actual hunger pangs and almost everything to do with psychological hunger. It is never about necessities—the idea of shoplifting a sack of potatoes has, I daresay, less than no appeal—and seems frequently to focus on trivial or frivolous items, such as cosmetics or lingerie. (Lipsticks, in particular, appear to radiate a welcoming light when sighted by the female shoplifter.)

The friend who was privy to my confession in front of the glass candies describes herself as having been a "heavy shoplifter" as a teenager, of everything from "little cubes of Laughing Cow cheese in the supermarket to rolling papers in head shops to a pair of Levi's smuggled under a floor-length Indian dress in the local army-navy store." She admits to returning to the habit of late, and although she muses whether, in her case, the timing has something to do with regression after childbirth, the most basic explanation she gives is echoed by all of the women with whom I broach the subject: "In the depth of my worst depressions it gives me a strange sense of accomplishment. I walk out and feel so good for a little while. It creates the illusion that the world is available for the taking." She goes on to recount her past year's cache in exacting detail, as though it were a jewel heist out of the movie *Topkapi,* but, in truth, her list of stolen goods (including a key chain, a stuffed monkey, and a Babar rattle) adds up to less than a few cab fares. Given how puny the average shoplifter's haul is, it may be hard to understand the thrill, but those who act on this impulse are unanimous in describing an accompanying high. That excitement—a release of tension that seems to be quasi-sexual in nature—is undoubtedly one of shoplifting's chief rewards, and helps explain why it holds a singular appeal for depressed women. (I've felt it myself, that moment that arrives out of the blue, like a surge of adrenaline, when I've been standing quietly in a store, waiting to pay for something, and suddenly find myself slipping some small item or other into my pocket.) Another woman I spoke with describes herself as having "the rationale without the courage"; she's shoplifted several times in her life but stopped for fear of being caught. "I've always wished I were less inhibited," she says, as though it were an admirable feat we were discussing instead of a disturbing compulsion. "When I was depressed, the physicalness, the rush of it, cheered me up."

Surprisingly little psychoanalytic theorizing has been done on the subject of shoplifting as a social disorder. What work there is connects it with depression and/or sexual frustration in women, ascribing "exhibitionism and substitutions for acts of passions" as its motives. One twenty-year-old paper from a British medical journal, replete with tables and statistics, concludes that "it is tempting to suppose that in a fair proportion of cases shoplifting is the first symptom of a frank depressive illness." Another paper from the same period, "A Contribution to the Psychopathology of Shoplifting," quotes analyst Otto Fenichel on the erotic associations underlying the act: "It is an unconscious formula, 'If you don't give it to me, I'll take it . . .' Stealing a penis is the principle fantasy of some women belonging to the 'revenge type' of female castration complex, who are afraid of open aggressiveness."

That argument, antiquatedly "male" and prefeminist in its logic though it may be, can hardly be written off as entirely inapplicable. Even the very-up-to-date Louise J. Kaplan, who, in her recent study of deviance, *Female Perversions,* distanced herself from the literal aspect of this kind of interpretation—"the psychoanalytic mythology that the stolen goods . . . are stolen penises"—agrees with its underlying premise, which is that shoplifting is a response to feelings of deprivation and loss.

This line of thinking connects to another motive that is touched on by many shoplifters—a sense of enraged entitlement. "I feel I've paid so much for things—whatever they cost, it's too much," says one such woman, "that I just cosmically had it coming to me. It's a sense of being psychologically ripped off, a helpless sense that you just have to have these things. Shoplifting," she concludes grandly, "is a neurotic response to what women feel they have to put themselves through as women in order to survive in the world." Interestingly enough, this feeling of being owed back by an exploitative marketplace seems to be shared on some level even by women who don't indulge: "Cosmetics," says one upstanding friend of mine, "are a great temptation. They're so little, so easy."

There wasn't a single woman I spoke with who didn't admit at least to dabbling in shoplifting as a teenager. "We all used to do it every Saturday," a therapist in her mid-fifties told me. "We'd go to the five-and-ten and lift everything in sight. Tangee lipstick and Mum deodorant and pens, and once when I was twelve or thirteen I stole pearls from B. Altman's and I got caught." But it is later in life, when peer pressure ceases to hold sway and the antisocialness of the act should, presumably, no longer give it a callow glamour, that the impulse calcifies and eventually poses serious problems. Amid all the descriptions of thrills and rushes of adrenaline, it's easy to forget that shoplifting places its practitioners in a potentially compromising situation, exposing them to humiliation and censure. For these women, hemmed in by the constrictions of bourgeois identities and a seeming allegiance to the normal order of things, it's their version of life on a dare. "My face flushes when I do it," reports my friend Lydia, an avid but mostly reformed perpetrator. "I'm a very cautious, good girl. This is my way of pushing the limits . . . it's the idea of

doing something wrong from time to time. I spend most of my life trying to do things right, not to make mistakes. The thrill is getting away
with it, whipping into a different identity from my usual play-by-the-
rules, dot-the-i's kind of person."

Long before *Thelma & Louise* packaged the fantasy, women have
dreamed of trading in their humdrum, Spic and Span existences for
something more action-packed, with at least the taste of blood. Suggesting, as it does, a controlled way of flirting with danger, shoplifting
has an unmistakable allure for women who feel they have retreated—or
been culturally conditioned to retreat—from the notion of life as an
adventure. "I've always been afraid of dangerous men, dangerous sports,"
Lydia says. "This was the one dangerous thing I did."

"Shoplifting," muses a writer who is intrigued when I bring up the
topic, "is sort of sly, like poisoning." She pauses and adds: "Poisoning
being a woman's kind of murder, don't you think?" At its core, the act
remains something of an enigma; one initiate refers to it, tellingly, as a
"secret society," with the traditional trademarks of silence and cunning.
And, like all secret societies, it reflects an uneasy truth: Ours is a culture
in which women, more than men, are dominated by the ruthlessly
depersonalizing ethos of materialism, what Louise Kaplan calls "the
tyrannies of the law of consumerism." We are, in other words, the face
—and clothes—we put on in the morning. It is this truth that one
woman must have had in mind when she spoke of shoplifting as something women need to do "in order to survive in the world."

Seen from this angle, shoplifting can be viewed as a means, however
misbegotten, of managing the tension induced by being at the beck and
call of the marketplace. We all walk around with a certain consciousness
about getting value for the dollar, no matter how economically secure we
are. Once money is not the issue, how much is too much to spend on a
new lipstick? And behind that valuation lies a more life-threatening
barter: How much am *I* worth?

For many people, of course, there is no mystery to upper-crust
shoplifting—other than why anyone would resort to it. The act is, trans-

parently, a bizarre, immature, and inherently self-defeating way out of the adaptations we are all called upon to make with reality. "My fear of imprisonment," says one censorious friend, "far outweighs any anxiety I would hope to assuage in doing it. I think it's masochistic, a not-so-subtle cry for punishment, for attention—like playing the bad little girl who gets away with it this time, maybe. I don't believe," she adds crisply, "in taking what isn't yours."

I suppose I don't believe in taking what isn't mine, either—except that the world appears to be crammed full of people, like corporate raiders and shifty lawyers, who take what isn't theirs in more socially acceptable ways. This sense of global injustice allows me to rationalize the shoplifting impulse when it occurs, and even tips me toward sympathy with the cosmic rip-off theory espoused by the woman quoted earlier, who sees the act as a female survival mechanism. (Although this kind of the-personal-is-political argument always seems suspect when it's invoked for the purposes of justifying deviance.) I suppose, too, I am more imperfectly socialized than my disapproving friend, more desperate and more angry. On the simplest of levels, taking something without paying for it provides a way of feeling victorious when I am feeling low, caught in the grip of a long-ago or immediate sense of deprivation. Although I have never shoplifted with any fervor and years have passed without my giving in to the urge, I will admit the impulse is always there, like a blip on my emotional radar.

What, then, of the women with otherwise impeccable moral credentials who move through stores with sidelong glances, ready to lift a lipstick here, smuggle a bra there? For them shoplifting may well be masochistic but it's also, I would argue, a mode—suitably covert in the timeless feminine manner—of fighting back. It is an ignoble act of defiance against perceived constraints.

In the end, the leitmotiv of this particularly puzzling misdemeanor would appear to be aggression played out by women who have been brought up to disdain, or fear, brute displays of force. If in the grander criminal scheme shoplifting constitutes a genteel violation, it is the outward "feminized" expression of very ungenteel feelings. Adolescent, sad, immoral, it is nothing less than an assertion of power over that which enslaves—a slap in the face of an ever more rarified and seductive marketplace. Buy me, sell me, take me for free. An easy offense to condemn, it is all the more difficult to understand, because beneath all the brio— the shoplifter's air of devil-may-care—lies a note of despair.

1992

Disorder and Early Sorrow

The Talking Cure Blues

It is difficult for those of us who have grown up in the last half-century to imagine a world unpermeated with Freudian ideas—with the free and easy use of such terms as *unconscious, oral,* and, of course, the famous *Oedipal complex.* Even at its most diluted, or parodied (as in the overused *Freudian slip*), the Viennese neurologist's daring reconception of human struggle as essentially interior—rather than exterior—in nature has entered the culture and forever transformed the way we look at ourselves. Accordingly, the "once upon a time" of our lives has become very much a matter of psychological, rather than behavioral, imagery. Where once we envisioned personality as an actively plotted construct, replete with the heraldic slaying of dragons, we no longer think of character as unfolding from triumphant or failed encounters with purely outward circumstances. Our plots have burrowed inward: Will the tender Ego withstand the onslaughts of the punitive Superego? Will the wily Id evade them both? What we have come to understand, for better or worse, is that the dragons that assail us are in our minds.

I say "for better or worse," but with the exception of the British, who have regarded this new mongrel of a science with a healthy degree of skepticism right from the start, we have all along taken it for granted that Freud's complex, highly abstract rendering of the forces that impinge on human existence is, in some simple sense, a good thing. But, one might well ask, *is* it? I mean, is it a verifiable improvement on previous ways of apprehending reality? Certainly it provides an intellectually more sophisticated model than earlier theories of character development, which looked to physiological or religious contexts for their organizing principles. But as anyone who has ever dipped a toe into psychoanalytic waters knows, there is nothing immediately to recommend it, either. For one thing, its premises (not to mention its solutions) as to the formation of character are frustratingly intangible; as Gertrude Stein once said of Oakland, California, there's no *there* there. Simply to be in therapy or to observe someone else in therapy is to have strong cause to wonder: *What does personality change actually look like?* How do you know when it's occurred? And is it worth several thousand dollars every month? For another, if it's consolation that one is after (and I would wager that, whether one's appointment is scheduled at the beginning, middle, or end of the day, this is precisely what most of us are looking for), the Freudian embrace is hardly a cuddly one.

The notion of ourselves as starting clean, as having entered the world innocent as babes (an image that the Victorians were the last to wholeheartedly embrace), free of "adult" emotions such as anger, envy, and lust, has been banished forever by the radical diorama of psychic development constructed by Freud and his followers. It seems that from the moment we exit the womb our psyches begin inexorably to take shape: Even while still tiny creatures suckling our mothers' breasts, we are rapidly evolving into beings riddled with conflicts and drives. Given this clouded-over view of our beginnings, the potential for malfunctioning is obviously enormous, and the requirements for proper nurturance —for "good enough" care and feeding—are difficult to come by. It's hardly surprising then, that the question that haunts our contemporary consciousness skirts the issue of potential resilience altogether, concentrating instead on our abject vulnerability to environmental forces beyond our control: Mirror, mirror on the wall, who's the most damaged of us all?

This is a question sure to occur to anyone who reads *Father, Don't You See I'm Burning?*, a recent collection of essays by Leonard Shengold. Its hefty subtitle alone, *Reflections on Sex, Narcissism, Symbolism, and Murder: From Everything to Nothing,* gives an indication of the book's pessimism, its persistently negative orientation. As befits an *echt* Freudian, Shengold's is an essentially tragic vision. The author's focus is on the unavoidable vicissitudes inherent in human development, which include often unbearable frustration over our never entirely relinquished wish for "everything"—"the wish," as he puts it, "to have exclusive possession of both mother and father."

Shengold, who has written two previous books, *Halo in the Sky* and *Soul Murder: The Effects of Childhood Abuse and Deprivation,* is a practicing psychoanalyst in New York City, and the patients he offers up (composites, to be sure) for clinical scrutiny are a plagued lot. Their histories range from bad to worse; as adults they yearn for what they can't have and are enraged about what they've been given. (Then again, one hardly expects contented, self-satisfied sorts to submit themselves to the expensive rigors of classical psychoanalysis.) Take A., the young woman who appears in the chapter entitled "The Metaphor of the Mirror": "The girl's initial complaints were of feeling unattractive, selfish, and unworthy. She suffered from suppressed rage and from bouts of sadomasochistically provocative behavior." During her treatment with Shengold, which involves much analysis of both actual and metaphorical mirroring (that is, the various means by which we catch glimpses of the reflected self), A. discovers that the mother she had once thought of as "wonderful" was, in fact, a bad introject—in layman's terms, a wretched nurturer: "a predominantly selfish, angry, irrational person . . . who required complete compliance and admiration from her daughter."

As if this weren't enough, it also emerges that A.'s mother (as is true of the parents of most of Shengold's patients) was given to exhibitionistic sexual displays—"fully displaying her vagina and anus," as well as masturbating in front of her daughter. Shengold postulates that in order to ward off "the terrible rage, felt as a magic murderous power," these experiences invoked in her as a young girl, A. turned to "the narcissistic promise" of the mirror. "To be in the bath water with mother, to gaze at her own image in the mirror (like Narcissus), would surely bring back 'everything': the timeless peace of the baby at the breast. . . ." Armed with this reconstructed knowledge of herself, A. goes off to live the life of "common unhappiness" that the unsanguine Freud, faced with *his* brood of roilingly unhappy patients, stipulated was the dim light at the end of the tunnel of "neurotic misery."

There are other patients in Shengold's account, all suffering from painful disorders of character that lend themselves to this psychoanalyst's particular version of What Went Wrong When. In contrast to the general theoretical trend, which has been to place key developmental issues in the oral (dependent) or phallic (Oedipal) stages, Shengold focuses on the anal (sadistic) phase—roughly equivalent to the Terrible Twos. The results are predictably woeful, although his insistence on inhabiting an anally focused interpretive universe can sometimes lead to comical, almost self-parodying findings: "Phones were always dialed in the years of F.'s childhood, and thinking about spinning the dial with fingers elicited his anal erogeneity and impulses toward anal masturbation. . . ." G., a homosexual, masturbates while on the telephone and remembers being frightened by the sight of his mother's "large, 'castrating' genitals"; and R. suffers from "low self-esteem" in spite of her "aura of self-confidence." (The latter's analysis reveals—but what else?— "intense rage and sadomasochism.") There is also the patient who leads "a life of inhibited, largely sadomasochistic heterosexuality" on account of his having been seduced as an adolescent by an older woman who made use of his bent knee (!) for orgasmic purposes, and yet another, V., who is symbiotically attached to his mother and has violent fantasies about the children he sees on the street.

Shengold intersperses the anecdotes of misery and pent-up fury provided by his clinical material with a more general portrait of a stark human trajectory—from a state of infantile narcissism ("the mindless everythingness of the womb") to one of adaptive unpleasure ("the something that lies between everything and nothing") to the final "beckoning nothingness" of death. In what seem to me to be some of the book's more satisfying chapters, he turns away from live subjects to literary examples. An assiduous reader and a resourceful critic, Shengold probes the regressive yearnings of King Lear and his painful arrival at self-renunciatory love at the close of Shakespeare's play to demonstrate his notion of the "hostile dependency" we are all born into, as well as the resolutions we can avail ourselves of while stuck in the predicament of living our lives. His dissection of Ibsen's conflicting pulls toward bourgeois caution and passionate abandon as enacted specifically in *The Master Builder* is illuminating in a way that his case histories often are not. Perhaps this is due to some innate theoretical bent in the author himself which makes him a better (that is, less reductionist) reader of texts than of people, or perhaps it is no more than that the tragic note is more sonorous when struck in literary masterpieces than when sounded in an office on the Upper East Side—where it too often turns to bleak music, and the unpaid listener is likely to turn a deaf ear.

I went to see Dr. Shengold not long ago, on a rainy Friday morning, to talk with him about his book and the current state of the psychoanalytic art. My appointment was for ten o'clock, and the doctor had made it clear on the phone that he was allotting me a hard-to-come-by spare therapeutic hour. Was I expecting to meet a man as grave as his pronouncements, adrift in the same fixations he perceived in those who came to him for help? If so, I am proven wrong. From behind his cluttered desk in a small office, the bearded and bespectacled analyst seems surprisingly matter-of-fact, even perky. It occurs to me more than once in my conversation with Shengold that doing this kind of work requires a thickened skin. Too much detachment, and you won't understand the emotional lower depths; too much empathy, and what use are you, wailing along with your patients that indeed your parents did you wrong and that there's no hope for the future?

Shengold readily admits that *Father, Don't You See I'm Burning?*, concentrating as it does on "the inherent primal discontents" of our existence, presents a "skewed point of view." "I think," he says, "this last book is a particularly gloomy book." He goes on to reveal that he's had "many complaints" about it from early readers, including friends and family. I am somewhat relieved to find that the book's unremitting misery has struck others besides myself—and that their instinct, like mine, has been to resist it. Still, Shengold maintains that this darkness of tone is the very nature of the beast, that "therapy contains unpleasant truths that people don't want to hear about." As a prime example, he points to child abuse, which, he says, with a poetic turn of phrase, "disturbs the peace of the world."

I mention to the analyst that I have been struck by his copious extradisciplinary reading; even when not explicitly about literary texts, his essays are full of the sort of determinedly bibliophilic analogies one doesn't ordinarily expect to find in psychoanalytical works. Shengold attributes his bookish bent to the influence of Lionel Trilling, whose classes he took at Columbia. Although he believes that Freud's insights are "deeper than what anyone else has come along with," he is quick to concede that "analysis isn't the treatment for everybody." I find myself wondering out loud why it is that often the people one would think would benefit from it most are least likely to be found partaking of "the talking cure" (as Freud called it), and Shengold suggests that both the "too well" and the "too sick" are unlikely to turn up on a psychoanalyst's doorstep. Paradoxically enough, you need both a certain amount of health to undergo this treatment, as well as a degree of acknowledged internal distress; in other words, those who are "too defended"—who have constructed enough armor around their problems not to feel discomfited by them—are less likely to seek help.

Interestingly, psychic health, from an analyst's point of view, is not the same thing as adaptive behavior, from the layman's point of view. ("Health," the author remarks in a footnote, "is even harder than pathology to account for.") It appears to be, finally, a more arbitrary call than one would have thought. To wit, given a requisite level of functioning, you are less likely to seek—or to be viewed as needing—psychiatric help the more you can get the world to fit around your particular set of needs. If you're Howard Hughes, for instance, and can afford the upkeep on your phobias, you're in luck. I ask Shengold for a baseline definition of psychological normalcy: "No life," he points out, "is free of shadow. . . . It's enough to feel 'I'm worthwhile' alongside 'I'm no good.'"

And what about the famously ameliorative phrase coined by the British psychiatrist D. W. Winnicott—"good enough mothering"— which Shengold keeps coming back to in his book, that all-important precondition which serves as a buffer against the slings and arrows of fortune? About its relevance Shengold leaves no doubt: "It's the most important aspect of psychic health, it provides the foundation." I am curious to know what precisely this critical nurturing consists of and how you know if the mother you've had is a Mommie Dearest or a Mommie Good Enough. Shengold obligingly explains that it hinges mostly on a basic feeling of self-acceptance, that "it's all right to be you." (Perhaps it can't be helped, but I wonder why there comes a point at which even the most abstruse of analysts begins to spout psychobabble of the "How to Be Your Own Best Friend" variety.) As to *good enough,* what that seems to translate into is "I'm loved by my mother, by and large." Since even the rosiest of maternal scenarios includes, according to Shengold, an inevitable falling-off from what he describes as "the postulated primal bliss at the breast," I deduce that, had there been a mother in the Garden of Eden, she, too, would have had her bad moments.

Still, the feeling that one has been insufficiently loved is so prevalent in our culture that Shengold confides he has written a paper about patients who misconstrue their childhoods as emotionally deprived when their parents have actually been *too* indulgent. They are encouraged in this view by their reading of Alice Miller, the Swiss lay therapist whose heated writings in such books as *Prisoners of Childhood* and *Banished Knowledge* suggest that the possibility of profound psychological harm occurring during even benign-seeming childhoods is more likely than not. This strikes me as an interesting development—due, undoubtedly, to a tendency in our culture to dilute complex ideas in the interest of popularizing them, only to then misappropriate them. (This phenomenon is also traceable, I can't help thinking, to the very laxness of meaning embodied in a term—corralled by Shengold himself—such as "soul murder.")

What remains unaddressed are the very real therapeutic issues of neglect or abuse—those patients for whom a sense of being damaged is appropriate rather than manufactured. I press Shengold: What if one didn't, in fact, get the requisite "loving care" without which separation becomes fraught with difficulty? Where does this leave one? Immured behind the high, unbreachable walls of a less-than-good-enough childhood? "Everyone wants everything," the doctor says solemnly. "The wish to murder can make one despair. It's hard to be good, to love. Rousseau was wrong." And what about those who *are* motivated to seek therapy, what lies in wait for them? Is there any alchemy—any far-off horizon of self-transformation—at the other side of the couch? From behind his desk, the analyst suddenly strikes me as sphinxlike, almost oracular: "As an adult," he allows, "you're no longer helpless. The fullness of the culture can rescue us from the damage of early life." As our session winds up Shengold holds out disconcertingly modest prospects, for both doctor and patient: "It's a long, slow battle, and some people can't bear to face up. All the doctor can do," he adds, "is suspend disbelief."

I make my way out of the lobby, past the doormen, onto Park Avenue in the nineties. It is a gray day, and the few people who are out in the street rush by under the shelter of their umbrellas. After so much speculation about interiority—conflicts that can't be seen so much as intuited, drives that are adduced by way of behavior—I am struck anew by the immutable *externalness* of the world, even at its dingiest. The sky hangs up above, as it always has, and the ground lies beneath my feet. As I walk along the avenue, past the whir and hum of traffic, I try and shake off a heavy feeling, a lingering sense of claustrophobia. And then I am suddenly taken by an irrepressible urge to run in the rain—that wily id acting up, no doubt—and I go bounding down the block, away from intrapsychic shadows into the grainy and very real light of late morning.

1991

A Family and a Fortune: Sallie Bingham's Revenge

"It will be a beautiful family talk, mean and also full of sorrow and spite and excitement."
—Ivy Compton-Burnett, *A Family and a Fortune*

The Drake Hotel on a chilly afternoon in early February is bustling with people. On a pair of couches located near the house phones, a family of Italians converses in rapid, high-pitched bursts, and standing at the far end of this group are what appear to be a father and daughter talking in weighty, Germanic cadences. The world as seen from inside a hotel on Fifty-sixth Street off Park Avenue seems to be full of families exhibiting their cordial relations in public places. Or maybe I am only struck by this because I am on the way to the nineteenth floor to see Sallie Bingham, whose newly published memoir, *Passion and Prejudice*, portrays in obsessive and fascinating detail the corrosive shadows lurking within the glorious House of Bingham.

I have not been sure what to expect on meeting its author. She is, after all, the precipitating factor in the dissolution of one of the last family-owned communications empires in the country. Her move to offer her shares of stock for sale catapulted the family into an internal but highly publicized battle, resulting in Barry Bingham, Sr.'s decision, in 1986, to sell the corporate holdings—including the Pulitzer Prize–winning Louisville *Courier-Journal.* Sallie and her family have been icily estranged ever since.

The rumors and insinuations swirl around Sallie Bingham as around a dervish—that she is "crazy," "difficult," "gay" (this last particularly amuses her)—so I am somewhat surprised to discover that the woman who opens the door to my ring is a contained and rather well-bred woman, very much a Southerner in spite of the fifteen years she spent in New York. (I note that she has the enviably straight-backed bearing of a girl who was reminded often about her posture.) Her straight blond hair is simply cut and there is a ready humor at play in her bright blue eyes.

For someone who has been depicted both in the press and by her own family as a loose cannon, Sallie Bingham is decidedly considerate in manner. She asks if I would like anything to drink and orders club soda for the two of us. Lying on top of the small table at which we sit are two copies of *The American Voice,* a literary magazine edited by Bingham and published by the Kentucky Foundation for Women, which she has endowed with $10 million of the $62 million she received for the family stock.

After a few minutes of chitchat, I lunge into the questions that have been pulling at me ever since I have read, burning several nights' worth of midnight oil, the book that has stirred such extraliterary controversy. The opening and most deadly volley in the war of words that *Passion and Prejudice* has aroused was reported in *The New York Times* and is the letter, signed by four members of the Bingham family, and its accompanying mass of documentation (neatly bound and labeled) sent to newspapers and book reviewers across the country protesting both the contents and interpretations of the memoir. The letter, written on the stationery of Mrs. Barry Bingham, Sallie's mother (Barry Bingham, Sr., died this past summer), asserts that "Sallie's view of the family history is maliciously skewed" and that "her claims rest on unsupported assertions, erroneous suppositions, leaps of logic, and in some cases, outright fabrications." There follows a lengthy refutation of more than three hundred points, replete with appendices, as well as a condensed, twenty-nine-page version of this same refutation.

Whatever one's take on the single-minded ferocity of the family's discrediting campaign—their blitzkrieg—the question still lurks: *Who is Sallie Bingham and why is her family saying these terrible things about her?*

"Not many people can afford to spend a quarter of a million dollars trying to discredit the writer in their midst," Sallie Bingham, the fifty-two-year-old maverick of her powerful clan, counters. "It all has to do with the fact that the Bingham family is used to controlling reality—and defining reality." (With a kindred zeal she has just put together a forty-page rejoinder to the charges, which she calls minor and petty. She will be making some small corrections, however, in the next printing.)

"The main problem," Sallie Bingham points out, "is saying anything at all. The issue of my grandmother was just a subterfuge."

I have asked her whether she thinks her family—and, in particular, her mother—would have been more accepting of the story she had to tell if she had left out the rumors of poisoning and syphilis and her own speculations about her grandmother, Judge Robert Worth Bingham's second wife, who died under mysterious circumstances within less than a year of their marriage. It was with the $5 million he inherited from a codicil belatedly added to his wife's will that the Judge (as he was called) was able to buy the *Courier-Journal,* thereby establishing the Bingham dynasty. An earlier book—*The Binghams of Louisville,* by David Chandler —that attempted to explore the allegations around the case had fueled the family's ire sufficiently so that Sallie's father had intervened to suppress the book's publication. (Its original publisher bowed out, although the book was already on the presses; it was picked up and issued by another publisher.)

Sallie Bingham narrows her eyes and assesses her grandfather, the Judge, as having had "a cold, reptilian charm." When I ask her how she feels about her mother today, she answers: "I am terrified of her. She has an awful combination of great intelligence and great distancing."

Although *Passion and Prejudice* is full of unsettling—albeit controlled—images of an antagonistic maternal figure, the only time Sallie comments directly on her mother's personality is when she confides, almost sotto voce, that Mary Bingham was "verbally incredibly abusive." I ask her why she didn't carve this aspect of her mother more incisively into the reader's imagination, and Sallie answers, with writerly pride, that she "did not want to turn her into a witch figure." It occurs to me later on, when reading up on the family, that the Bingham siblings, opposed as they may be each to the other, don't disagree about things as much as they think: Barry Bingham, Jr., the dislodged heir to the newspaper empire, who has referred to his sister's "craving for attention" as the source of her dissatisfaction and has held her responsible for the fall of the empire, has a curiously similar view of their mother. "She's a very harsh person," he was quoted as saying in the immediate aftermath of the sale of the papers to Gannett, "a very damaging person."

Inevitably, one comes to wonder whether the whole Bingham disaster might have been averted had perceptions like this been shared, had the siblings not been raised as pawns in a parent-directed game of crucial silences and unspoken filial preferences. But, like cogs in some vast, well-oiled machinery, the Bingham children—with the noisy exception of their eldest sister, Sallie—seem to have ended up seeing themselves as she insists to me their parents saw them: "not as individuals but only as part of a system." As she describes it in her memoir, in a somewhat chilling moment of reflection concerning her reaction to the freak death of her older brother Worth, who was driving in an open car with his wife and young child when a surfboard that was standing in the rear swung around and broke his neck (an earlier accident had claimed the life of her younger brother, Jonathan, who was electrocuted while trying to connect power lines for a Cub reunion at his house), even the fatal glitches within the system worked to keep its members divided: "Worth's death did not lead me back into an examination of our shared past. I tried to put this new horror behind me, terrified of being infected by the fatal family virus."

Sallie Bingham describes her family to me as practicing "that old black magic—the myth of the liberal family." The children were brought up to believe what was said (that you should treat people as equals, including Jews and blacks) rather than what they saw: After George, the adolescent son of the Binghams' black yardman, went swimming in the family's large pool along with two of the Bingham children and their friends, Mary Bingham had the pool drained. In her book about the Binghams, *House of Dreams,* Marie Brenner quotes from a letter Mary wrote her husband, then in the Pacific overseeing press coverage of the war effort, about the incident: "It amazes me that any child brought up in this part of the world would not have taken in through his pores a sense of the mores which forbid inviting nigs to swim in the pool." Likewise when George's younger brother, Luke, started to use "bad language" and became interested in playing with Sallie's younger sister, Eleanor, Mary found the yardman and his troublesome brood a job farther out in the country.

Sallie Bingham talks about the allure of her parents: "They were people who never sweated, never argued, were perfectly groomed." She describes her father as a "charming, powerful man" (who, in some tacit fashion, seems to have endorsed his rebellious daughter and undermined his compliant, proud-to-be-a-Bingham son Barry Jr.). She calls both her parents "gifted manipulators" and claims that journalists—such as Brenner, when she came to interview them for the article in *Vanity Fair* that became the basis for her book—were "invited in" and dazzled by the "incredible appointments, the glass, silver, and food."

■ ■ ■

"Children who are born to power and money," muses Bingham late in her book, "must learn, and learn well, several fierce lessons. They must give up most signs of independence or originality that conflict with the family's view of itself, whether it is the long hair and shabby clothes of the adolescent army, or the vocabulary and accent of poverty and rage, or the questions born of acute observation or the ideas that challenge the status quo."

It seems to me that the issue at stake here is, in stark terms, one of survival: Conform, or resist at your own peril. It is an idea that gets planted within pliant children in hope of making compliant adults of them. You can learn not to see what you think you're seeing, and thereby win the family's seal of approval. Or you can risk a tidal wave of disapproval and censure—risk being deemed "crazy"—and permit yourself to perceive. A not uncommon way out of airtight, suffocating families is to self-destruct: Edie Sedgwick is a famous, lurid example, and several years ago there was the death by overdose of David Kennedy, scion of another golden clan. The more common resolution of the double bind such families present is to *stay in*—to identify with the aggressor-parents at whatever cost to one's psychic life. (In the case of Christina Onassis, the effort to perpetuate the family's Dionysian myth arguably cost her her life.) To step drastically away from one's own family and dare to tell it as you saw it—as Sallie Bingham has done, in spite of the arched-eyebrow critics sniffing about "dirty linen" and "poor little rich girls"—suggests a kind of reckless pugnacity. Because the truth is that no one really wants to hear the truth about families. The family remains, where almost all else has fallen, an American icon—imbued with sentiment and guarded from demystification. It may well be the last taboo.

All families, poor ones and rich ones, negligible as well as powerful, exist somewhere between an ideal and a reality. The ideal has everything to do with blissful, sun-kissed images of loving adults and carefree, loved children; with the unconscious but tenaciously held belief that people are somehow transfigured once they reproduce, when they really only stay themselves. The reality, in turn, has everything to do with the compromised ideal: childhoods that were terrible, or good enough, or obligingly forgotten. Somewhere along the way, most of us learn the value of pretense. In families where the stakes are high, where the parental reach is long and influential, the value of pretense is still greater. Calling up the resolve necessary to separate—*to unlink from the family system*—becomes an all but impossible feat, for the system is eerily pervasive. To use an admittedly immoderate metaphor, it is as though one has finally escaped from a concentration camp only to find that the rest of the world is run by the Nazis.

Perhaps people with intractable, unobliging memories also, paradoxically, have the most loyalty to those memories: *Passion and Prejudice* is dedicated to Lucy E. Cummings, the beloved "Nursie," who, Sallie Bingham tells me ardently these many years later, "saved my life." "She gave me vision," Sallie says. "She gave me a message that *you can see and survive.*"

The very last page of the memoir has Sallie visiting Nursie's grave, which she had earlier not been able to locate: "She is buried beside her mother . . . in a section of Cave Hill Cemetery that looks like a field." I had the sense while reading this that the spirit of this proverb-spinning countrywoman of Scottish and Irish descent was being evoked as a shield against the isolation this rebellious daughter and sibling felt then, and still feels. One of the more problematic aspects of Bingham's memoir— its almost desperate use of an implacable and sometimes shrill feminist reading of history—seems to me to be directly traceable to this feeling of loneliness. It is as though Sallie has discovered "sisterhood" where once she had Nursie, a clump of fierce women in place of the lap she once had to sit on. Of course, aspects of Sallie Bingham's analysis of women's role in the South and, especially, of women and money, are both feminist *and* cogent. But there is something unconvincing about her application of a politicized overview to what is, at heart, a deeply personal view of one family's contradictory history. Still, her search for company is understandable: If to be a renegade is lonely, to be a rich renegade is doubly lonely. This is, after all, a woman who walked away with $62 million in the process of standing up for the rights of womankind (as she might like to think of it) or (as I prefer to think of it) for the rights of Sallie Bingham.

The fascination with the Bingham saga has, clearly, a lot to do with the fact that they are enormously wealthy. We are, naturally enough, far less inclined to be intrigued by the unrest in Joe Rizzo's family in Bensonhurst or Joe Stein's family in Nyack than by the malfunctionings behind the enviable facade of Joe Kennedy's compound over in Hyannis Port. Few, if any of us, really believe in the adage that "money doesn't buy happiness." At the very least, we are convinced that it pads *un*happiness and protects one from the griminess of certain experiences. Yet this seems to me to be just another of those convenient falsehoods, like the myth of family life, that works to keep us on the straight and unexamined road. For one thing, money certainly doesn't buy happiness for children, who have to be taught to understand its significance—whereas they intuitively comprehend the meaning of love given, or withheld. For another, I tend to agree with Sallie's Bingham's comment on the unredemptive aspect of money: "I don't think any amount of money," she said with a wry smile, "can save you from experience."

And yet, if we are more than willing to grant the rich the benefit of our rapt attention, how much less willing we are to grant them comprehension—or sympathy. Being asked to take the emotional pain of people who happen to be rich *seriously*—as opposed, say, to our mindless indulgence of the farcical maneuverings for power among the endless crystal water decanters and silver trays of *Dynasty, Falcon Crest,* and *Dallas*—is like adding insult to injury. We look to the wealthy for escapism, and to this end willingly consume good yarns about them. But we rear back at being asked to consider the rich as versions of ourselves. In this regard, Sallie Bingham has committed not one but two crucial errors and thereby guaranteed herself a mostly hostile reading: She makes a genuine bid for reader identification, in spite of the glitter of her family.

Even more egregiously, she has presented her story not as a yarn but as nonfiction. Family secrets, however bald, most often come encased in the thick hide of fiction, leaving the reader free to fantasize and project at will. Autobiography (when it doesn't come gracefully veiled as a "novel") has, of all the literary forms, the thinnest skin: There is a certain artlessness, no matter how artful the prose, to writing a nonfiction book about one's unhappy family, an insistent tugging on the reader's emotional sleeve.

In the end, what Sallie Bingham has inherited from her family, along with her slightly elongated jawline, seems to be a confusion about public versus private vendettas as well as a somewhat showy propensity for communicating with the public about private matters. The fatal "failure of communication" that Barry Bingham, Jr., referred to as the motivating cause for the family's dynastic collapse has resulted—in that strange fashion by which nature redresses such imbalances—in a loquacious act of communication with people outside the family.

Passion and Prejudice is, to my mind, "a beautiful family talk" in the ironic, Ivy Compton-Burnett sense of the phrase. It is an immediate, accessible instance of that queasy-making phenomenon alluded to by George Steiner in a recent review of John Boswell's *The Kindness of Strangers,* about the abandonment of children from late antiquity to the waning of the Middle Ages. With great and mordant understatement Steiner observes: "Throughout history, men and women have known how to be less than kind to their own kind." To read Bingham's memoir is to learn about the sheen of brutality, the cunningness of wealth, the power of silence, the efficacy of ruthlessness ("So much of success," Bingham writes, "is the ability to imagine success"). But most of all to read this book is to absorb the lingering hurt and anger of a little girl who discovered, perhaps too well, how to see.

Several days after I interview Sallie Bingham at the Drake, I attend a small celebration for her at the home of Julia Miles, who has produced two of her plays. I enter the apartment just as Sallie has begun to read from her book. This is the first time I've been to a book party where the author has taken it upon herself to give a reading, and I am struck by the oddness of the notion, half naive and half imperious. I wonder why no one, not her agent or her publicist or her editor, has thought to gently coax her away from this plan. She reads extremely well, in her warm Southern accent, but there is something strained about it, something strained about the audience's appreciative laughter. After the reading is over, the assembled guests drink wine and pop hors d'oeuvres and make book-party talk, as they always do. Bingham's third husband, Tim Peters, who looks like a less chiseled version of Tom Selleck, is there, a protective and very masculine presence.

But what I am struck by most of all is how dazzlingly alone she seems to be, a creature made impenetrably alien by virtue of her background and by the fierceness of her need to cure the malady of the Bingham past. I think of one of the last things she said to me: "To this day," she remarked as we sipped our club soda at her room in the Drake, "kindness makes me cry."

1989

When She Was Bad: Anne Sexton at Home

Mothers, unlike lovers or spouses, come one to a customer: If you don't like the mother you have, you can spend a lifetime banging your head against the wall, protesting your misfortune in being of the wrong woman born. Much writing—gifted and not so—has come out of this gravely consequential accident of birth. (Fathers, even in this score-settling, gender-bending day, still seem to come in for disproportionately little assignment of blame.) Depending upon how convincingly an unhappy daughter evokes a not-good-enough-to-hellish mother, the reader's response may range from impatience to receptivity to a rush of empathic identification. And yet, although wholesale censure of the materfamilias may be the reaction literary daughters secretly long for, it seems to me that the more fine-tuned the memoir or novel, the more complicatedly good-and-bad a given mother is likely to come across as, and the more mixed one's emotions as a reader will be. True Mommie Dearests, wielding wire hangers and banishing offspring from their wills, tend to be rare; it's no coincidence that Joan Crawford was a larger-than-life figure, not just in her daughter's mind but in the hyper-reality that movie stardom endowed her within the minds of her fans.

Anne Sexton, who killed herself in 1974, shortly before her forty-sixth birthday, cultivated as neon-lit a persona as a poet could have. Her impact, unlike that of many female writers, had nothing quiet or recessive about it. Of her obsession with suicide—which she attempted nine times over a period of eighteen years—Sexton crowed, "I'm the queen on this condition. / I'm an expert on making the trip / and now they say I'm an addict." Openly sexual in her use of metaphor, she was also openly seductive toward male mentors and poets. Unlike the *Redbook*-homemaker persona of her fellow-suicide Sylvia Plath, Sexton projected an aura of glamour: Tall and slim, green-eyed, dark-haired, and frequently tanned, she sported bright lipstick, cigarettes, and glittering rings. When she gave poetry readings she dressed as if for the opera, in flamboyant evening gowns. The drama of her art, it appeared, was matched by the drama of her looks, almost as if she were trying to envision herself, as played by Anne Bancroft, in the forthcoming movie version of her life: Tormented suburban wife and mother is released by psychiatrist into the world of poetry writing, where she ascends to the pinnacle, taking time off between mental hospitals and Pulitzer Prizes to flash her gams.

Even before the appearance several years ago of Diane Wood Middlebrook's biography of the poet, with its controversial use of material from Sexton's psychiatric sessions and its uneasy-making revelations about Sexton's penchant for inappropriate cuddling and role-playing with her daughters, one might have guessed that being the child of so flashy and self-plundering an artist was not a fate to be envied. With the publication of Linda Gray Sexton's memoir, *Searching for Mercy Street: My Journey Back to My Mother, Anne Sexton,* it becomes clear just how long a maternal shadow Anne Sexton casts.

The details of Sexton's life are familiar to many readers: Born Anne Gray Harvey, she was raised in upper-crust Massachusetts, the third daughter of appearance-conscious, hard-drinking parents whom she remembered as cold and unavailable. She eloped at nineteen with her boyfriend of only one month, Alfred Muller Sexton II (called Kayo), and they had two children, both girls, by the time Sexton was twenty-six. She played briefly at being the perfect, cake-baking fifties wife, but she seems to have been deeply unhappy from the outset, and in 1955 she started seeing a psychiatrist. It was after her first suicide attempt, which came on the eve of her twenty-eighth birthday, that she began her life-long effort to write her way out of her anguish, at the suggestion of Dr. Martin Orne. She was quick to take herself seriously as a writer, and she enrolled in John Holmes's well-known poetry workshop at the Boston Center for Adult Education, where she met, among others, Maxine Kumin and George Starbuck. Soon thereafter, she won a coveted place in Robert Lowell's poetry-writing class at Harvard, and in 1960 her first collection, *To Bedlam and Part Way Back,* was published.

As a late starter, Sexton brought to the writing of poetry neither the erudition and technical skill of Lowell nor the sheer rhetorical force of Plath, who was briefly her classmate in Lowell's seminar. (The conclud-ing lines of Plath's "The Applicant," for example, "My boy, it's your last resort. / Will you marry it, marry it, marry it," have infinitely more res-onance than the final lines of a poem Sexton wrote about witnessing the sudden onset of Lowell's madness, which display a similar use of repeti-tion: "Or the prince you ate yesterday / who was wise, wise, wise.") Yet Sexton succeeded for a while in spinning gold out of her deficits—her rawness and her ignorance of literary tradition. And she had extraordi-nary energy, producing ten volumes of poetry before she died. There would always be troubling self-indulgences in her work and, increas-ingly, toward the end, a lack of the tensile aspect that makes for effec-tive poetry, but there was in her best poems a breathtaking immediacy. She had an inimitable way of starting a poem as though she were gazing out beyond the page and talking aloud, and her ability to objectify emo-tion with a childlike, near-at-hand image is almost unrivaled: "I am drinking cocoa, that warm brown mama." Her early poems, written at a time when Adrienne Rich was still wearing a good cloth coat and pearls, retain their blistering directness, their startling air of autobiographical impropriety, even after more than three decades of reflexively "confessional" poetry. (Peter Davison points out in *The Fading Smile,* his recently published memoir of the poets who gathered in Boston in the late fifties, that the term *confessional,* which is so often associated pejoratively with poetry by women, was first used in a review of Lowell's groundbreaking *Life Studies.*) Sexton's place in the hierarchical scheme of things may be debatable, but her genuine accomplishment is not; even the competitive Plath conceded in her journal that to have her poetry compared with Sexton's was "an honor, I suppose." Sexton managed to break down the walls of a calcified, highly attenuated art form—one that accommodated the birdlike natterings of a Marianne Moore but not the lumpen realities of menstruation and menopause—with courage and wit. Put more crudely, she rammed her unpretty and very personal vision up poetry's elegant ass.

Linda Gray Sexton is Sexton's older daughter, whose budding adolescence was immortalized in her mother's poem "Little Girl, My Stringbean, My Lovely Woman." (Sexton always had a way with titles.) She is also the daughter who chose—or was chosen—to follow in her mother's artistic footsteps. As her mother's literary executor, Gray Sexton has edited a volume of Sexton's letters and three books of her poetry, and has played a crucial part in the shaping of the Sexton mystique. It is she who has made the judgments about which private documents to release into the public domain—whom to risk hurting or affronting. The hue and cry following her decision to give Middlebrook access to tapes of Dr. Orne's therapy sessions with Sexton resulted in a prepublication front-page article in the *Times,* which took up the issue of patient confidentiality; after the biography was reviewed in the *Times Book Review,* two of the poet's nieces signed a letter to the *Book Review* which vehemently questioned Middlebrook's sources and her account of, among other things, Sexton's childhood and her relations with her parents and sisters.

Linda Gray Sexton has also written four novels, two of which concern a daughter's relationship with a difficult mother. She explains in her new book, "The urge to write about my life with Mother had been there throughout all these drafts and pages, and in all these words." The shift from traveling under the cover of fiction to walking out into the open field of nonfiction—where authorial intentions are more transparent and no one will be fooled into thinking that the destructive mother figure in your book is not your own—can't have been an easy one. And, indeed, this memoir has an urgency about it, an impelled rather than volitional quality, as though feelings that had been buttoned up for years were clamoring to be let out. "I needed an exorcism," Gray Sexton writes. "Although Mother had killed herself when I was twenty-one, my thirty-ninth birthday had come and gone and she still rose each morning from the tumble of my sheets. She still lay down to sleep by my ear at night." Two paragraphs later, she elaborates: "To write about Mother and me would enable me to take control of the demons inside and let them know who was boss. I would be my own witch doctor."

I suppose it's possible to view *Searching for Mercy Street* as an act of unconscious one-upmanship, a kind of grand-slamming "Take that!" from someone who until now has been watching from the sidelines—providing others with tips but keeping quiet about intimate information that she alone possesses. And yet the really interesting thing about this book is not what awful domestic truths it reveals—given the exhibitionism of Sexton herself and the exposure that her life has received, it seemed unlikely that there were any more skeletons in the closet—but the halting, even provisional manner in which the person who wrote it has come to terms with those truths. The need to forgive one's parents and let go of the past has been endlessly aired in our twelve-step "recovery" culture, but few of us have any real sense of how childhood damage is redressed. With the exception of those creative or ambitious enough to recycle their pain as serious art or, even, raucous entertainment (which would include everyone from Louise Bourgeois to Roseanne Barr), the rest of us are expected to sustain our early wounds as best we can and get on with it. So if on no other level but the one of offering a peek at the behind-the-scenes gruntwork of psychic repair, this memoir is absorbing to read. "I loved my mother when she was alive," Gray Sexton writes toward the end of the book. "I love her still—despite anger, despite her mental illness and the things it allowed her to do. I never wanted her to seem like 'a monster' to anyone. She was loving and kind, but she was also sick and destructive. She tried to be 'a good mother,' but in truth, she was not."

We watch as a very young Linda becomes infatuated with the unpredictable but vivid mother who leaves her child with relatives for months at a time because she's overwhelmed (albeit not too overwhelmed to lunch with friends or have her hair done), spanks her with a sneaker, and tunes her out for hours on end while she works at the typewriter. This same mother plays Monopoly, makes hot cocoa, and bakes ginger snaps —in her daughter's words, "Not the richness of chocolate chip. Ginger snaps: an exotic mix of sugar and bite, just like Mother." Sexton's messages were no less mixed when it came to matters of class and tradition. She may have disdained housewifely virtues, sleeping away the morning as it suited her, but she also embraced some of the more sniffy values of her Yankee upbringing: "Mother carefully taught us finger-bowl etiquette and the use of the correct fork, and how to scoop soup from the back of the bowl to the front." With the help of a female psychiatrist, who encouraged Linda to resist her mercurial parent's invasions on every front, a tentative adolescent distance was forged: "Gradually I stopped confiding in her and stopped listening to her secrets in exchange." This was replaced by genuine enmity when Linda went off to Harvard: "And so, I began to hate her. I hated her selfishness and her sickness, and I could no longer tell where one stopped and the other began."

The summer before her senior year, Linda got a job working in the production department of Houghton Mifflin, Sexton's publisher, while her mother, newly divorced, was sinking further and further into the mire: "All the boundaries of decency had been permanently erased: my mother slept around; my mother drank as much as she wanted whenever she wanted; my mother did as she pleased regardless." That fall, as Linda lay reading *To the Lighthouse* in her dorm room, she received a call from Loring Conant, her doctor at Harvard Health Services and a friend of her parents, inviting her to his office, where he informed her that her mother had committed suicide. "*I wished for my mother to die,*" she confesses. "As much as I dreaded her suicide, I also craved it. I longed for freedom from the tyranny of her many neuroses that seemed, in that last year, to have overtaken her personality."

If the book had ended on this note, it would have read more cleanly —and even, perhaps, more satisfyingly—than it does, enabling the sympathetic reader to shout "Down with Anne Sexton and Her Kind!" But then, too, it would have been easier for Linda to make a clean break with her mother if there hadn't been moments of maternal sweetness and nurturing as well as exploitation and cruelty right up to the end. ("As August waned toward September and I planned my return to school, Mother and I had one final talk. It was, I believe, the last time we ever spoke intimately. She was sitting in her study, drink in hand, talking to me as I stood ironing the clothes I would take back to Cambridge.") It is to Gray Sexton's credit as an honest and largely unselfserving narrator that throughout this memoir she has chosen to forgo the primitive gratification of scrawling over the picture of her childish mother-worship with a fat black crayon; instead, she continues to add strokes of color and lightness to an ever-darkening portrait. By the book's end, she will have made her way valiantly back to her mother, passing through the portals of rage and despair before she glimpses the possibility of separating out Anne Sexton's perverse influence from her legacy of delight in words and experience.

As I read *Searching for Mercy Street,* I found myself feeling oddly protective of Anne Sexton's daughter—almost as though I were putting myself in the role her mother had so dismally failed to fill, and trying to reverse the ethic of violation that she was raised on. "She deemed nothing too minor nor too inconsequential nor too private—neither her own passions, adulteries, womanly crises, nor her daughter's nightmares, shy questions, changing body," her daughter writes. "Reach out and grab what you see and hear, said her example: be greedy with life, and for God's sake don't ask permission." Of course, Sexton set an unmatchable standard when it came to grabbing. At one of the family's Sunday dinners, she announced that she couldn't stand to eat any of the roast, and then insisted on having the "prized beef juice" that her mother-in-law, Linda, and her sister Joy's beloved Nana, had put aside for them. Linda recalls the scene, with herself forced into the role of mediator:

> "Anne, you know I save the juice for the children," Nana
> says quietly.
> "It's all right," I interrupt anxiously. "We don't mind."
> "Well, *I* mind. You children are the ones who need the
> nutrition here. You're the ones who are growing."
> "I need it too," Mother insists. "They're already healthy. . . .
> I can't eat any meat, and it should be mine."

Gray Sexton's tone, in the face of so much incriminating evidence, is artless and unassuming; she presents the case with so little adult posturing that she encourages blind acceptance of her story, flaws and all. But critics and readers are not meant to be therapists or good mommies, and it must be said that, for a woman who learned how to string metaphors practically at her mother's knee ("I had been weaned on the power of the word"), there is too much slack writing. Within three pages Sexton's death is called "an old wound that ached on rainy days" and Gray Sexton describes herself as revising the page of a novel "as if I were a dog worrying an old wound." We are told twice that the author's second son was born "ten years to the day" after her mother's suicide—a detail that I noticed because it had stood out so compellingly the first time. And we could certainly do with less of the dutiful jargon of the overtherapized: "We both understood, intellectually at least, how those who are wounded seek unconsciously to recreate the original trauma," and "As a child I had learned to split off what I was feeling: when emotions overwhelmed, they had to be gotten rid of." One has come to expect such psychobabble from the guests on *Oprah* or *Sally Jessy Raphael* but not from serious writers.

There are also problems of a more substantive nature. A faint but discernible whiff of what has come to be known as false-memory syndrome hovers over this book, as though the subject of Anne Sexton's incestuous behavior had filled so many of her daughter's psychiatric sessions that it no longer seemed important for her to sort out fantasy from reality. "You don't have to be raped by your father to call it incest," Linda's analyst reassures her, in a sweeping generalization, when she questions him about how much to trust her own recollections of her mother's behavior (which serves to remind the reader that, in the end, shrinks have only their patients' versions of events to work with). In this regard, there is something inauthentic about the reconstructed scene of Sexton masturbating in the presence of a young Linda, who had been watching TV in her mother's bedroom: "Naked from the waist down, she is making noises and her fingers curl through her crisp black hair. She pushes her long clitoris back and forth against the thick lips of her vagina." Would an adult woman really remember herself, as a child, dissecting the process of masturbation in such technical detail? Aside from the fact that she would have had to be straddled over her mother with a magnifying glass in order to be afforded such a bird's-eye view, how would a little girl know from clitoris size? (And what is a "long" clitoris, anyway?)

Then, too, *Searching for Mercy Street* has strange omissions, which, given its general note of openness, make for an unsettling, and slightly unbalanced, account. Linda's father, Kayo, is a ghostly presence, despite the fact that he seems to have been good to her. Referred to generically as "handsome and charming," he is Mr. Anne Sexton: the put-upon Mrs. Tolstoy of this inverted tale, clearing the path for his wife's genius by taking over many of the domestic tasks. (Not that he had much choice in the matter; once Sexton spotted the glimmer of fame on the horizon, there was no stopping her. Much though she benefited from the role reversal of their marriage, she apparently felt a fair amount of contempt for this feminist partner of hers, calling him "a little old maid" during one of their many marital fisticuffs.) I could not find much trace, either, of what Linda describes as "a tight emotional bond" with her younger sister, Joy; she seems to have dealt with "the interloper in the bassinet" by mostly ignoring her presence. From the information that's given, one can deduce that this second daughter got less of their mother's sting but also less of her honey; if Anne is "the star," as Linda calls her, of the family show, Linda is assuredly the starlet, while poor Joy appears to have been relegated to the role of understudy. Although Linda describes herself as her mother's "watchdog," her sister, who went on to become a nurse in adult life, seems to have literally internalized their mother's incessant demand to be cared for.

A number of details are dropped in disconcertingly, out of nowhere. We discover in casual asides that Linda, in her twenties and married, has been trying unsuccessfully to get pregnant, using fertility drugs, and later on, after her children are born, that she and her family have moved from a suburb of Manhattan to the West Coast. The suicide of Linda's aunt Jane, Anne Sexton's oldest sister—referred to within the family as Jane Jealous—which comes within a decade of Sexton's, is also mentioned in passing and pleads for amplification. What did this event—and, in particular, its timing, for it occurred soon after Linda had written letters of introduction on behalf of Diane Middlebrook and her projected biography of Sexton—mean to Linda? Did she see it merely as a corroboration of her mother's dramatic view of her own upbringing, "her vivid depictions of a miserable childhood punctuated by rejection and physical discipline"? Or did she feel some guilt at having roused sleeping dogs and stirred up in her aunt a deep apprehension about what might be revealed if she was interviewed?

The really signal issue that isn't dealt with, however, concerns the

whole question of what's come to be called, in the world of English professors, the anxiety of influence—the problem of writing Romantic
poetry, say, after Byron, Keats, and Wordsworth. As the designated
inheritor of an artistic legacy, Gray Sexton has no choice but to be a living exemplar of this phenomenon. "A facility with words and language
was the only gift I ever believed I possessed," she writes. But what does
it *feel* like to be the less attention-grabbing (and less talented) daughter
of an overweening literary parent and precursor? She doesn't tell us, but
she reveals that, time and time again, Sexton was willing to sell her life
ruthlessly down the river in order to secure the perfection of her art. "I
strongly resent the fact that you feel I am using Linda," she wrote to one
of the doctors in what her daughter calls "the parade of her psychiatrists,
pompous as kings." Sexton went on, "You so winningly said, 'People
come first' meaning before the writing. You forced me to say the truth.
The writing comes first." And in a letter she wrote to Linda on Linda's
twenty-first birthday (accompanied by a thousand-dollar check) she
comes to the defense of this position: "You and Joy always said, while
growing up, 'Well, if I had a normal mother . . . !' meaning the apron
and the cookies and none of this typewriting stuff that was shocking the
hell out of friends' mothers. . . . But I say to myself, better I was mucking around looking for truth."

Gray Sexton's way of dealing with this flammable—and potentially
illuminating—issue is to tamp it down by presenting herself as a ready
and able acolyte in what Sexton called "the black art" of writing: "Without knowing it . . . Mother passes on to me her powers of observation;
she shows me how to watch, how to see, how to record what transpires
in the world around me. This is how I inherit her greatest gift." The
truth of the matter is that, alas, creativity can't be acquired so conveniently; it's not a habit to be passed on from mother to daughter, like
taking care of your complexion or packing your suitcase a certain way.
Perhaps it's too much to ask of an emotionally hungry child that she
question the one form of sustenance she did get—and, if Anne Sexton
was consistently generous about anything, she seems to have unstint-

ingly encouraged Linda to join her in "this business of words." But Gray
Sexton's disinclination to examine her own role in the mother-daughter
act of being writers together begs more questions than it answers. She
declares, "Writing was the balancing bar both Mother and I carried
across the tightrope of our daily lives, a weight that kept us upright."
There is something touching about this; but does the author mean us to
equate her with her mother in terms of native ability? Or just in terms
of vocation? Perhaps what this finally amounts to is a form of wishful
thinking—a willed alignment with the best part of her mother.

Linda Gray Sexton's eagerness to put the worst behind her has enabled
her, paradoxically, to fashion a likable book about an unlikable parent.
Anne Sexton, who flaunted her honesty both on and off the page, was by
all accounts none too sympathetic, her abundant charisma notwithstanding. (A friend of mine whose apartment the poet stayed at after giving a reading at the Whitney Museum remembers her dominating the
scene in orange chiffon, spreading out her array of pills at the breakfast
table.) *Searching for Mercy Street* is suffused with a complicated kind of
love; even as the author tries to shake off the grip of the past, it tugs
enticingly. Along the way, the book reminds us that poetry once mattered a great deal more than it does now: Sexton not only behaved like a
celebrity but was treated like one, drawing an audience of three thousand for a reading. Most of all, though, one comes away with the sense
that there are different types of honesty, some more destructive than others. Despite the apparent and soul-wrenching candor of this memoir, the
family romance, as Freud called it, dies hard. I was left with the feeling
that Linda Gray Sexton has shielded her mother from being judged too
harshly. She has written the opposite of a tell-all: In the end, there's as
much discretion as there is revelation.

1994

The Fall of the House of Gilmore

Somewhere across a desolate American landscape out of Edward Hopper, a child—born in 1940, in a tiny Texas oil town off Route 67—is being beaten. On the fringes of down-and-out neighborhoods in Portland, Oregon, and Salt Lake City, his family is taking violent shape: a father, a mother, four good-looking sons, and a "legacy of negation." The second son has wide, light eyes, which, on the evidence of photographs, go with the passage of time from a gaze of receptivity to one of chilly wariness. At the age of fourteen, after several years of delinquent behavior, he will be manacled to another errant youth by the state police and driven to reform school. Among other corrective brutalities, he will take part in "cum fights" (in which the object is to ejaculate first, onto a nearby opponent's face) and be subjected to a punishment known as "spats," whereby the offender's naked buttocks are pounded with a Ping-Pong paddle "that had holes drilled in—to lessen the wind resistance."

The boy is Gary Gilmore; there is something memorable about the pleasing alliteration of his name, or perhaps it is the blueness of his eyes. Twenty-two years later, in January of 1977, he gripped the public imag-

ination when he was executed—after adamantly rejecting all interces-
sion on his behalf—by a firing squad in Draper, Utah, for killing two
young Mormon men on consecutive nights, in July of 1976. Gilmore's
death restored capital punishment to the American scene after an
absence of a decade, and became the focus of intense legal interest. His
execution also became the center of a media circus the like of which had
not been seen before: The stirring and surprisingly articulate (surprising
given that Gilmore never finished high school) mash notes that the
celebrity outlaw wrote to his honey-haired "elf"—the virginal-looking
Nicole, who by nineteen was thrice divorced and the mother of two—
became the stuff of daily newspaper reading; Johnny Cash sent Gilmore
a copy of his autobiography, *The Man in Black;* the rights to Gilmore's
story were expertly negotiated by the convict himself, acting as impresario through his uncle Vern; and an eight-year-old boy wrote to
Gilmore that he had no right to die, signing his letter, "With all the
malice in my heart." Within several years of Gilmore's death came *The
Executioner's Song,* orchestrated by Larry Schiller and written by Norman
Mailer. This "true-life novel," as it was coyly billed, ran to more than a
thousand melancholy pages. The culmination of exhaustive research
(taped interviews, recollected conversations, legal papers, scores of letters), the book transformed the grubby facts of the matter into an existential whodunit that tried to solve the mystery of a killer who wanted
to be put to death. Later came the made-for-TV movie, with Tommy Lee
Jones and Rosanna Arquette, but, whereas Mailer's impassive prose had
captured the psychic destitution of Gilmore and the people who surrounded him, the film's flatness reduced the story to a minor tragedy, a
skirmish among deadbeats.

I was in my early twenties in 1976, when Gary Gilmore sauntered into
notoriety, dressed in raffish prison whites, his muscular arms decorated
with tattoos. Like many other people, I followed the case with rapt
attention, partly because of Gilmore's sex appeal, and partly because it

was the first time I had encountered the phenomenon of the killer as superstar. Gilmore had a quality, a sort of negative charisma, which suggested that we on the other side of the prison walls were moral idiots and he was the visionary from Hell. This perception was reinforced by his determination to bid adieu to the world—to the world of incarceration, that is, which was almost all he had known since the age of fourteen. He wanted no more of us, no more of our belated offers to lend a hand, no more of our judgments or our morbid curiosity. Our curiosity about him was, of course, an intrinsic part of Gilmore's steely allure: The wish to die—to reach "the darkness beyond," as Gilmore jocularly referred to it —in someone as young and physically healthy as he was, even though he surely would have been fated to live out his years in prison, is still jarring enough to give pause.

Then, too, there was Gilmore's personal style, his infinite hipster bravado. He had mastered the art of cool, which A. Alvarez once described as "the art of controlled and detached delinquency." Undoubtedly, it was this aspect of Gilmore that attracted Mailer, who has declared his admiration for deviance time and time again, and, in an early essay called "The White Negro," noted in the magisterial third person that "the decision is to encourage the psychopath in oneself." If we had to choose a psychopath, Gilmore—with his mordant wit and no-holds-barred romantic passion—made a fine one. In the nearly two decades that have passed since he was executed, the need to penetrate the mind of killers has become something of a national preoccupation, but few of them speak to the imagination quite in the way that Gilmore did —with his talent for drawing (his subjects were ballet dancers, boxers, and children) and his predilection for Shelley and J. P. Donleavy. More than was true for most of his kind, the downward trajectory of his life suggested that somewhere, somehow, something human and precious had been irretrievably mangled.

Years after I read *The Executioner's Song*, I was still carrying around in my head the echo of Gilmore's reported last words: "Let's do it"—a terse directive that seemed to me the ultimate in poise and dignity, a final assay at self-regard. Interestingly, according to Mikal Gilmore's riveting and immensely moving memoir, *Shot in the Heart,* those were not Gary's last words. Rather, they took the form of the more opaque and haunting sentence "There will always be a father." The reader learns this near the book's end, when the significance of the remark both is—and isn't— clear. It is a tribute to Mikal Gilmore's scrupulous honesty in recounting the story of the ill-fated Gilmore clan that clear-cut explanations come to strike the reader as insufficient and, finally, beside the point. "There will always be a father" could mean that Gary was pointing back to the rage he felt at his abusive father. It could mean that there will always be fathers who cause damage or fathers who incite a love they fail to respond to. Or it could mean none of these things.

Shot in the Heart is, in the starkest sense, about the ties of flesh and blood, and how ties of flesh can turn, literally, to blood. Gary was not the only Gilmore to come to an untimely end: Gaylen, the third brother, "died young of old wounds"—from stomach perforations that were probably the result of a stabbing by a cuckolded husband, who left him for dead. Mikal, the youngest of the four Gilmore boys, and Frank, Jr., the oldest, are the sole surviving members of a family whose saga reads like a cautionary tale. The author seems to be coming to terms with the full extent of the wreckage in his own mind even as he is describing it. "Sitting there that night, I realized I had grown up in a family that would not continue," he writes. "There were four sons and none of us went on to have our own families. . . . It's as if what had happened in our family was so awful that it had to end with us, it had to stop, and that to have children was to risk the perpetuation of that ruin." Although the observation that damage breeds damage is not in itself a new one, the specifics usually make for mesmerizing reading. Part of the fascination of reading about destructive families is that there is a way in which any such history points up our own relative good luck, our sense of "There, but for the grace . . ." For, certainly, whether we are loved well or not enough or not at all, the world begins at home for each of us, and even houses of horror have their tranquil moments, their shafts of sunlight.

There is, for instance, a photograph from Gary Gilmore's childhood that shows him as a little boy sitting on a swing: He is carefully dressed, and his hair is neatly parted. It might be stretching things a bit for the average reader to say, "Gary Gilmore, *c'est moi,*" but it's not hard to recognize in his childhood the shadowy traces of what we might consider a normal upbringing.

Long before *dysfunctional* became the operative word in every discussion of parents and children, Bessie Brown, a young woman from a large farming family in Provo, Utah, attempted to escape the long arm of her impoverished and authoritarian Mormon past by marrying the dashing —and, as it turned out, impoverished and authoritarian—Frank Gilmore. The ceremony was conducted by Frank's eccentric mother, Fay, who dabbled in spirits (card-reading and fortune-telling as well as "the serious stuff: séances, summonings, materializations") for fun and profit. Frank rapidly proved to be not only a boozer but a petty criminal who conducted various scams under assumed names until his luck ran out in a particular city, at which point he would take to the road with his wife and growing brood. "The day the Japanese attacked Pearl Harbor," Mikal Gilmore recalls grimly, "my father was sitting in a dirt-water jail on a bad check charge." Frank's past was littered with a slew of different identities: He was much married, with scattered and intermittently acknowledged offspring from these unions, and the details of his own birth were obscure. (One theory had it that he was the illegitimate son of Harry Houdini—a theory promoted by Fay, and one that Frank himself believed, but whose veracity the author doubts.)

During Frank's disappearances and prison stays—shortly after he was married, he was sentenced to five years for running a confidence game—Bessie would move back in with her parents, who disapproved of her choice of spouse and of her non-Mormon ways, and made her stay in a shack out back. Gary Gilmore was born into the middle of this turmoil. From the very first, he aroused his father's ire. ("Like *hell* we're going to call him Gary," Frank announced. "No son of mine is ever going to have that name.") Gary's father beat his mother, leaving "her face knotted with ugly, black lumps and bruises." She, in turn, hit her two young children—so much that her own mother threatened to take them away from her. And when his father wasn't pounding Bessie he was beating Gary and his older brother. He administered spankings when they were very young, and then moved on to belts, razor strops, and fists, sometimes not stopping until they bled through their jeans: "On an at least weekly basis, my father would whip either Frank Jr. or Gary, or more likely both of them at the same time, until my mother would insist that the beating stop. Usually the punishments were the result of small matters—for example, one of the boys forgetting to mow the lawn behind the backyard tree—but just as often they seemed to occur as the result of my father's bad whims."

There is in this story—narrated in prose that is almost translucent, and that only rarely breaks out of its restraint to take on a tone of self-conscious melodrama—a sense of the inexorable. Through the accretion of detail, Mikal suggests that Gary Gilmore was an accident waiting to happen—a deeply wounded creature biding his time until he could wound back. Here is the author's description of a photograph of Gary and his father alone together:

> In the picture, Gary is wearing a sailor's cap. He has his arms wrapped tight around my father's neck, his cheek pressed close against my father's, a look of broken need on his face. It is heartbreaking to look at this picture—not just for the look on Gary's face, the look that would become the visage of his future, but also for my father's expression. In that moment, my father is pulling away from Gary's cheek, and he is wearing a look of barely disguised distaste.

But there is also a sense that Gary Gilmore's fate—and the fate of his brother Gaylen as well—was propelled by circumstances that went beyond the chaos of the Gilmore home. Much of the pain of *Shot in the Heart* seems to emerge from the unbearable sadness of being white trash, of being disenfranchised outsiders—"outcasts," Mikal calls them— looking in on a fifties culture of Norman Rockwellian smugness. This sadness is a reminder that on the other side of the panorama of endless choice which constitutes the American dream lies a dreary vista of choicelessness. Our Emersonian belief in boundless self-transformation doesn't leave room for the possibility that people may be psychically wedded to the constricted conditions of their past even as the future opens up before them.

The Gilmores were, at least for the first half of their life as a family, poor and on the move. More than that, they were out of step with the cheerful, upwardly mobile world beyond their own devastated one, and wary of any ethos that hinted at a more benign order of things. Although the general tone of the house was strictly do-as-I-say-or-else, there was lit- tle effort made by the parents to instill in their natively intelligent off- spring any sense of purposefulness, of the rewards of achievement. One of the author's few memories from his early childhood involves being sent by his mother to wake up his then-adolescent brother. While other teenagers were safely in school, Gary was holding sexual court in his room:

> Gary was sitting up in bed. On his right side was a girl with black hair, naked. She was bent over him, her head over his lap, bobbing up and down. On his left was another girl, with long brown hair. She was on her knees and she had one of her breasts in his mouth. Gary looked up and saw me, then tapped the girl with black hair on her head. She stopped sucking my brother and then settled down on the pillow next to him. "This is my lit- tle brother Mike," Gary said.

But even after Frank Gilmore does an amazing turnaround and becomes an honest and fairly substantial provider—he moves his family to a house on top of a hill, bordered by "elaborately-patterned flower gar-

dens" and filled with "fine furniture imported from Europe and Japan"
—the family's metaphorical setting remains essentially unchanged. Psychically speaking, they are always to be found "on the far outskirts of a
dead-end American town."

It is a landscape half tumescent, half stoned out of its mind, as
though *Lolita* had walked into *Naked Lunch:* There seems always to be a
TV going in the background, and a carport where girls in tight cutoffs
are being nuzzled. Their parents may have moved into the nicest house
in the best neighborhood—"old money, old ways, no disorder or dis-
ruption"—but clearly it's too late for these Dead End Kids to buy into
the promise of Pledge. Gary, for one, is already committed to the underside of life. "He was twenty-one years old," Mikal says, "but he dressed
like a man at the end of middle age, in a shabby black raincoat and curl-
brim porkpie hat—junkie wear." In the brief interludes when he is out
of jail, he uses drugs—"uppers, grass, cough syrup, some heroin, plus
plenty of alcohol"—and sits around in his car with ominous-looking
thugs. Frank Jr. drinks a lot, and so does the seventeen-year-old Gaylen,
while their mother is subject to crazed fits about linoleum patterns. "A
few days before, when she had picked this tile, she declared it one of the
most handsome domestic designs she had ever seen," Mikal recounts.
"But now, viewing the new floor under her feet, she decided the pattern
was actually a product of somebody's hellish vision." Seven years after
her husband's death, Bessie Gilmore lost the fancy house that had meant
so much to her and moved into an un-air-conditioned trailer in a court-
yard park in Oak Grove, down the highway from their old neighborhood
of Milwaukie, a suburb of Portland.

Pulled by too many demons from below to maintain a foothold on
the ladder to well-being, the family would cohere into tableaux of ordinary domesticity, only to rapidly drift apart once again into mayhem and
disorder. During Christmas of 1961, after Gary has returned home from
the Oregon State Correctional Institution (and before his youngest
brother got to shake the hand of John Glenn, who was touring the Seat-
tle World's Fair), we see the clan come together around a tree decorated

with blue lights and ornaments. Bessie Gilmore, who is an excellent cook, has prepared a holiday dinner, and Mikal recalls that she and Frank distributed generous presents: "Both Gary and Gaylen, I believe, received cars." Lest the reader get carried away by the vision of a family gathered around the upright singing carol after carol, the author remarks that this was the first and last such celebration.

Two-thirds of the way through his memoir, Mikal erupts into an unmodulated—and uncharacteristic—denunciation: "God, I hate families. I see them walking in their clean clusters in a shopping mall, or I hear friends talking about family get-togethers and family problems, or I visit families in their homes, and I inevitably resent them. I resent them for whatever real happiness they may have achieved, and because I didn't have such a family in my life." In this moment of truth—self-pitying, to be sure, but also self-revealing—the writer suggests that the greater damage has been inflicted not on those who are gone but on those who have been left behind. "Gary and all those others who had joined the dead—the members of my family, the men Gary murdered—they were the only ones in this story who had any claims to closure, the only ones who had completed their parts, who had finished paying for or escaping the legacy. The rest of us were still living the lives that had to go beyond final pages."

One of the singular achievements of *Shot in the Heart* is the way it subtly deglamorizes the nature of criminal rage—the way it cuts down to size the "little boy outlaws" who grow up into clever, cool felons of the type admired by Norman Mailer. In a society that increasingly dances attendance upon its deadliest members—as though we saw in their psychopathology a grim clue to who we really are—probably only those who have lived alongside the twisted and deadly know the full price such people exact, and how little they offer in return. Here's how Frank Jr. recalls Gary's temper, some fifteen years before his brother let off a final burst of steam, pointing a gun at a twenty-six-year-old gas-station attendant and then pulling the trigger, once "for" Nicole and once "for" himself: "He was brutal. . . . He got mad at you, and his terms were that he could kill you or hurt you or injure and ruin you. You could not reason with him and he could not punish you enough. It was like being around Mussolini." And, in an anecdote designed to show the extent to which Gary was both gifted and destructive, Mikal describes a conversation they once had in which he tried "cracking Gary's indifference, telling him I thought he could be a notable and successful artist if he wanted to." Gary's answer to this plea for his redemption is startling in its wanton, blithe nihilism. "'You want to learn how to be an artist?' he said. 'Then learn how to eat pussy. That's the only art you'll ever need to learn.'"

There are two heroes in this gruesome tale, and neither of them is Gary Gilmore. One is the author, who admits that he experienced a different father from the one his older brothers knew—a father who whipped him only once, and cocooned him for most of his childhood in an aura of paternal care: "Nowhere else in life have I known such safekeeping and such love." The reasons for Mikal's being singled out for affection remain murky, though the explanation may lie partly in the fact that he was the baby of the family, a late as well as a last child; his father was sixty-one when he was born, and his mother thirty-eight. Then, too, Bessie Gilmore suffered from what today would surely be diagnosed as a postpartum depression after Mikal was born, and her active hostility toward this new baby—at one point, she was found standing over his crib with a pillow, getting ready to smother him—permanently engaged Frank's protective feelings for his youngest son. As the youngest, he was in a position to bear witness to "the ideal of ruin" that "was a family covenant"—or, as he puts it in a less elegant moment, "the whole fucking tragedy"—and he does so with piercing dignity. Only occasionally does he give way to the sort of grandiloquent statement ("When I look at this photograph . . . I see the face of a broken angel") that he elsewhere goes to such pains to avoid. The other hero is the writer's oldest brother, Frank Jr., to whom the book is dedicated; he seems to have survived the same battering treatment as Gary with his humanity bruised but intact.

Shot in the Heart is a gesture of sustained courage that just happens to be a page-turner. The memoir has several haunting subtexts, one of which revolves around the question of what Gary Gilmore—with his "long and lively conversations about literature and art . . . his fine mind and his impressive vocabulary"—might have become had he not been derailed, beaten into a permanent state of deflected parricidal fury. "My father was the first person I ever wanted to murder," he told his uncle Vern shortly before the end. "If I could have killed him and got away with it, I would have." But truth is always many-angled. It must be noted that the complex man who savagely pummeled his son also hired the best lawyer available whenever his son got into trouble. And that a counselor who evaluated Gilmore when he was at the Oregon State Correctional Institution thought that one of the reasons for the twenty-year-old prisoner's poor adjustment was his parents' *over*indulgent attitude: "Outside relationships and contact were solely limited to subject's mother and father who continued to excuse, condone, and indulge their son without end." Proponents on either side of the nature-nurture debate could use this inside scoop on the evolution of Gary Gilmore to buttress their cause. Was he genetically doomed, the product of two tainted bloodlines? Or was he emotionally flung askew, the product of a devastating home life?

Early on, Mikal Gilmore managed to put distance between himself and his woefully tangled roots. Undoubtedly because of his father's emotional backing, he was alone among his brothers in being able to withstand his mother's "formidable madness and unpredictability." Whereas the three other boys were caught between Bessie's dark outlook and Frank's savage discipline, Mikal was groomed to cross over into fresh, unhaunted territory. After his father died, his mother decided to induct him into the Mormon heritage that she had formerly eschewed, and shortly before his thirteenth birthday he was baptized into the Church; he embraced its teachings for several years. He came of age in the sixties, idolized the Beatles (whom his brothers despised), and won a scholarship to Portland State University. "For a long time," he writes, "I did not look back." During this period, he saw Gary—who was serving fifteen years for armed robbery—very little, and when his brother Gaylen was dying in the hospital, he didn't visit him at all. "It would have been like visiting Gary: I could not go see people in places that were built to carry them to death."

Eventually, though, Mikal's history caught up with him. Gary was paroled from the federal penitentiary in Marion, Illinois—as a result of his pleas that he wanted to help take care of his sick mother, and at the urging of his cousin Brenda, who offered herself and her family as custodians—and within four months on the outside had committed the murders, at about the same time that Mikal, who wanted to be a writer, had his first piece of music journalism accepted by *Rolling Stone.* When Mikal realized that his brother was serious about wanting to go through with a "state-sanctioned suicide," he reluctantly got involved in trying to obtain a stay of execution—until he confronted his brother face-to-face and accepted that for Gary death was the "final scenario of redemption, his final release from the law." The last time Mikal saw Gary, they conversed by phone, on either side of a glass divider, and then, because it was their final visit, the warden agreed to Mikal's request that the two brothers be allowed a moment of physical contact. After they shook hands, the older leaned over and kissed the younger on the cheek. As Mikal left, Gary yelled after him, "Give my love to Mom. . . . And put on some weight. You're still too skinny."

The making of art is supposed to be cathartic, but often the catharsis does more for the audience than for the creator. Mikal Gilmore writes, "There are memories of rage and loss and longing that are so ruinous and transforming, you can carry them to your grave before they will leave you alone." One wonders if the fashioning of *Shot in the Heart* has brought its author any peace—a partial exorcism of the clamorous ghosts within. Shortly after Gary Gilmore was arrested, Mikal visited his sixty-three-year-old mother in her trailer. "If I had been there, he never would have killed those two boys," Bessie Gilmore said to Mikal. "I know I could have stopped him, I could have calmed his heart." It would be nice to think that this memoir has, in some small way, calmed Gary Gilmore's youngest brother's heart.

1994

In My Tribe

Jerusalem, Under a Low Sky

Everything hangs low in Jerusalem, even the sky. The weather seems close at hand, though it is less of a constant theme than it is in New York, where nightly the news is stopped dead so overcommunicative and gimmick-laden weather people can expound on atmospheric conditions. If life were more of a teleological process, Jerusalem could be said to be a city of primary causes: love, war, death, bullets, milk, children, newspapers, bread, sun, rain, water, children, car crashes, children, children, children. Don't you see a lot of *soldiers carrying guns?* people who've never been to Israel always want to know. But once you're there you get used to the soldiers and the guns slung casually across their backs like knapsacks. What you don't get used to is the pride Israelis take in their young, the way adults seem to bestow a uniformly indulgent glance upon them. The rare instance of teenage violence aside (several months ago two fifteen-year-old boys from an affluent suburb of Tel Aviv killed a cabdriver for kicks, in a case eerily reminiscent of Leopold and Loeb) and the occasional article on the problems of adolescence notwithstanding (the cover of *The Jerusalem Report* for the week of March 10 proclaimed, "Don't

Judge a Kid by His Leather," promising to divulge "The Surprising
Truth About Israel's Much-Maligned Youth"), the concept of Generation
X is inconceivable in Israel.

I had arrived with my four-year-old daughter at the end of February,
looking for a way out of New York and its self-involved buzz—out of my
life and its cramped dramas, as well. There was nothing further I wanted
to know about Tonya Harding or Nancy Kerrigan (by the time I returned
the latter was already parodying herself, gotten up in blond Valkyrie
braids on *Saturday Night Live*), and nowhere further to go for the moment
in the divorce proceedings I was enmeshed in. Israel beckoned like a clean
slate—surely, that has always been part of its appeal. And sitting on the
TWA flight, waiting to take off, I felt I had been right. While the American crew explained everything to do with seat belts and emergency pro-
cedures and life rafts at exhaustive length, the Hebrew-speaking steward
came on with a few succinct, slightly mocking instructions, as if to say,
You know the rules. Try and stick to them, okay, bubeleh?

It was a cool, clear Monday afternoon when we got into Ben-Gurion
airport, where the luggage carts were free for the taking; no fumbling
for dollar bills and trying to coax them through some gizmo. I had come
to Israel looking for a vacation, but that may have been my mistake to
begin with. (May the Israeli Department of Tourism forgive me, I wish
the country more visitors who can be served those overwrought hotel
breakfasts, mile after buffet mile of herring and scrambled eggs and rolls
and cheeses and more brands of yogurt than would seem economically
viable.) The vicissitudes of jet lag and traveling with a young child could
have explained why I took sleeping pills for the first few nights but
didn't quite suffice to explain why I continued to take Ambien—a
friendly white pill with little hangover effect—for my entire stay. Perhaps it was something in the air, an atmosphere of vigilance that enters
the nervous system of all but the most thick-skinned visitors, making it
hard to let down one's guard and allow sleep to knit the raveled cares of
the day. "You don't come to Israel for a vacation," said a friend I called
late into my second restless night. "It's too tense here." For the first few

days it rained, and on the fifth day, a Friday during the Muslim holy month of Ramadan which also happened to be the Jewish holiday of Purim, Baruch Goldstein (née Benjamin, "Benjy" to his friends) opened fire, with or without an accomplice, on the bent-over Arab worshipers at the Ma'arat HaMachpela (the Cave of the Patriarchs) in Hebron.

News in Israel travels like brushfire; official reports lag behind even more than they do in larger, less incendiary countries. The thirty-nine-year-old physician had started shooting at five-thirty in the morning. It was only eight-fifteen on that same morning that my nephew, who studies at a religious high school in Efrat—a settlement founded a decade or so ago, situated midway between Hebron and Israel—was standing in my sister's kitchen with the grim report. The first accounts making the rounds put the number of dead higher than it actually turned out to be (forty instead of twenty-nine), and, more curiously, had Goldstein committing suicide in a final deluded act of martyrdom. Perhaps that second, incorrect touch was wishful, a way of transmuting a disastrous, explosive act into something more profoundly self-sacrificial, however misguided. Whatever the explanation, the full import of the event was sensed from the start. Israel is a Jewish country, after all, and there is nothing more endemic to the Jewish sensibility than a tragic sense of consequence. How would this affect the nascent, infinitely fragile peace process? What use would Hamas, the radical Palestinian faction that was growing stronger all the time and that spat on Arafat's efforts to claim himself as representative of the people's will, make of this solitary act of butchery? *What would the neighbors think?*

The birds were twittering outside my sister's apartment on a street in Jerusalem filled, like many others, with wash hanging out to dry, garbage bins, scavenging cats, and everywhere the color of yellow stone. Whereas vast areas of Tel Aviv are made up of concrete resembling nothing so much as the gray cardboard backing that comes with shirts from the laundry, this yellow stone—the cost of which varies depending on its gradations of pink, white, or beige—has been the mandated building block of Jerusalem since 1948. A conference-hopping Rumanian architect whom I have lunch with across the street from the King David Hotel at the YMCA dining room—no plebian institutional mess hall this, but an airy, glass-paned venue for the city's nonkosher cognoscenti—explains that there is something about Jerusalem stone that apparently refracts the light differently. (He is part of the opposition to an ongoing civic movement agitating to use a variety of materials for construction.) If you respond to Israel, if you overlook its many unpleasantnesses, ranging from scratchy toilet paper to the all-powerful "Bezek"—the nationalized phone company which periodically goes on strike, scrambling numbers and making it impossible to confirm flights into or out of the country— it is my personal belief that sooner or later it will be the color of those yellow stones you are responding to. It will linger in your bones, like an ache, making it difficult to write the country off as a contentious and divisive mirage otherwise known as a Jewish homeland.

After the massacre, the blitz of accusations and recriminations began within what seemed like a matter of minutes. Who was to blame? And for what? Americans, for producing this strange breed, this "neta zar," which were the exact disdainful words Rabin used, pointing a finger at all those unwholesome immigrants with their deranged allegiances to Meir Kahane et al., which a chronically people-hungry country like Israel was forced to take in—to welcome, yet! Or maybe it was the government, for allowing the settlers to think their expansionist vision had a particle of reality. . . . Or maybe it was Shimon Peres himself, for pursuing an accommodationist, possibly self-destructive peace policy—and in the process giving fuel to those who were waiting for an opportunity to prove him wrong.

Amos Oz, Cynthia Ozick, and Abe Rosenthal weighed in on the *New York Times* op-ed page with widely divergent, panoramic views, suggesting either that Israel was too aggressive or that Jews were too contrite. Meanwhile, Israeli commentators tried to study the tragedy under a microscope, providing a closer examination of the volatile intertwining of biblicism and nationalism that led to the redemptive theology of the tiny "Kach" movement to which Goldstein belonged. Aviezer Ravitzky, a professor of Jewish thought at Hebrew University, suggested in *The Jerusalem Post* that within any given society and every religion—including Orthodox Judaism—there will always be a fringe group of people whose core identity comes from demonizing the Other: "'If I have an enemy, I know who I am. I am different from the Other. I am superior to the Other.'" Ravitzky, who has plumbed the literature of the fanatic anti-Arabist Meir Kahane and his adherents, went on to explain, "You don't need Judaism to understand Kahanism. Kahanism is the Jewish expression of a universal phenomenon." And an Israeli professor of Jewish history who is interviewed on the evening news from his cozy post at the Wilson Center for International Studies in Washington, D.C., solemnly advanced the theory that Kahane's adversarial politics had its origins in urban street encounters between Jewish working-class youths and "African-Americans." Listening to him, I wondered how many Israeli viewers recognized either the *au courant* rhetoric of rage or the equally *au courant* appellation "African-Americans." What is clear, in any event, is that the long shadow of political correctness has fallen across the sunny groves of Israeli academe.

"It's fashionable to be on the left," says Naftali Lavie, the former consul general to New York and Shimon Peres's closest aide from 1974 to 1977. Lavie, whose younger brother is the controversial Chief Rabbi of Israel, has recently published a widely praised memoir of his grueling escape from the Nazis and of his years advising those at the helm of power, from Dayan to Begin to Peres. Its title, *Am KeLavi (Nation Like a Lion)*, is a witty pun on his own last name, and the book contains the juicy revelation that King Hussein met with Prime Minister Golda Meir in 1973 eleven days before the start of the Yom Kippur War in order to warn her of Syria and Egypt's impending attack. Lavie's British-born wife, Joan, serves us coffee and homemade cake in the living room. "Give the Arabs everything they want," Lavie says. "It's an illusion. Those Arabs who are involved in the peace process are not in a position to deliver peace." He speaks with the slightly jaded fluency of someone used to dealing with philanthropic, know-it-all Americans. "The bosses of the masses are religious fanatics. . . . Their leadership is blackmailed by extremists, of which Hamas is the established expression. For religious and nationalistic reasons, they won't accept the peace process. . . . We Jews are helping Arabs to use the massacre. . . . It's a certain weakness on the part of Jews—wanting to appease the whole world."

Theodore Herzl convened the first World Zionist Congress in 1897 in Basel, Switzerland—a peaceful and verdant spot. How differently might the question of Jewish statehood have played itself out had the early Zionists accepted the British offer of a homeland in Uganda a few years later, rather than holding out for that small piece of the parched and beleagered Middle East known as Palestine?

The day after the massacre, late on a Saturday afternoon, I pay a visit to my uncle, Mordechai Breuer, a historian of modern German-Jewish culture who lives in the leafy, quintessentially Jerusalemite neighborhood of Rechavia. There is something about both the neighborhood and my uncle's apartment that is serenely unchanging. Rechavia was originally settled by Central European and German immigrants in the late twenties and thirties (the historian Gershom Scholem lived there). Many of the buildings are Bauhaus-inspired, and they are still largely inhabited by elderly natives of proud cities like Frankfurt or Prague, who have adamantly less of the Levantine about them than the other immigrant groups who flowed into Israel in the wake of World War II. To fully understand the sociology of a neighborhood such as Rechavia—dotted with tiny flower stands, the air filled with the strains of classical music, including that of the once-taboo Richard Wagner—one would probably have to be familiar with the work of Israel's Nobel Prize–winning novelist, S. Y. Agnon. It is an area redolent of a more cosmopolitan, less polarized time in the city's history, when the secular and the sacred coexisted in relative harmony, and people of vastly differing levels of religious

observance lived next to each other instead of in segregated enclaves. As
for my uncle's apartment, it is equivalent in size to a small two-bedroom
in New York City. He and his wife have raised seven children (who
among them have given him fifty-eight grandchildren) here, and I cannot remember it ever looking very different than it does now with just
the two of them living there: ordered and immaculate and unprepossess-
ing, its greatest luxury an absence of ornamental distraction.

Shortly after I arrive, my uncle dashes off to attend the *mincha* service which ends the Sabbath, and I pass the time in conversation with
my aunt. When he returns he performs the *havdalah* ceremony. One of
the briefest in the panoply of Jewish rituals, this blessing made over can-
dle, wine, and perfumed cloves marks the distinction between the
imposed inactivity of the Sabbath and the start of the workaday. After-
ward, we sit down to talk, but our conversation is interrupted by a constantly ringing phone: Congratulations are pouring in on the birth that
day of a new grandchild, his youngest daughter's tenth-born.

I ask my uncle his opinion of the recent debacle, and he gives a pained
shrug. Referring to the shrill note of blame sounded by Rabin on down,
he comments that it is all too easy to finger American Jewry for export-
ing misfits on the order of Goldstein and Meir Kahane. Still, he points
out that the combination of education and violence that characterizes
many of Kahane's followers is rarely to be found among Israeli opponents
to the peace process. "Of course we have our thugs," he says, "but they are
mostly primitive people, from poor or uncultured homes. Someone like
this, a doctor . . ." He stops and shakes his head. Then he laughs and confides that he has succeeded in avoiding a fellow synagogue-goer this
evening, a man who disapproves of my uncle's involvement with Oz
VeShalom, the religious branch of the peace movement. My uncle is sure
that the man wanted to engage him in a debate about Goldstein's action.

The next day it rains again. For abstruse calendrical reasons, Purim
is officially celebrated on Friday in Tel Aviv and on Sunday in Jerusalem.
Custom dictates that the traditional Purim meal, the *se'uda,* is held in
the afternoon, so in the late morning I venture with my daughter and

some American friends into downtown Jerusalem. The annual pre-
Purim festivities—a three-day street fair featuring clowns, face-
painting, cotton candy, and balloons—have been markedly less riotous
than usual. Today many of the galleries and boutiques selling ceramics,
jewelry, and silver in the artsy, Soho-ish area known as Nachalat Shiv'ah
are closed; those shops that are open are eerily empty, and one kiosk
owner tells me that business is off for this time of year. In the taxi on the
way home I decide to conduct an on-the-spot survey of the average
Israeli's—as opposed to the intelligentsia's—response to Goldstein's
action. The cabdriver, who is of Yemenite extraction, seems bemused by
my effort to engage him in serious conversation about events that neither of us have any hand in. "Your Hebrew so good," he says. "You like
Israel?" He wants to talk about his own yearlong stay in Queens, but
when I press him, he says quietly, with another of those shrugs that I
will come to think of as a national tic: "Haya beseder." *Beseder* is the
Hebrew equivalent of the English *okay,* except that it is a fraction more
affirmative than a mere *okay,* meaning something closer to "as it should
be." He goes on, "They kill us, and sometimes we kill them."

Was it ever different? "The spirit of hatred and fanaticism imbedded
[*sic*] in the heart of the Arab Muslims against everything that is non-
Muslim has been perpetually nurtured by the Islamic religion." This
statement, from a letter written to French Prime Minister Léon Blum in
1936, signed by, among others, Sulayman al-Asad, the father of the current President of Syria, continues: "There is no hope that the situation
will ever change." The authors of this document were six prominent
members of the Alawite community, a breakaway group from Islam situated in northwestern Syria, and they adduced the condition of the Jews
in Palestine to be "the strongest and most explicit evidence" of Islamic
intransigence.

Naftali Lavie maintains that in the face of such historical antago-
nism, the right questions aren't being asked. "Should we evacuate the
settlements for peace?" is less to the point than asking "Is Arafat really
in a position to deliver peace, when he can't even deliver on his promise

to annul paragraph nine of the PLO covenant, which affirms the organization's commitment to the destruction of the state of Israel?"

We went to Eilat all the same. Eilat is Israel's fling at being a genuine tourist destination for European sun-seekers, its pretend resort-by-the-sea. In my almost three decades of traveling in Israel, I had never deigned to visit Eilat, so intent was I on imbibing the climactic, Zionist-fostered scenarios of my upbringing: Masada, Rachel's Tomb, Ein Gedi, and in those pre-Intifada days, the Ma'arat HaMachpelah. This time I had planned on stopping at the resort, on acting as if Israel were the sort of country you could actually, wholeheartedly *vacation* in, and I wasn't going to let Baruch Goldstein stop me, even if it meant suspending vast amounts of disbelief.

At three-thirty on Monday afternoon we—my sister, her fifteen-year-old daughter (who had successfully begged off from school in our honor), myself, and my daughter—left for the central bus depot to pick up the van that would take us to Atorot, the airport about half an hour outside of Jerusalem which services Arkia, Israel's sole domestic carrier. (Since Eilat is a five-hour drive from Jerusalem, we had decided to fly.) Inside the van the curtains were drawn: "Israelis love curtains everywhere," my sister says cheerfully, but the curtains are not just a characteristic decorative touch. When my daughter tries to pull them aside, the swarthy man sitting up front next to the driver turns around and sharply tells her not to. I had noticed this man immediately upon entering the van; I had also noticed the anxious woman sitting in front of us, who wanted to know if anyone had checked the unclaimed piece of luggage on the seat next to her. (Someone does so.) Plastic bags and other such innocuous-seeming stray items are Israel's Achilles' heel: There is always the chance that they could be artfully disguised lethal weapons rather than prosaic repositories for groceries or toiletries. In the days following the massacre—as is true each time there is a violent flare-up—the tension heightens around the possibility, unspoken but omnipresent, of terrorist retaliation. (A month after I return to New York, a nineteen-year-old Arab detonates an explosive-filled car in the northern town of Afula, killing himself and seven Israelis, and wounding forty-five other Israelis, many of them children. Hamas promptly claims him as a member and calls the bombing a reaction to Hebron.)

On the way to the airport we pass through the Arab village of Shu'afat. Through the van's curtains, the village looks rundown and underoccupied; there are men standing in clusters around doorways and young boys in shapeless sweaters who gaze after our Israeli license plate with undisguised hostility. The atmosphere in the van thickens with apprehension. (Several days later, on the way back to Jerusalem, there will be another long moment of held-in breath, the same precarious assumption that we are entitled to pass through enemy territory unharmed. It is nighttime when we return, and the low-built Arab houses emit a lurid blue glow. My sister tells me she has heard that Arabs tend to paint at least one of their walls turquoise to ward off the evil eye and that they actually prefer this slightly melancholy lighting effect.)

Atorot itself is small—approximately the size of the airport on Nantucket Island. This being a Jewish country rather than a WASP stopover, there is a kiosk standing ready with food (candy bars, soda, and ice cream as well as the characteristically Israeli sandwich known as *shakshuka*—pita bread containing an egg, onion, and tomato) to ease any hunger pangs that might strike on the fifty-minute flight to Eilat. In the interval between having our passports scrutinized, checking in our luggage, and answering a barrage of security questions ("Did you leave your luggage unobserved at any time? Has anyone given you anything to put in your luggage? Do you understand why we are asking you these questions?"), I talk with Eli, the security guard who accompanied our van driver and is now waiting around the airport, puffing furiously on a cigarette. I ask him if his presence is standard procedure, or whether extra precautions are being taken in the wake of Hebron. He gives a dazzling gap-toothed smile by way of polite resistance to discussing the situation. One of the stranger aspects of being in a country that operates under as high a level of strain as Israel does is that everyone feels compelled to act as if this strain were normative. He is joined by Itzik, the driver, and in the tacit way such things are decided, the two of them agree that I can be trusted. They take me outside and show me the dents in the side of their van, the shattered rearview mirror. Eli seems almost apologetic: "Only boys throw rocks," he says, "never grown-ups." When I inquire how and when they will decide that the situation has cleared—that Israeli vehicles will no longer be vulnerable going through Arab areas—he replies: "L'tzorach ha'inyan."

"L'tzorach ha'inyan": *According to the need.* There is something about Eli that is enormously reassuring. It could be his un-macho yet securely masculine manner, or perhaps it is something more superficial, something having to do with his melting eyes and aquiline features, which remind me of Omar Sharif's. At any rate, I don't point out that his answer is in the nature of a tautology: The situation will no longer require it when the situation no longer requires it. It occurs to me that tautologies have a Zen-like logic all their own, providing a solace that is grounded in a passive acceptance of a fate as unknowable as it is inevitable: Peace will come when war is over.

If the Middle East were a movie set, I would want to write in a part for a good-looking, multicultural Israeli like Eli, who goes on to ask with charmingly inverted syntax, "What does it help, war?" Then, too, if the Middle East were a movie set, Eilat would be perfectly cast as a wannabe tropical getaway, with its ominous Graham Greene touches (security guards who loom at the exit of the hotel in order to check your key) and its dated, slightly tacky notion of the deluxe. Think of Miami Beach before its renaissance or of a third-class Caribbean island. The wonder of it is that Eilat exists at all, with a strip of hotels fronting the water, where tall drinks with little parasols bobbing in them are served up poolside and time-share schemes are pushed on the unwary.

HERE BEGINS YOUR VACATION, announces a sign in the Eilat airport, ENJOY IT. Ah, I can relax at last, book myself a manicure at the hotel salon (never mind that I am blithely given an appointment only to discover when I show up for it that there hasn't been a manicurist in residence for six months), watch television (never mind that cable has not yet come to Eilat and that the only clear reception is on the channel carrying a promotional video for the hotel), take hot baths or long showers (never mind that the water is lukewarm and the water pressure varies from low to nonexistent), and eat myself happy at the Brasserie, a kosher French restaurant where the rolls are proffered in no-nonsense descriptions of "brown" or "white" (no sourdough or seven-grain flights of fancy here). The chef, married to an Israeli, is one Manfred Hanover from Germany. When he comes around to our table in his white apron and toque, he enters into an intense conversation with my sister about how far innovative cooks can stretch the limits of kosher cuisine, which dictate that milk and meat, as well as their most attenuated derivatives, be kept separate; there is much praise for Rich's nondairy creamer, a soy-based American product that has been available here only in the last year.

My room at the King Solomon—nominally a five-star hotel (a *kibbutznik's* idea of a five-star hotel, I think huffily to myself) and considered to be the best in Eilat until it was eclipsed by the isolated and understated Princess—looks out on a Holiday Inn, beaming its sign into the night in green neon Hebrew letters. Green lights, be they beckoning or garish, always remind me of Gatsby, but Gatsby would surely be staying at the Princess—all snobby and white with the reddish Edomite Mountains rising outside its sheer glass walls. Walking around that hotel's undeniably elegant marble lobby and peering at its pools and sundecks, whirlpool and water chute, intricately connected by Venetian-style bridges, I have my first real glimpse of *calme, luxe et volupté*. But perhaps such grand pleasure palaces are contrary to the real spirit of Eilat. After all, the Princess is rumored to be cold and badly run, and with its ambitious rates (ranging from about $350 per day for a regular room to nearly $900 for more lush accommodations), it is hushed and empty compared to our own package-priced King Solomon, where they've run out of poolside chaises by ten o'clock in the morning. As we drag some abandoned lounge chairs into the sun—self-service appearing to be the order of the day—my sister, a resident of Jerusalem for eight years, waxes nostalgic for the glory days of Taba and the casually chic Sonesta hotel. Taba, which sat on a much-disputed piece of land at the southernmost tip of Eilat, is within spitting distance of both Jordan (King Hussein's summer residence is in Akaba, which flanks Eilat on the east) and Egypt, and was finally, after international arbitration, given back to Egypt in the late eighties.

Around the pool there are swimming contests and live music and all sorts of desperately festive, Poconos-like touches. My daughter insists on my accompanying her into the water, which seems to have a film of dirt floating on it. Beyond the hotel there are official tourist sights: the Yellow Submarine, where for the equivalent of twenty-five dollars you can descend deep into the Red Sea and look at coral reefs (which turn out to be gray and brown in their natural state), and the underwater observatory where you can watch the fish go by. One fish looks like it's wearing a striped sweater, and another looks, as my niece astutely observes, like Yassir Arafat, with a trailing headpiece (his trademark *kaffiyeh*) for a fin. True, there is a soft sonic boom that, for a moment, frightens people in the observatory's café, where we stop to have Cokes and some cloyingly sweet chocolate cake. And it's hard to ignore the irate German woman who argues loudly with the security guards who stop her on the promenade outside the King Solomon that anyone who might vouch for her identity is already *inside* the hotel. But Eilat is, withal, a reprieve from the sustained watchfulness of Jerusalem, a vigilance so quiet and efficient—so routine—as to be almost indiscernible. However surreal it may strike one when set against the blood-stained backdrop of the Middle East, Eilat is a place where French, German, and Dutch tourists mill around, searching out tans and shopping bargains. It is proof positive that, along with the carnage and anxiety, an ordinary country is going on, with key rings imported from China and trashy television shows imported from America.

One could even wish, at times, for *less* ordinariness—less, at any rate, of the cultural debris that advanced Western civilization throws up in its inimitable wake. If the glitzier forms of entertainment have of necessity been slower to develop in this war-torn nation, with each of my successive visits Israel appears to be catching up. The country has always relied on hit American shows—*Dynasty, Dallas, L.A. Law, Beverly Hills 90210*—to distract the attention of its overstressed citizens, but with the addition in the past few years of cable television and, more recently, a new channel of original programming, there is more to choose from. Talk shows are all the rage: Dan Shilon's gets the highest ratings, and with his deliberately motley crew of guests (Naftali Lavie tells me that he appeared as a guest along with a petty criminal) Shilon seems to qualify as an Israeli Charlie Rose and Arsenio Hall rolled into one, provocative in a *haimish* way. The week I return from Eilat to Jerusalem the Miss Israel Pageant airs; I watch it with my two American-born nieces and am surprised by the wobbly, untoned thighs of many of the contestants—dumbstruck as well by the frenzied nature of Israeli television commercials. The ads are numbingly overt, as in one for Asuta breath spray, in which the concept of "dragon breath" is literally enacted while curvaceous, barely dressed actresses swoon in horror.

Call waiting has come to Israel, which is a wearying prospect in a country where people feel free to telephone before seven o'clock in the morning, and there is a twenty-four-hour supermarket adjacent to the Jerusalem Plaza Hotel. The Ben & Jerry's in Jerusalem's new, multilevel shopping mall next to the soccer stadium and across the street from the biblical zoo is, down to the napkins, an exact replica of its American counterparts except for the Hebrew lettering. I sit there on a Saturday night with my nieces and nephews, who crave ever more scoops of Cookies & Cream, and watch Jerusalem's self-conscious high-school set—the girls with their identical platform sandals and long hair, the boys with earrings and brush cuts. They dance around near the jukebox, which plays songs that were hits several years ago, with an emphasis on the work of Meat Loaf and Joe Cocker. "Do they think this is a disco?" my younger niece asks indignantly. The concept of the *disco* as signifying all that is glamorous, risqué, and very American still floats around here, confirming the sense I have that I am adrift in a gentle time warp—that Israeli popular culture is a pesky little sister, forever tagging behind and trying to copy attitudes that have already been abandoned by its disdainful older sibling.

This sense grows even stronger when I take a taxi into Tel Aviv for the day. Tel Aviv is said to be the city of choice for the artistically forward-looking or the merely sophisticated, but I have never found it to be quite as cosmopolitan as it is strenuously imitative. I've arranged to meet a friend, the writer Ida Fink, for lunch at the café in HaBima, the national theater. Fink is the author of two scrupulously unsentimental accounts of evading the Holocaust's grasp—the first of which, *A Scrap of Time,* won Israel's Anne Frank Prize. It is almost a week since the massacre, but when we aren't discussing the vexed lives that writers lead or whether Israel has a literary mafia, as one novelist here has charged, the massacre is the subject that dominates our conversation. Like most writers who live here, Fink has no sympathy for fundamentalist thinking—whether Islamic or Jewish; she is a secularist through and through and cannot conceive of a politics based on historical principles.

One major difference between Jerusalem and Tel Aviv is that while in the former city the predominating attitude to the ongoing conflict is that the answer lies in getting tougher with the Arabs, in the latter it is that the answer lies in getting tougher with the Jews. Everywhere I went in Jerusalem, I encountered what I suppose could be thought of as neoconservative views of the massacre. Judicious and self-protective, these views are espoused, in the main, by Israel's religious and Sephardic Jews. *No one raises a fuss when Arabs kill Jews. They've never stopped killing us. Has the PLO ever publicly apologized for any of its terrorist attacks? Have any of its leaders taken out an ad stating their apologies on behalf of their people the way Rabin did in their papers?*

In Tel Aviv, where a Peace Now rally is being planned for the upcoming Saturday, I find the attitude of wholesale condemnation and self-laceration that one has come to expect from those on the Israeli left —secular Jews, academics, and artists. It is an attitude meant for consumption by the foreign press (indeed it plays better outside the country than within it) and for anyone, Jew and non-Jew alike, made uncomfortable by the idea that the people of the Book have made themselves familiar with the nonbookish enterprise of war. *Look what we've gone and done now, with our crazy capitulation to religious fanatics who don't want to make peace with the Arabs. How can we protest the enemy's terrorist attacks when we can't contain our own settlers? We should go into mourning, and then we should throw the settlers out.*

But Tel Aviv also means—and it is this aspect of it, I think, that makes it easier on the nerves than Jerusalem—forgetting the state of the country's soul in pursuit of the state of one's inner chic. It means being taken to Alexander's, Tel Aviv's place to eat and be seen, for dinner. I'm told it's impossible to get into Alexander's for lunch on Friday unless you're a regular. The restaurant may lack pepper mills, but there are magazine racks near the front door as well as coy touches in the industrial-look toilets upstairs, so coy that I have a hard time figuring out that the pedal on the floor is how you flush. At the table behind us a group of Manhattan-thin women and several men who look like variations on Jean-Pierre Léaud in *The 400 Blows* avidly discuss movies. Are they in them? Do they make them? Or simply see them? Spielberg has just been here in a blaze of publicity to open *Schindler's List*. In one of the many interviews he's given to the Israeli press, the director ruefully conceded that "Jerusalem of Gold," which closed the American version of the film, struck a wrong note with Israeli audiences (for whom the song is a tired anthem) and has been replaced with the more fittingly elegiac "Eli, Eli." Although Spielberg himself in all his newly Jewish celebrity has been embraced by the country, his movie was given a distinctly less enthusiastic response—mostly on account of what were seen to be sentimental and inauthentic touches.

Is it possible to go away for two weeks and come back only to find that one has ceased relating to the context one left behind? I came home and forgot to watch the Academy Awards until they were half over, I who had always looked forward to them for weeks ahead of time. I went to a brunch at my brother's house in Englewood, New Jersey, where conversation turned to the open declarations of anti-Semitism made by Louis Farrakhan and Khalid Abdul Muhammad. We discussed how for people like us, Jews born after World War II, such racist invective comes as a shock in a way it wouldn't have for the generations before us—that we had grown up in a period of post-Holocaust goodwill which seemed destined to come to a close. As I listened, I wondered to myself why the creation of the state of Israel had not, over the span of nearly half a century, more crucially altered the landscape of Jewish identity—at least for those Jews like my brother and his friends, who chose to live in Orthodox suburbs. Was the cushiness of life in America so much more attractive a prospect than the complex allure of life among one's own in a foreign, troubled land? By what accounting had one kind of vulnerability—that of being a Jew in a non-Jewish country—been deemed less costly than the vulnerability of being a Jew in a Jewish state, albeit one fringed by enemies?

I went to two Passover seders where we concluded, as we do every year, with the axiomatic recitation of "Next Year in Jerusalem"—as though Israel were still Palestine and the whole country no more than a mirage.

It's been a month since I've been back in my native city, where the sky is something whose existence you take on faith. I'm back to reading the paper and returning the messages on my answering machine, back to frantically hailing cabs or descending into the subway, chasing after my own life as one does in New York. In my head I'm slouching toward expatriation, not sure I have the courage or the energy to do so. At a book awards ceremony, I mention to someone that I'm entertaining the thought of moving to Israel, and she says to me confidently, "You couldn't, you have too much at stake here." But do I? I find myself fighting with old friends, impatient with the image others have of me. Are all dreams of expatriation no more than dreams of exiting the self as circumscribed by all-too-familiar others?

Like a glimpse of a truer reality, I keep before me the image of a quiet street in a distant country—ordinary in an extraordinary way—where the sky hangs low and the stones give off an ancient, yellow light. I will find my way back someday soon, and thereby wander home.

1994

The Last Yom Kippur
of Yaakov Riegler

Borough Park, a neighborhood of ultra-Orthodox Jews in the heart of Brooklyn, has a certain insular appeal. With its rows of faded redbrick homes—one- and two-family houses of pre–World War II vintage next to three- and four-family houses, built in the late fifties and early sixties to accommodate an expanding population—and its narrow streets lined with double-parked cars, its porches filled in sunny weather with playpens and baby carriages, this Brooklyn enclave presents a self-contained image of family and community life.

There is nothing aesthetically pleasing, given its garish mixture of architectural styles, about the area. Its charm is of a different sort: the charm of stasis. In its very removal from the hurly-burly, it speaks to our imagination, wherein we dream of worlds more orderly and controllable than the ones that generally greet us. For those who live in less sheltered communities, who imbibe the chaotic air of contemporary New York City, there is something poignant about the timeless, religiously ordained atmosphere of Borough Park, something enviable about its willed distance from the world beyond its borders.

■ ■ ■

To most of the denizens of Borough Park, the rest of us—less rigorously observant Jews included—are fatally secular, *goyish*. As a young girl growing up in a modern Orthodox environment, I used to be struck whenever I visited the neighborhood by its fiercely separatist, world-within-a-world quality. I felt as alien in my clothes and outlook as a Zoroastrian; however religiously observant my family might have been with their strict adherence to the laws of Sabbath and *Kashrut,* I was clearly and immediately not one of the Borough Park community. In their eyes, we who live on the outside are tainted by the infidel nature of American culture itself, whether as overt as *Penthouse* magazine or as seemingly innocuous as a TV game show. The price these Jews—both Chasidim and non-Chasidic "black hats" (so-called to distinguish them from the more middle-of-the-road Orthodox)—pay for their separateness ranges from dress restrictions (women wear stockings and long sleeves even on the hottest summer day) to their eschewal of English for Yiddish. Such self-imposed exclusion would appear to come with the implied promise of a morally superior way of life—one less marked by the vicissitudes of the "outside" world. And indeed, as the American-Jewish community, in all its assimilationist glory, seems to cleave ever less to Jewish values and is beset by the same nondenominational problems that afflict other communities, it becomes all the more tempting to believe in the possibility of a haven, a virtuous refuge where black-frocked men and bewigged women stroll in their finery on Sabbath afternoons, a shiny-eyed, Nintendo-immune flock of children in tow.

With what a sense of disappointment, then, did we recently discover that this perceived haven was as vulnerable to the forces of human calamity as the unlawful world beyond its borders. Several weeks ago, an incident of domestic violence took place in the heart of Borough Park, on one of those narrow streets with double-parked cars where the women visit one another on weekdays dressed in bathrobes and housecoats.

■ ■ ■

The day in late September on which eight-year-old Yaakov Riegler was brought to a Brooklyn hospital in an irreversible coma was not a weekday: It was a Saturday, *yom Shabbos kodesh;* it was also Yom Kippur, the holiest day of the Jewish calendar. Two weeks later, Yaakov Riegler died, a victim of child-abuse syndrome—a recognizable pattern of head injuries and broken bones. His mother, thirty-three-year-old Shulamis Riegler, six months pregnant with her fifth child, was charged with second-degree murder.

The facts that emerged in subsequent news accounts added bits and pieces of dismal history: that Yaakov was mentally retarded and attended special classes at a public school in Bensonhurst; that his mother had been sentenced to five years' probation in August 1986 for assaulting another son and was required to undergo psychiatric treatment; that in April 1986, the two boys and a third brother had been placed in foster care under the supervision of the community-run Ohel Children's Home; that they were returned to their parents' home in October 1989 by family court; and that neighbors, Ohel social workers, and school officials suspected abuse and contacted welfare officials at various points. It was, in other words, one of those tragedies that gathers momentum while it waits to happen. The warning signs were all there, not ignored, but not sufficiently heeded, either.

A medical examiner has determined that Yaakov Riegler was fatally injured sometime between seven A.M. and noon on Yom Kippur, September 29, 1990. He was at home with his mother and his thirteen-month-old brother, while his two older brothers attended synagogue. It was initially alleged that no other adult was home at the time, but it since has become a contention of Shulamis Riegler's defense that the father was present as well. Not much else is clear about this case, partly because the Borough Park community is singularly effective at closing ranks in moments of crisis, and partly because it is in the nature of many child-abuse cases to retain an aura of opacity, of impenetrability.

A community, needless to say, is only as healthy as its healthiest members; one can safely speculate that the Rieglers, under cover of ultra-Orthodoxy, were a severely disturbed family well before the bruises appeared on Yaakov's body. One can also speculate that the eight-year-old's aberrant status did not help him in a world that values cleverness and conformity as much as this one does. Listen to Rabbi Simcha Srohli, a yeshiva principal acquainted with the family, as quoted in *The New York Times:* "From day one, when the child was born, he had problems."

There is, of course, a dark side to separatism. Beyond the dictates of religious ritual loom the strictures of inbredness, a fear of any sort of difference—even in so small a matter as interior decorating (ornate chandeliers and glass-paned breakfronts displaying silver kiddush cups and *havdalah* holders are *de rigueur* dining room fixtures)—and a suppression of individual needs. One of the less exemplary imperatives of so insular a society as that of Borough Park is an intricate form of keeping up with the Joneses, of maintaining a facade so one's family name will remain unblemished and one's children will marry well. It is a community whose focus is relentlessly generative, where the warning cry about airing problems, emotional or otherwise, is *shadem dem shiddech* (it'll hurt the marriage) and there is intense pressure to keep any and all skeletons firmly in the closet. To speculate once more: Shulamis Riegler must have had a larger share of problems than most, and her husband must have had his own problems. But the custom—inviolable as law—of the community of which they were part has it, among other things, that women are meant to be mothers and that families are meant to be large. If Shulamis Riegler showed the strain of being a mother after her first child (or her husband the strain of being a father), undoubtedly the best face was put on so she had another child, and another, and was expecting yet another as her least acceptable child was battered to death.

This is one of those bewilderingly sad stories where any attempt to assign blame seems beside the point. The community tried to help, and the secular, *goyish* world tried to intervene, but at some moment the ball was dropped. Between the cracks of public concern, a private madness erupted and eight-year-old Yaakov Riegler, who could not read and who could speak only in one-word sentences, was killed.

Meanwhile, an eerie silence has descended; the news out of Borough Park is nil. That community—given to a siege mentality at the best of times—is adept at protecting its own against the intrusive curiosity of outsiders, especially in circumstances such as these. To try to ferret out information from people who know the family or about the case is to come up against the tribal instinct at its most oppressive, *us* against *them*. In the eyes of the world into which Yaakov Riegler was born, any attempt to clarify what happened is viewed with grave suspicion. In the end, however, insularity is no proof against tragedy or shame. Skeletons will have their say, even in Borough Park, and no one is spared the ravages of the psyche, not even people who put God's interests before human distress.

1990

Ecclesiastes:
A Depressive's Lament

Ecclesiastes, or as it is also known by the nom de plume of its author, *Kohelet,* opens with a great sputter of protest, an exhaust fume of indignation let off against the motoric insensateness of life: *"Havél havalim,"* intones Kohelet, *"Havél havalim, hakól hevel"*—"Vanity of vanities, Vanity of vanities, all is vanity."* The Hebrew is remarkably sonorous in its repetitiveness, but it is nonetheless grim; there is no denying the opening message of raging futility. We read on and discover that this message runs throughout the text, pumping its sentences with the strange sense of invigoration that sadness can bring.

I cannot imagine what it is like to read Ecclesiastes on a sunny day under a clear sky. It is, however much the pious commentators bustle in with their ready assuagements, a depressive's lament—perfect reading for a gray day. I began to explore Ecclesiastes on such a day, on a wintry after-

---

*The Jewish Publication Society's translation of the Bible is used in this essay.

noon, and immediately found myself colored by its plangent melancholy: "All words fail through weariness"; "There is nothing new under the sun!" Of course, it is precisely from such a miscomprehending reader as myself that the sages wished to protect this slim book, potentially the most subversive of the thirty-three in the biblical canon. Midrashic literature (those disparate, post-Talmudic interpretations of the Bible known collectively as "midrash") resounds with anxieties about the heretic influence of *Kohelet,* quoting a Rabbi Benjamin who declared that the sages originally wished to conceal the text, and a Rav Samuel ben Isaac who maintained that its reading could easily lead to unbelief. That Ecclesiastes got in under the wire of religious censorship at all is due to its alleged authorship at the hands of King Solomon—a construction now discarded by most biblical scholars—and also to a somewhat startling elasticity of spirit on the part of those who dictated the shape of the Tanach, or Bible. But its negative power was certainly not lost on those who decided in favor of its inclusion.

For a Jewish text, Ecclesiastes is almost unconscionably jaded, brimming over with the most romantic and sophisticated sense of *Weltschmerz.* Kohelet, who takes for himself the persona of the wealthiest of Jewish kings, is at ease among the glitterati. (The midrash rather cunningly points out that, had a poor man uttered the words *havél havalim,* we would have scoffed at him, but since they come from King Solomon, whose vessels were all of gold, we pay attention.) No withdrawn, ivory-towered observer he, Kohelet is someone who vies with competitive zeal and has tasted of excess: "I bought slaves and slave girls, in addition to my household retainers; my possessions of cattle and sheep also were greater than those of all who had preceded me in Jerusalem, I amassed also silver and gold, such private treasure as kings and satraps have. I provided myself with male and female singers, and with the pleasure of the flesh, concubine after concubine. As I became greater than any who have been before me in Jerusalem . . ." And yet nothing suffices for this acquisition-happy malcontent, this biblical character blessed with the dazzling "lifestyle" of a corporate raider but burdened with the wrong soul—the soul of a Flaubert. Like that other great connoisseur of ennui, Kohelet is acutely aware of the "boredom and ignominies of existence," and would, I suspect, agree with the nineteenth-century writer's calibrated assessment: "I admire tinsel as much as gold: indeed the poetry of tinsel is even greater, because it is sadder."

Although the corpus of Ecclesiastes is carefully appended with a statement of religious exhortation (generally thought to have been composed by a later, uneasy editor)—"The sum of the matter, when all is said and done: Revere God and observe His commandments!"—its twelve segments contain little in the way of homiletics or even of the platitudes of Jewish faith. Similarly, the idea of an afterlife, in which the good are rewarded and the bad punished, is questioned—"Who knows if a man's life-breath does rise upward and if a beast's breath does sink down into the earth?"—and specifically contradicted: "But the dead know nothing; they have no more recompense, for even the memory of them has died. Their loves, their hates, their jealousies have long since perished; and they have no more share till the end of time in all that goes on under the sun." So much for the consoling childhood images we carry with us—those neatly polarized depictions of heaven and hell, golden-haloed angels and pitchfork-wielding devils.

More interestingly still, Kohelet proposes that as far as *this* life goes, moral stature and earthly status not only don't necessarily follow on each other practicably—"Sometimes an upright man is requited according to the conduct of the scoundrel; and sometimes the scoundrel is requited according to the conduct of the upright"—but also they may not bear any but the most oblique relation to divine will: "To the man, namely, who pleases Him He has given the wisdom and shrewdness to enjoy himself." The phrase *shetov lephanav* ("who pleases Him") is, to my mind, a provocative one, for it suggests that God may be seducible by an attractiveness of aspect—a simpatico quality—that has nothing to do with inner probity, and may be entirely arbitrary. The progression is clearly spelled out: *First* one finds favor, *then* one merits His bounty. Given the almost Calvinistic preselection of the process, how are we to know if God might not indeed stand up for (attractive) bastards after all —fall head over heels, that is, for the wrong man?

Known as "the most modern book in the Bible," Ecclesiastes is undeniably the most heterodox. Although even the least cautious of critics is quick to point out that Kohelet's skepticism is only the topmost stratum of his core identity as a monotheistic Jew, there is no getting around the fact that the ideas he espouses—in a pithy and proverb-based style that has been called "Oriental"—are informed by the pressure of nullity. Kohelet comes to us having faced down the existential void, the hollowness at the heart of the getting and spending that is the human enterprise: "The race is not won by the swift, / Nor the battle by the valiant; / Nor is bread won by the wise / Nor wealth by the intelligent, / Nor favor by the learned."

No wonder it is the Old Testament text most cherished by secular readers, by non-Jews and even by those who are faintly anti-Semitic in their sentiments. Tennyson proclaimed it "the greatest poem of ancient or modern times," and so unlikely a reader as Havelock Ellis suggested that you could spare yourself some unhappiness in the world "if, beforehand, you slip the Book of Ecclesiastes beneath your arm." Even more sweepingly, there is the verdict of Ernest Renan, the French historian and critic, for whom *Kohelet* is "the only charming book ever written by a Jew."

There is, to be sure, a bracing—even healing—aspect to the stark realism of the writer's vision, a way in which his resolute emphasis on the transience of all things human can be said to be a cloud-chaser. Still, the "charm" of Ecclesiastes is a tonic charm, a somewhat bitter-tasting dose of our own dust-to-dustness. (For some readers, the atmosphere of skull-rattling verges on the lurid, like those Elizabethan revenge-tragedies where Death puts in an appearance as a character onstage: "The book has indeed," mused one biblical exegete, "the smell of the tomb about it.") But the appeal of this work stems primarily, I think, from its tone of mercurial intimacy—from the narrator's almost defiant credo of personalism. The stakes here, unlike the stakes set by the "other-directed" Prophets, are very private ones: What is the formula for achieving success? Do or don't I find happiness in this life? What use is *carpe diem* if disaster may strike as readily as good fortune?

Of course, with his healthy respect for money and his palpable indifference to the idea of community, Kohelet seems to be speaking far more than the usual biblical protagonist on behalf of the *real,* rather than the *ideal,* self in all of us. If, as recent psychological research indicates, personal happiness derives less from our sense of how close we come to our idealized inner selves and more from how content we feel with ourselves as we are, it becomes understandable why Ecclesiastes has been embraced in all its cold and gnomic comfort. "Wedged in among resplendent priests, ecstatic psalmists and implacable prophets," as the biblical critic Robert Gordis so aptly described him, Kohelet cuts a less-than-imposing, recognizably human figure. Shamelessly inconsistent in his reasoning, though always a bottom-liner, with what relief we fall upon him!

It must be fairly noted, however, that a lonely perusal out of season is not what the sages had in mind for this pickled dish of a text. Such a reading can only lead away from the larger ritual purpose, the instructive calendrical context, that the rabbis who agreed to include Ecclesiastes had presupposed. As is true of so much of Jewish life, the specific occasion designated for its reading—the festival of *Succot,* or Tabernacles, which falls, in our hemisphere, in the brilliant days of early autumn—evokes a dialectic and therefore a deliberate state of tension. Set against the gaiety and plenty of the holiday, which commemorates the ingathering of the harvest, the book of *Kohelet* casts shadows that lengthen and darken.

■ ■ ■

Succot is an eight-day festival during the course of which Ecclesiastes is read aloud in the synagogue. It stands out in my mind as the favored holiday of my childhood. The biblical injunction concerning its practice stresses enjoyment over decorum. Following as it does upon the heels of Rosh Hashanah and Yom Kippur—those sober, prayer-inundated, and self-abnegating Days of Awe—*Succot* struck my youthful imagination as decidedly and atypically carefree. Given that my attitude toward the minutiae of Jewish observance was an admixture of resentment and a not wholly unappreciative compliance, I had a perhaps overdeveloped sense of the prohibited (what I wasn't allowed to do on *yontev,* or "good" days, as they were called: turn on lights, write, listen to music) and not enough of the celebratory as a factor in religious life. *Succot,* with its light touch and cheery tone, was just the right corrective for me—nearer, or so it seemed, to the Christian ideal of holiday than to the Jewish.

For starters, the holiday is deeply sensual: aromatic with the branches of *s'chach,* the pine or evergreen that crowns the makeshift dwelling of the *succah* (a reminder of the portable huts the Jews built while wandering the desert), and pungent with the scent of the *esrog,* the ritual citron resembling nothing so much as a wrinkled and obese lemon. Then there were the decorations within the *succah* itself: the painstakingly lettered and curlicued drawings, like Hebrew versions of kitchen samplers, that my siblings and I had worked on for days. These were hung on the thin wooden walls of the *succah* next to ancestral photographs, alien-looking relatives who stared out from their frames with mournful sepia gazes. In between the branches of *s'chach* nestled vivid touches of fruit—apples, oranges, and an occasional banana. If you looked more closely, you could glimpse the tiny glass bottles of oil, flour, and wine (symbolizing the harvest) that stirred in the breeze, catching the light.

Although both the holiday itself and its representative text constitute a warning against being too at home, too comfortable in the material universe, *Succot* is also very much about the aesthetics of improvisation. True, we may die or lose everything at any time, but we can dance rings around that fact, festoon it with all manner of ingenuity. In a family where the spiritual impulse often seemed to get buried under layers of German formality and propriety, *Succot* drew on my mother's strengths—her genuine love of beauty, her pleasure in tasteful adornment. It is all the more curious, therefore, that when I think of the message of Ecclesiastes, I think not of myself or my family but of Teddy, the Irish handyman who fixed leaking ceilings and faulty plumbing. It was he who, within the course of a single afternoon, put up the *succah* in the space allotted for it in the driveway—just under the basketball hoop.

With nothing more than a mouthful of nails and four planes of green-painted plywood, Teddy worked the sort of magic my brainy but impractical brothers and father could never have managed. He built us a house, one with curtained windows and a plastic roof that could be raised and lowered over the fragile covering of *s'chach* in case of rain. It was a real house, with room inside to seat twelve or fourteen, but one that also partook of the meta-real—a house appearing suddenly in the woods in a fairy tale, providing shelter from storms both metaphorical and actual. Teddy, whose face was always slightly ruddy—from wind or from drink, or a bit of both—seemed to understand the implication of Ecclesiastes deep inside his bones: Everything that happens has happened before, will happen again. Alone among us, he seemed to take the world precisely as it came, was caught up in a race against no man or clock. Free of the morbid self-consciousness that marked the members of my family, he was satisfied with his own inner synchronism.

Who was Kohelet? Who was the person behind the persona, the man behind the philosophy? Although as contemporary readers we might wish to psychoanalyze his malaise—to make guesses about his temperament and upbringing—there is too little to work with. The paucity of personal allusions in this self-revealing yet elusive document spares him. We deduce that Kohelet is an older man, looking back on his life from a position of material success as well as spiritual disappointment. The book is generally believed to have been written in the second to third century B.C.: From the author's casual reference to attendance at sacrificial rites, scholars have presumed that the Temple was nearby, and that he probably lived in Jerusalem. Ancient Jerusalem appears to have been no easier a country for old men than Yeats's modern Ireland—"an aged man" there, too, "but a paltry thing." In one of the last and more lyrical passages of the book, the writer describes the humiliations of senescence so vividly—with an almost Yeatsian intensity—that it suggests his own biography.

"So appreciate your vigor in the days of your youth," opens Chapter 12, "before those years arrive of which you will say, 'I have no pleasure in them. . . .'" Then follows an allegory composed of a series of startlingly beautiful metaphors in which the slow deterioration of the parts of the body is likened to the closing down of a once-bustling village: "When the guards of the house become shaky" (i.e., the arms); "And the men of valor are bent" (legs); "And the maids that grind, grown few, are idle" (teeth); "And the ladies that peer through the windows grow dim" (eyes); "And the doors to the street are shut" (ears). This terrifying vision of decrepitude and impotence concludes with the painful reminder: "And the dust returns to the ground / As it was, / And the life-breath returns to God / Who bestowed it." Like "the old, old men" in Yeats's poem—titled, with grim humor, "The Old Men Admiring Themselves in the Water"—Kohelet flashes before us a mirror in which is reflected an image of our eventual fate: "one by one we drop away."

There are other traits we can adduce about this biblical *cahier*-keeper, habits of mind and intellectual biases (although any critical theory constructed about this most protean of texts immediately produces a countertheory: Greek influences have been equally asserted and denied, and one lone scholar claims to see a Buddhist influence). Deeply skeptical as he may be, Kohelet is a political conservative, a believer in the sovereign power of the state as reflected in the king. "Money," he says at one point, "answers everything." There are limits, then, to this writer's philosophy, entrenched as it is in the mercantile culture of the early Hellenistic period and bounded by rationalist, egotistic considerations. He is a man for our time, a private-sectorite. But being a personality who wears contradictions without discomfort, he has another side, one that suits another realm—the realm of the artist, where a restless spirit of inquiry soars beyond the walls of the status quo.

Like Voltaire and his *Candide,* the author of Ecclesiastes engages in an exercise of constructive fantasy. The book has scarcely any narrative to hold on to; it offers little of the systematic construction of Job. What we get instead are the squiggles of an implied quest, a classical quest that can also be put in the most contemporary of terms: If you were rich as Croesus—as Kashoggi—how would you choose to live? Through the reversals and inconsistencies of Kohelet's paradoxical reasoning (examples of sloth in Chapter 10, for instance, are followed by examples of too much caution in Chapter 11) emerges the curve of a critique, a testing of the standard notions of pleasure. The consolations Kohelet remains with have mostly to do with the actual producing of wisdom—the making of however pessimistic a philosophy. Then, too, it is possible to find a dim comfort in the thought that catastrophe itself is part of the experiential spectrum: "For there is a time for every experience, including the doom; for a man's calamity overwhelms him."

But even these small victories snatched from the jaws of despair cannot be granted without qualification. Given his acute awareness of the role hubris plays in human affairs, Kohelet is convinced of the ultimate uselessness of intelligence, its tragic lack of effect: "For as wisdom grows, vexation grows; / To increase learning is to increase heartache." Later in the text, describing an underpopulated city which might have been spared its ransacked fate had anyone thought to seek the counsel of a wise but poor inhabitant, he concludes: "A poor man's wisdom is scorned / And his words are not heeded."

Thinking about who the author of Ecclesiastes might have been and who scholars historically perceive him to have been brings me to an even more literal-minded linking of the figures of Teddy and the writer of the book. Although my mother used to quote a phrase from *Kohelet* as an argument in favor of getting married ("two are better off than one"), I now realize she did so slyly and knowingly out of context. For one thing, the reference is to business and not marital partners; for another, notwithstanding the traditional view—which proposes that the author of Ecclesiastes is King Solomon, with his many wives and many children —I envision Kohelet as a bachelor, a very early case of what today we might call the uncommitted male. Although he commends matrimony in the abstract—"Enjoy happiness with a woman you love, all the fleeting days of life"—his distrust of women's wiles verges on misogyny: "Now, I find woman more bitter than death; she is all traps, her hands are fetters and her heart is snares. He who is pleasing to God escapes her, and he who is displeasing is caught by her." Who can say what circumstances in his own life led to this extreme position: Was Kohelet perhaps thrown over by a woman he loved for someone less implacably dark-natured? Or was he the son of a dominating mother whose clutches he felt even in old age? One can only guess.

But what I, as a female reader, cannot help being especially struck by, more than his probable bachelorhood, is the *childlessness* of the narrator. For a Jewish text, Ecclesiastes is remarkably and singularly devoid of the urge to perpetuate. The sense of futurity and continuity—both familial and racial—that the idea of posterity guarantees is wholly absent in Kohelet. Always conscious though he is of his own mortality, he never succumbs to the allure of having children as a means to ensure *im*mortality. When Kohelet speaks of "the case of the man who is alone, with no companion, who has neither son nor brother," one can reasonably speculate that he is talking of himself. And "the case of the man who is alone" brings me back willy-nilly to Teddy. For in a childhood where all the grown men I encountered were married, and mostly saddled with kids, Teddy was single. It must be said in his behalf that he didn't begin to share in Kohelet's rampant hostility; he seemed to like women, albeit from a safely flirtatious distance. But Teddy certainly hadn't been inspired to tie the connubial knot; nor, so far as I knew, had he sired offspring. As an unprocreative male, he was spared one of the prevailing anxieties in Ecclesiastes: the fear of producing offspring who will fail you, of "toiling for the wind."

In the years that have intervened between then and now, Teddy has aged imperceptibly. He has never married—he is, I think, proud to have abstained from so routine a decision—and he appears to be childless. Although I connect him with my childhood, he still comes around to painstakingly repair windows and stop up leaks. The present has caught up with him, as it has with me, but in a sense it will never overtake him. He will not witness the fruit of his labor despoiled by future generations, a son who builds houses on shaky foundations, or a grandson who scoffs at his skill with a piece of wood and nails.

As a daughter in an Orthodox household, I had no text to call my own. In contrast to Jewish sons, who are raised with a proprietary relationship to the Bible, Jewish daughters have at best an oblique connection to the sacred volumes of their heritage. When each of my three brothers turned Bar Mitzvah, at the age of thirteen, they recited the weekly Torah portion as well as the selection from the *haftorah* Shabbos morning in *shul*. The arduous months of preparation—the bearded teacher who sat with them, ceaselessly going over the *"trop,"* the half-chant, half-melody in which the lines of the text are sung—paid off handsomely in that hour of glory up on the *bima,* before a jam-packed congregation that hung on to every syllable uttered. When I turned Bas Mitzvah, at the age of twelve, my family went out to dinner at Lou G. Siegel's, a kosher restaurant. I wore a light-blue dress that had belonged first to my sister, and I recited nothing of greater consequence than a litany of thank-you's for the presents I received.

In retrospect, I think that as a young girl with a marked tendency to depression and no great conviction about the particulars of the faith in which I was reared, I would have warmed to Ecclesiastes. I might even have chosen it—its antifeminist aspect notwithstanding—as my text, my very own out-of-season *haftorah,* to be recited before an admiring public not on *Succot* but on my birthday, which fell in May.

The message I take from *Kohelet* is that sadness flows under the skin of things, like blood. It is a part of life—Freud's "ordinary unhappiness," what we are left with even after "neurotic misery" is cured—not to be avoided, but to be recognized and understood. Once understood, it becomes possible to contain the sadness within circles of light: orbs of warmth against the encroaching chill. When I look back on the *succah* of my childhood, it stands out in my memory as one of those circles, a confining but also cozy haven. If it makes me somewhat wistful to realize that I am now irrevocably outside the radius of the *succah*—that I have moved away from its green smell and flickering candles, its food and conversation—I also realize that for me it was a necessary, liberating step. Still, who knows if there won't come a day when I will once again step inside under the canopy of *s'chach,* together with my daughter, and inhale the complex religion of my upbringing as it wafts by me?

If the news that the sober, immensely clear-eyed writer of this book brings us is that there are no second acts, even in Jewish lives, who is to say what twists and turns the first and only act holds in store for us? Perhaps the single most famous sentence in Ecclesiastes is: "There is nothing new under the sun." What else can this mean except that possibility is recurrent; nothing is surprising, nothing is absolutely unprecedented. In our leavetakings are the stirrings of return.

1987

Enter the Shulamite:
How Sexy Is the Song of Songs?

1

Everyone lies about sex, more or less, to themselves if not to others, to others if not to themselves, exaggerating its importance or minimizing its pull.

Perfect sex is like some Platonic essence, taking place only in our heads, safe from the incursions of an always-blemished reality. Sexual reality demands that we bury our erotic disappointments and leads us to credit a moment's tremorous fulfillment with the whole earth-shaking shebang. We cannot experience sex except as it is acted upon us, and we can only imagine the erotic life of others. As befits the workings of fantasy and guesswork, the mythology of sex tends toward florid stereotypes: Men in general are supposed to prefer their sex served straight up—like strong drink, without the diluting agent of affection. Lower-class men are supposed to be either quick and unsubtle or, like Lady Chatterly's lover and the shepherd in the Song of Songs, unexpectedly gifted in the sensual arts. Then there are rich men, gone soft with too many pleasures, men on the order of King Solomon, who chase skirts frenetically, showering gold coins, but who ultimately lose out to poorer and more potent rivals.*

Women, the whole lot of us, are a mystery, insistently confounding. ("What do women want?" Even Freud threw up his hands.) Supposedly incapable of sex without intimacy—of physical ardor without at least the whisper of love—we insist from time to time on following our baser instincts and thereby put the whole tentative patriarchal order in jeopardy. Just look at Eve. Ignoring the compliant Adam's lead, she bit covetously into the infamous apple and thereby sundered carnal and spiritual desires forever.

When speaking of erotic matters, it seems we are always at pains to guard against gender anxiety, to differentiate between subject and object, between the *he* and the *she:* who's on top and who's on bottom. From biblical times through the present secular moment, the power play of lust—frivolous but telling—remains a constant if encoded theme. A strict division of behavior along male (designated as active) and female (designated as passive) lines runs like a hidden thread in the Judeo-Christian narratives that have been passed along, pulling them tight against homosexual and/or androgynous encroachment. (This is in distinct opposition to the construction of morality put forward by the ancient Greeks and Romans, wherein boys and women were treated as interchangeable objects of male desire, with the former culture glorifying homosexuality and the latter accepting it as a matter of course.) Thus, down the slope of religious history it is unmanly to seek fulfillment where none is forthcoming, but it is just like a woman to long for what she cannot have.

Accordingly, the Judaic formulation of the world—which was the only one of the archaic civilizations to prohibit homosexuality per se—provides us with clearly demarcated territories: The godhead is kept rigorously unanthropomorphized, while the sexes are kept in their

---

*Throughout my piece, I have referred to three translated versions of the Song of Songs: the Anchor Bible, the Soncino, and the Jewish Publication Society. In each case, I chose the specific translation that struck me, purely subjectively, as most in the spirit of the original Hebrew.

places at opposite ends of the seduction equation as the sorely tempted male and the dangerously blandishing female. There have naturally been some lapses or detours along the way—most notably the kabbalistic strategy of investing the Jewish concept of divinity with erotic power. But the kabbalistic mode, which embraced mysticism and its attendant sacral devices, calls attention to itself by the very audacity with which it went against the mandated principles of the religion it sought to invigorate.

Enter the Shulamite, whoever she be, love object or subject, bestride (or ridden by?) this frisky colt of a text—canonical glitch or deliberate oversight, Jewish original or Persian derivative, holiest of holies or pure, unadulterated smut—called, with arrant hyperbole, the Song of Songs. Enter the dusky-skinned Shulamite ("I am black but comely"), filled with boundless longing, just like a woman. . . .

Or is she in fact just like a man? The pinprick of gender anxiety haunts the reader almost from the moment one begins reading this most sacrosanct piece of erotica. All the ordinary mooring points of identity are so tentatively established in this famous love poem—a dramatic dialogue with remarkably diffuse boundaries—that the reader is left feeling deeply uncertain as to exactly *who* is doing the talking, much less what sex the person is.

This first sliver of doubt brings others in its wake, revolving around the basic dyad of Self and Other upon which the enigma of amorous choice is based: Are you me, am I you, are you there, are you gone, are you worthy, are you ridiculous, who is the male (i.e., dominant-aggressive) and who is the female (i.e., subordinate-receptive)? *Who is the lover and who is the loved?* Indeed, the emotional lability of the writing—all in a dither over the Other, but the Other as representative of aspects of the Self—is so omnipresent that one could easily imagine it being presented, in another context, as psychiatric evidence of dangerous symbiotic yearnings on the part of two mental patients, the "David and Lisa" of biblical times.

It is one of the givens of literary interpretation that there will be almost as many perceived contexts as readers, and what looks like signs

of pathology to one reader may seem indicative of the greatest psychological health to another: Turn unhealthy symbiosis on its head, in other
words, and you end up with blissful mutuality.

Feminist biblical critics, ever on the lookout for hidden textual per-
suaders, have been quick to adduce progressive—that is, antipatriarchal
—signs from the Song's suppleness, or sexual amorphousness; there is,
among this crowd, glowing talk of the narrative's "egalitarianism," as if
its author, unbeknownst to him/her, was a hoary prototype of the contemporary jargon-infused orthodox-feminist reader.

So you have one academic reader like Ilana Pardes, in an essay full of
opaque theoretical stratagems ("'I am a Wall, and My Breasts like Towers': The Song of Songs and the Question of Canonization"), referring to
the Song's "metaphoric fluidity, whereby the lovers use the same vehicles to interpret one another in their cocourting [sic]." With similar
pyrotechnic ease at overlooking time warps and bending a given text to
her will as a reader, the French psychoanalytic critic Julia Kristeva, in an
essay entitled "A Holy Madness: She and He," comments passingly on
"the listless quality of the woman lover," only to go on, rather confusingly, to hold said listless lover up as a domestic woman warrior: "The
amorous Shulamite is the first woman to be sovereign before her loved
one. Through such a hymn to the love of the married couple, Judaism
asserts itself as a first liberation of women [!]."

Of course, the hunger of female Bible scholars to find some trace of
their own predicament in the onion-peel layering of the Old Testament is
entirely understandable. This ongoing need helps explain why Marcia
Falk, a feminist biblical scholar who's written an audacious translation of
the Song, seems compelled to locate in this perplexing artifact echoes of
her own concerns—although she's just gotten through admitting that the
poems don't offer much in the way of gender specificity, much less valida-
tion. To this wishful end she distorts, however eruditely, parts of the original material beyond recognition on more than one occasion. There is, for
instance, the implausible opening line of stanza 13 as Falk renders it—"At
night in bed, I want him"—which suggests that the zipless fuck was

invented way before Erica Jong came along to coin the phrase. It also explains how like-minded readers have managed to hear a sanguine "collective female voice" in the "daughters of Jerusalem" to whom the Shulamite addresses her warnings about love, in spite of the fact that these unwilling soul sisters are as likely to jeer at the Shulamite's advice as to applaud it: "What is your beloved above another, / O fairest of women, / What is your beloved above another, that you thus adjure us?"

Perchance one can discern in the Shulamite's predicament an early instance of sexual harassment, replete with unconscious racist overtones. . . . So long as we are merrily throwing caution and credibility to the winds, we might as well go a step farther. Who knows but that biblical times had their wily subversives just as we do—their Princes and Madonnas who had a say along with the clean-living, God-fearing Pat Boone types. What if this most famous of love poems, preserved in the amber of a deeply paternalistic tradition that is yet canny enough to give the opposition its due, constitutes a stab to the heart of the very androcentric religion in which it nestles? "His hands are rods of gold / Studded with beryl; / His belly a tablet of ivory, / Adorned with sapphires." Any putatively male love object described with such a decided lack of virility and such a decidedly female sense of adornment presents ripe territory for study. Could it be that what we have before us is nothing less than a daringly prescient ode to bisexuality? *The Male Lover as Odalisque: Gender Inversion in the Song of Songs*. Chills run through one at the exegetical possibilities such a hypothesis would open up, whole graduate departments trained to spot the semiotics of kinky doings in the late biblical period.

2

There is, patently, nothing straightforward about the Song of Songs. Even before you get to the text itself, you encounter controversy. While one historian has argued that "the Song of Songs has suffered basic neglect in modern scholarship," Marvin Pope begins his introduction to his thickly appended translation for the Anchor Bible series with the following observation: "No composition of comparable size in world literature has provoked and inspired such a volume and variety of comment and interpretation as the biblical Song of Songs."

Then there is the vexed issue of authorship. The time-honored conservative view, which attributes the poems to King Solomon, has an undeniable (if unprovable) logic to it. Who better to pen poems with a prurient undertone than the Bible's own homegrown voluptuary? Less tradition-bound scholars have tended toward a looser theory of authorship, though there is little consensus as to which reconstruction is the most persuasive. In the past generation or two, as the field of biblical criticism has come into its own and its methodolgy has been refined, a wide variety of historical influences have been discerned in the poems, each in turn cast aside as soon as a tantalizing new lead presents itself.

Along with Ecclesiastes, Proverbs, and Psalms, this slim collection of verses—also known as the Canticle—occupies a much-disputed position in the biblical canon; the book has inspired a flurry of interpretive strategies bent on controlling if not outright dousing the fiery passion contained within. These strategies have themselves been looked upon with a suspicious eye: Gershom Scholem, for instance, in his *Origins of the Kabbalah,* cites one Meir of Narbonne, who, in the 1240s, thought that "the commentary on the Song of Songs deserved to be destroyed in order to prevent simple souls from being ensnared by it." Fears of the common reader's misjudging the book are rife: Rabbi Akiba is quoted as saying, "He who trills his voice in chanting the Song of Songs in the banquet house and treats it as a sort of song has no part in the world to come." Staunchly defended as the "holiest of holies" by this same Rabbi Akiba (also known for indulging himself in the farther shores of mystical speculation and emerging with his belief unscathed), the book remains a strange contender for inclusion and has generally been conceded to be a bit rich for less-than-sophisticated palates. "It is like a lock," observed Sa'adya Gaon in the early tenth century, "whose key is lost or a diamond too expensive to purchase."

Reader, in other words, beware. But who can resist a challenge? The intelligentsia least of all. Precisely because of the difficulties it poses, the Song of Songs is beloved of theorists, traditional and nouveau alike. The postmodernists, especially, warm to its "charming confusion," as Pope calls it. And with good reason: If ever there was a narrative cut to fit the current fashion in dense literary speculation, this one qualifies. Various special-interest groups—be they religious, deconstructionist, or feminist —have tried to get in on a piece of the heterodoxical action, all laying claim to a unique relationship with this avowedly independent-minded text, all attempting to fudge the question, How did so conspicuously ungodly a composition—a piece of undeniable erotica, filled with enough sexual punning ("Your lips drip honey, bride," or "Let my love enter his garden. / Let him eat its delectable fruits") to make Shakespeare blush— slip by the defenders of the faith, the old men with beards?

And then, like dominoes toppling, a whole slew of questions comes in the wake of that first one: How could the rabbis of the first and second centuries have failed to sound the alarms and allow the Song to secure for itself a sanctified niche, right up there with the creation of the world and the destruction of the Second Temple? Were they duped into stretching the category of sanctity wide enough to let in a bastard text? Or did they discreetly look away, recognizing that a religion based on 613 commandments could do with a little leavening, a welcome touch of sensuality?

What is clear in any event is that it is well-nigh impossible for the contemporary reader to approach the Song of Songs in a virginal spirit; the book's fame—or, more rightly, infamy—as the *I Am Curious, Yellow* of Jewish literature precedes it.

3

The notion of the taboo in Jewish thought has always struck me as hazy, underdeveloped in its implications.

Unlike Catholicism, a religion that comes with a firmly entrenched sense of sin—and a concomitant sense of religious confession—Judaism makes, perhaps, insufficient fuss about the mysteries of the flesh. In the Old Testament everything is handled in a matter-of-fact, so-called naturalistic fashion, from Noah's drunken near-incest with his daughters, to David's wandering eye, to Kohelet's sexual malaise. This inclination to regard the promptings of the id with a certain bemused tolerance is true of rabbinic literature as well: If a man can't handle his urges, advises the Talmud, he should go to a neighboring town and seek relief. It is important to note, in any discussion of the Judaic treatment of eros, that it is the only religion that historically had no specific sexual rites. As Gerson D. Cohen has been credited with observing, the love of the couple *sanctified by the law* has always been at the core of the Jewish stance toward lust and its consequences. This emphasis on demystifying the erotic by placing it in an ongoing conjugal context is a canny and subtle one; without fully disavowing its power, the focus on situating sexuality within marriage works toward weakening the hold of the unattached woman, as well as the hold of the carnal in general. Yael S. Feldman, in an essay that maps out a psychoanalytic reading of the Bible, argues along these lines: "It is therefore no accident that the domestication of the sexual drive is a major theme throughout Genesis, rivaled only by the analogous gradual sublimation of the aggressive drive." If Judaism can be said to be about the contextualization of problematic drives, then anything that is inherently outside the law of religion—the wild landscape of eros, for instance, a region without recognizable markings—must be brought inside and given boundaries.

Yet with all its emphasis on the connubial satisfaction of libidinal claims, there is in Jewish tradition a shrewd recognition that marital life and the business of ritual observance will not fully tame the stirrings of desire. So it seems entirely in keeping with this sense of realpolitik to allow the unrulier passions some representation. Which goes a long way to explaining the acceptance not only of the crazy-for-your-body lyrics of the Song but the groanings of the eponymous Kohelet, who, with his nihilism and decadence, might have found greater outlet for his frustrations had he lived in the latter half of this century.

But leave it to the rabbis to gyp us hapless readers. See them wink knowingly at one another behind their *s'forim,* their big black books of learning, getting ready to renege on their offer. Watch as they pat themselves on the back for their sense of embracing irony about the human animal, stuck forever between the worldly and the transcendent. The rabbis—of whom it can be said, as the critic George Steiner said of Freud, that they had "a mastering bias toward solutions"—were, after all, stuck themselves between appeasing the more absolutist among their constituency and keeping the less inflexible of their followers within the fold by attending to their wishes. And so we are handed a bill of exchange in which a Shulamite virgin is meant to stand in for Israel and a tumescent Solomon is meant to stand in for God, their passion to be acknowledged but never gratified. (Renunciation as a form of holiness is something those sniffy WASPs Henry James and Edith Wharton would surely have cottoned to.) What at first might have appeared to be a blistering piece of amatory literature turns out to be, via the magic of hermeneutics, a dutiful homiletic; instead of gaping at a skin flick, we find ourselves watching a video made for the annual synagogue dinner.

How like a people who have God in the head to insist that God is in their loins, too!

4

I have never been a true believer, not even as a child brought up in an Orthodox Jewish family. For one thing, I never understood my role in the religiously ordained hierarchy, other than to mutely observe and admire. I think of myself on Saturday mornings, standing in the women's balcony with my mother and two sisters, at a careful remove from the men's club going great guns downstairs. All those patriarchs and their sons busily thumping around with the Torah, carrying it aloft and singing its praises, opening and closing the curtain of the *Aron Hakodesh,* the Holy Ark, where the Torah scrolls were stored, or officiously dispensing *aliyes,* calling up young and old to the *bima,* the raised platform in the center, for a bit of momentary glory. That club included my father and three brothers, included anyone who wasn't female and excluded anyone who was: me, for instance, blusher carefully applied, the essence of self-conscious, unblossomed girlhood.

At what point did I stop listening to the text of the service, my years of Jewish day school and immersion in Hebrew endured for naught, the better to concentrate on the subtext—the palpable sexual tensions I sensed around me in the synagogue? All those dolled-up women, dressed and made up to kill, *their eyes like doves', their hair as black as goats, their teeth like a flock of ewes all shaped alike, their lips like woven threads of crimson silk, their breasts like twin fawns.* Why did they gleam and glisten so, I wondered, only to be cordoned off from the objects of their ministrations: the men downstairs, who cast appreciative glances upward and then went back to their noisy activities?

The burden of sexuality—both its allure and its danger—is placed on women, this much I see. Can it be that if the men venture upstairs, come too close to the expensive scents wafting through the women's balcony, they'll be bewitched, throw their marital vows out the window? Perhaps they'll cheat or, worse yet, leave their wives and families altogether; perhaps they'll go crazy with fleshly greed. Down the corridors of my mind, doors open upon a flurry of long-ago, briefly glimpsed images, scenes from a synagogue on the Upper East Side of Manhattan: sudden divorces and shamefully short marriages; older, prosperous husbands paired with younger, blond wives; trade-ins and -ups. The doors close, and order is restored. All is once again as it should be: We are here, the matriarchs and their daughters, stuck behind the *mechitza,* that inviolable dividing wall, whether balcony or curtain, consigned to an attitude of expectant readiness.

There are other questions that go unanswered because to ask them would be to imply that the bourgeois verities of life are up for grabs, and thus their very asking is taboo. How interesting, really, is *fulfilled* desire? What happens, that is, after you get the girl, find yourself actually bedding the Shulamite? How sustainable is erotic passion once you place a ring upon its finger? How sustainable is erotic passion, period?

The Song of Songs is read aloud in synagogue at the end of the long eight-day Passover holiday. It is doubtful I was present to hear it at an age when I could most have appreciated its uniquely untheological nature; once I had put in an appearance in my spring finery on the first two mornings of the holiday, I generally forswore further *shul* duty. But even if I was to be found in my seat in the women's balcony, I doubt I was listening anymore by the time I could have grasped its message, the secret it clutched to itself, behind its reputation for smuttiness.

It would be years before I stumbled upon a true consideration of what the secret was, before I teased out that sexual desire is a lie we tell ourselves, more or less. Romantic enamorment is a fabrication that serves to conceal the immense relativity of all passion and the virtual invention of the love object. "How sustainable is erotic passion?" *It was a question nobody asked because nobody wanted to know the answer.* Tell the truth about it and you did so at your own peril, as I discovered when I heard the tale of my great-uncle Raphael Breuer. Simple artistic soul that he was, he undertook in 1912 to write an interpretation of the Song based on a literal rather than allegorical reading—that it was merely a love poem. So strong was the reaction of the German-Jewish community of which he and his family were an influential part that Breuer not only had to rescind the introduction to his commentary but the gaffe is said to have cost him one of the most prestigious chief rabbinates in Germany.

And so, burdened by my particular history as a woman, I come to reacquaint myself with this infamously titillating text. How well will it live up to its reputation as the dirty, red-hot book of Jewish literature? I must admit that, after several readings to make sure I haven't somehow missed the climactic moment as I used to do when I read the late novels of Henry James, I don't find the poem particularly sexy. Resoundingly lyrical, yes; intimate and charming, undeniably; in the nature of an aphrodisiac, hardly. Perhaps it is the overwhelming rusticity of the amorous imagery—love that is like the crocus of the plain, the lotus of the valley, the apple in the wood; love that leaps over mountains and bounds over hills—that leaves me, a constitutionally urban creature without much direct experience of flora and fauna, at a loss. Perhaps it is all those trailing flocks of goats and ewes come up from the washing that give the narrative a faint whiff of barns and cow manure. I muse upon the possibility that allusions to the bestiary once carried a greater erotic charge than they do now. At any rate a zookeeper's vision of loveliness is not mine. Nor, for that matter, is a banker's; otherwise the persistently mercantile notion of comeliness that the Song advances—the lover's beauty is compared to gold, gems, ivory, sapphires, and marble—would undoubtedly move me more.

I find myself without sufficient frame of reference in the jumble of other metaphors as well. Lebanon. The tents of Qedar. Carmel. Clusters of grapes. More Lebanon. True, there is praise for a vulva that smells, improbably, of apples, but what is one to do with *that* piece of information?

Which leads me to the tale itself, rather than the telling. Goethe was supposed to have viewed the Song as "the most tender and inimitable expression of passionate yet graceful love that has yet come down to us." Nice words, although they still don't help me get a grip on the story.

Like, what exactly *happens* in it? I look ahead a couple of centuries and come upon this, from Julia Kristeva: "The Song of Songs gives Judaism the unique trait of being the most erotic of abstractions, the most ideal of sensualities." Nice words again, although they leave me with a blurry feeling around the edges. All this obscure, high-flying description, and I'm beginning to feel like the proverbial Hollywood philistine who prefers his plots pitched in one sentence or less.

Here, for better or worse, is what I've made of this "enigmatic parable," as it's been called. Once you've put the credos aside, you're left slipping around in the liquid atmosphere of the text without a foothold. Interestingly enough, what almost all of the readings of the Song have in common is a notion of union, marital or merely consensual, presumed to be implicit within the poem itself. This interpretive bias can be discerned as much in the various secularist stances as in the religious-allegorical approach, which raises the bawdy goings-on of the poem to a spiritually correct level by treating Israel as the symbolic bride and God as the symbolic husband—a familiar sacral conceit, used by the prophets Hosea and Jeremiah.

But to this reader the whole predicating idea of a union is never quite persuasive, perhaps because the Shulamite never comes across as an actual breathing specimen of womankind, just as Solomon and his lowly shepherd rival never emerge as fully embodied malehood. The verses, I propose, speak not to the idea of union, either literal or metaphorical or, God help us, "depatriarchalized," but rather to its virtual opposite: the solitary, wholly interior churn of ambivalence, expectant desire entwined with melancholy longing. Inherent in the very nature of erotic presence is absence—the looming loss of the lover even as he/she is glimpsed.

How to "own" the love object, how to pin down another beyond the fleeting moment: The possibility of sexual gratification is at least as threatening as it is pleasing, with its inevitable shadowy denouement of withdrawal and further longing.

I choose, then, to think of the Song of Songs as a story about the risks of passion—about being a fool for love and all of that. A particularly overlooked aspect of the text, to my way of thinking, is its recognition of the lover's vulnerability. To fall in love is to open oneself up to potential ridicule. The Shulamite's thrice-repeated bleak admonition about the dangers of falling in love seems most significant in this regard: "I adjure you, O / daughters of / Jerusalem, / by the gazelles, and by the hinds of the field, / That ye awaken not, nor stir up love. / Until it please." Under its Zen-like absolutism this refrain points to the fear of rejection implicit in all extensions of self. There is, too, the implied fear that once you've gone ahead and fastened your hopes on some designated other, the world will rush in with scabrous comparisons and invidious remarks of the "Who, him?!!" variety.

Radical as its inclusion in the canon of Holy Scriptures may appear to be, I suggest it is less surprising if one sees this amorous dialogue in the form of a warning—a prophylaxis, as it has been called: Caution, ye seekers of passion, lest you end up lost and wandering, in a city with no name, reduced to calling on the help of anonymous and hostile "watchmen." Caution, in other words, lest you end up lovesick, shades of Truffaut's Adele H., the woman consigned to an unfulfillable longing for the absent, ever-fleeing male.

5

The final section of the Song begins by alluding to the yearning for a pre-eroticized period in life in which a young boy is free to suckle on his mother's breast and a prepubescent girl ("Our sister is young / And breasts she has none") is free to kiss her brother without risk: "none would scorn me." It is a curious scenario for a purportedly heavy-breathing amorous dialogue to end on, but an entirely reasonable conclusion for the conflicted, push-me/pull-you recitation—a monologue in several voices—that I take this text to be. Perhaps, with just the smallest of shifts in emphasis, we might read the Song of Songs as an internalized argument *preceding* the taking of romantic action, a sort of amplified version of Hamlet's famously indecisive soliloquy: To love or not to love, that is the question.

At the core of the Song of Songs, under all its waffling, is an erotics of restraint, even of stasis. Someone, a woman perchance, longs; someone else, a man perchance, responds, but is ultimately unattainable. It is a game, a lie, an elaborate ruse: A case for adult heterosexual passion is presented in the guise of two amorphously defined lovers who never come close to consummating their relationship. Once the dust the poem is designed to kick up has settled, its stark secret is revealed: Stay upstairs in the balcony, Shulamite woman, for withheld consummation is the best kind.

But even as I write this, it becomes clear to me that I am writing out of my own idiosyncratic tastes. As such, it must be pointed out that my imagination is drawn more to the prospect of erotic doom than to sensual rapture, to Jean Rhys and her abandoned boardinghouse creatures than to daredevil dames astride one stallion-lover-husband after another. It is, in the end, a matter of personal accounting whether any passion is worth the price of that passion. So, too, in the end, the Song throws one —in the most parodied of postmodernist theories of reading—upon oneself as Author.

It would seem, finally, that one brings to a text about love all that one was taught to read into it, an amorous imprint stretching back for generations: unto mothers and grandmothers, and behind them ancestors galore. Some of us are destined to exalt love and others to demonize it; some rise to its occasion and others shy away for reasons unknown even to themselves. Lineage counts—Noah was the son of *x,* the son of *xx,* the son of *xxx*—even in matters of the flesh and heart. What you recognize as the siren call of love I may have learned to fear as the siren call of imminent abandonment. Someone must have scared off the author of the Song of Songs in the porousness of childhood, whispering sweet messages of caution: "Bolt, my love / Be like a buck, / Or a young stag, / On the spice mountain."

1994

Dreaming of Hitler: A Memoir of Self-Hatred

1

For a number of years during my adolescence, I dreamed about Hitler. These dreams occurred irregularly, but they always took place in a verdant setting—the same green glen to which I summoned other male figures, Bob Dylan and Franz Kafka, whom I longed to meet. In these dreams I stood at the end of a long field of grass, and from the other end a man walked toward me. The man was dressed in a khaki uniform and tall, glossy black boots; his eyes were a piercing light-blue with tiny pupils and he sported a perky, abridged mustache. The man coming toward me could have been anyone, a father or a boyfriend, but he was recognizably none other than Adolf Hitler. Adolf Hitler was smiling at me!

What took place in these dreams amounted to a miracle, a miracle performed not by God's hands, but by my very own: I convinced Hitler that he didn't really hate the Jews. I did this by talking to him softly, against a sun set low in the sky. Our conversation seemed to take up in the middle, as though we had been interrupted only recently. It involved a lot of gentle argument, of the sort two lovers might engage in. At one point during our conversation Hitler even stroked my hair—the hair of a Jewess, I remember thinking deep within the dream, the wrong color hair, not an Aryan blond. The thrust of my argument with Hitler was very personal, almost embarrassingly intimate. It had little to do with what I considered to be the pompous male line of thinking about the world, with theories of a humiliated post–World War I Germany or of an entrenched national anti-Semitism. I believed entirely in private wounds. After all, I had enough rage in me to decimate whole races, and I was a girl. Having been fascinated by Hitler for years, I had read enough about his background to know that the real object of his fury was his father, Alois, who had beaten him with Teutonic conviction (although I am not one of those who believe, as the analyst Alice Miller has argued, that Hitler's genocidal impulse can be attributed to a single cause, such as child abuse).

"Don't you see," I said, "it's not us you can't stand, not me. It's your anger at your childhood that makes you want to kill all the Jews."

Oh, the serene imperialism of dreams, where Adolf Hitler nodded his head, comprehending, and 6 million lives were about to be spared! How much we can undo in dreams. I would wake up with a secretive glow, a sense of mastery that I never experienced in my everyday life.

I first learned about the Holocaust at an age when I had difficulty assimilating it as anything other than a natural extension of the hostility I felt from my own parents, siblings, and schoolmates. The effect of that hostility—as perceived by me—had landed me in a hospital for extended psychiatric observation at the age of eight. The given reason for my two-week stay was that I suffered from anemia, but my siblings were not fooled by the medical cover my mother put on my emotional distress. They looked at me strangely when I returned home and started referring to a "brain operation." Nothing much changed after this—nothing that would have alleviated the family situation—except that I started seeing a psychiatrist. The second psychiatrist I went to believed in "play ther-apy," and I remember my frenzied beating-up of dolls in her office.

Although I don't connect the growing despair of my childhood with anything so remote from it as Hitler's destruction of the Jews, I think an awareness of that massive, external effort contributed to my innate feel-ing of houndedness. For children, the world begins at home, and in my home there was a lot of terror. My parents were both German Jews, of authoritarian inclinations. I was one of six tightly spaced children who pretty much toed the line, except that in my case a sense of internal protest expressed itself in incessant tears, and I was sent off for repairs. It seems to me now that the fact of the Holocaust did not come to me as a revelation so much as a confirmation of something I already fatally knew: The world was full of pain, might made for right, and everywhere lurked insinuating ironies. ARBEIT MACHT FREI—Work Will Set You Free—was the inscription mockingly emblazoned on the entrance gate to Auschwitz; if there was no actual gate to our apartment, there might as well have been, for ours was an unusually isolated family enclave, bar-ricaded by money and religion.

Even before I learned about the specific brand and virulence of Hitler's hatred, I was aware of a certain fragility about the whole enter-prise of being Jewish. The Upper East Side of Manhattan, which is where I grew up, was—and still is—a bastion of genteel money. The Jews who live there are a fairly assimilated bunch, given to stringing Christmas lights along with their Christian neighbors. My family, on the other hand, was strictly Orthodox, given to lighting Hanukkah candles and to the observance of deeply separatist religious laws. In the late six-ties, the years in which I reached adolescence, there were few like-minded Jews in the neighborhood who shared my family's ways. To walk along Park Avenue on Yom Kippur in dressy clothes and the requisite sneakers (this was well before the age of Reeboks) induced in me a state of morbid self-consciousness: *Everyone* could tell I was Jewish, as clearly as if I were wearing a yellow star.

But nothing was clear about the subculture of being Jewish in the larger culture of America: There was no direct route to unambivalent ethnic pride, because there was something I imbibed very early about the possibility—even in my highly identified family—of seeming *too* Jewish. My father wore his yarmulke at home but not outside or at business, the better to mingle with the populace. If being Jewish was all right, why wasn't it *completely* all right? Why, for instance, did I detect an admiration in my mother for an aesthetic that was quintessentially "WASP," a love of understatement, and a disdain for flash? My brothers wore Eton suits—gray or navy wool shorts and jackets—in the tradition of the sons of the British upper classes, and my sisters and I were outfitted in the guileless smocked dresses favored by patrician mothers everywhere. Floating always among us was an awareness of the importance of avoiding, if one could help it, "too Jewish" an appearance, the dreaded stigma of "too Jewish" a voice. My sisters, accordingly, emerged with carefully modulated accents that sounded vaguely foreign, a mix of German and British. I, by some cruel twist of fate, developed an accent that sounded unmistakably, harshly "Noo Yawk." My mother and sisters wanted to know why I talked as if I came from Brooklyn, but somehow I must have wanted to shed all vestiges of the dominant culture and get back to the lusty Jewish core. Most resoundingly of all, everyone I knew admired the sort of looks—in both men and women—that are thought of as classically non-Jewish: the Irish handsomeness of a John Kennedy, the sweet prettiness of a Donna Reed. My sisters and I venerated the blond and blue-eyed child actress Hayley Mills. Who among these icons displayed the strong features, darker coloring, or intensity of gaze I associated with being Jewish?

As I grew older and the first, fumbling dance of the sexes began around me, this perception of an elusive ideal of golden beauty would only deepen: I never met a Jewish girl or woman who didn't take it as the highest accolade to hear it observed that she didn't look Jewish. Perhaps the resolution of what seemed to me to be a historically vexed sense of identity was simply a matter of aesthetic reshaping! Certainly this issue lay at the core of something even more disturbing that I noticed in my early twenties. This was a phenomenon I will call "shiksa hunger": the longing for non-Jewish, crystalline Christian women on the part of Jewish men. And what Jewish men they were! All the best, most creative ones—Woody Allen in his movies, Philip Roth in his novels—steered clear of the classical, mother-polluted Jewesses and cast yearning eyes upon the blond, Aryan fantasy. In a toss-up between having Anne Frank or Eva Braun as a date, it was clear to me whom these men would choose.

Can racial self-hatred be passed along, like a bad gene?

In a theater on the Upper West Side, somewhere in the middle of *Hotel Terminus,* Max Ophuls's movie about Klaus Barbie—the infamous "Butcher of Lyons," a rabid Nazi but also the father of a pretty, blond daughter who speaks lovingly of him—the following statement is made: "Only Jews and old Nazis are interested in Jews and old Nazis." It is an observation that stays with me after the film is over, another of those insinuating ironies, chilling the night air.

Only Jews and old Nazis are interested in Jews and old Nazis: a relentless, claustrophobic thought, like being stuck in an unhappy childhood even after one has chronologically grown out of it. Certainly, many of the Jews I know are ceaselessly interested in reading about the Nazi period, myself included. Goebbels and Göring, Himmler and Hess, Mengele— the names mean something; one can put them together with faces and idiosyncrasies. Julius Streicher and his inflammatory cartoons, Eichmann and his clerklike personality, wives and children filling out the background . . .

The person I saw Ophuls's film with was struck by different aspects of it than I was. A friend of long standing, she said she hadn't noticed the pervasive, cool anti-Semitism expressed by many of the Americans and Europeans interviewed in the film. I accused her, as we waited for the light to change along Broadway, of insufficient Jewish self-awareness, a cultivated disinterest inherited from *her* deracinated parents. It occurred to me, even as I pointed this out, that ethnic consciousness of a high order —who is less or more Jewish—is a relative luxury. In Lyons, in the early forties, my friend and I would have been equally vulnerable, equally prey to Klaus Barbie's arbitrary acts of brutality. But is such a realization conducive to a sense of solidarity or of isolation? To be pressed into a group identity by animus alone, by the sheer weight of ostracism, is probably sustaining cause for de-identification. The old Groucho Marx line about not wanting to belong to any club that would have him as a member could only have been said by a Jew. In a way, it is a dead man's joke, the sort of hopeless truth that could make one scale barbed wire.

There is a stifling quality to enforced tribalism, a negative airspace, like being in a gas chamber. Perhaps to be Jewish is to be trapped always with *other* Jews, even with others Jews one doesn't like. It is difficult, for instance, to conceive of disliking the person piled next to you in a train bound for the death camps. Still, must one embrace one's fellow victims? The Resistance survivors in Ophuls's movie, the heroic men and women, Jews and non-Jews, seem to harbor deep suspicions one toward the other. Combating a greater, evil force did not seem to bring these people closer together. Under circumstances of extreme duress, do untrusting souls become more trusting? Or is the larger Jewish family akin to the smaller, nuclear one in which I have been raised—a worthy but untenable concept?

I have dreams of making Hitler pay attention to me, but in waking life my father is permanently out of reach, a figure who mostly frightens me, a German Jew whom I eye with distrust, who is given to ear-splitting displays of temper. Sometimes I think inside every German Jew—like the proverbial thin man trying to get out of every fat man—is a German trying to get out: a Nazi manqué. Around my father I feel the helplessness of appeal; the attack dogs of his derisive impatience are barking inside me, straining at the leash, ready to jump if I make the wrong move.

■ ■ ■

Questions that occur to me over the years about the Holocaust:
- Would I have survived?
- Would I have *wanted* to survive?
- What did you have to do inside your own head in order to survive?
- What did you do with the wish to die?
- Would anyone I know in the present have tried to hide me then?
- If it happened now, would any of the non-Jews I know be willing to risk their own lives in an attempt to save mine?
- Would *I* have been willing to risk my life to save another?
- What was it like to wake up in the morning in a concentration camp?
- What did you do with your memories?
- What did you do with your hopes?
- Did you, sooner or later, stop dreaming?
- If you did dream, did you dream of the concentration camp, or was it doubly shocking to wake up and find yourself there?
- How bad was the smell?
- If you couldn't adapt, did that mean you were weak?
- If you adapted, did that mean you were bad?
- Why did the act of survival seem to confer an honorary status?

The basic question, of course, is this: Do the good survive? (Primo Levi survived to write about his experience in an everyday voice, with a searing directness, only to commit suicide.) As Claude Lanzmann's mercilessly long film, *Shoah,* demonstrated over and over again, the Holocaust was nothing if not a precise equation, a particular set of circumstances, a certain brand of lethal gas, a certain number of people per train, the perfection of logistics. Against such calibration, what hope has goodness? More questions occur to me, questions addressed from a different angle, as though another twist of the evil kaleidoscope might bring a better picture or truer colors:

- Can one generalize that no Jewish mother will henceforth name her son Adolf?
- Did all the Nazis have a fondness for music, dogs, and chocolate?
- Did any of the Nazis have sleepless nights?
- Did the hum of German efficiency ever falter?
- Was a messy Nazi viewed jokingly as a kind of Jew?
- Did Nazis work an eight-hour day in the death camps?
- What did a Nazi think about when he stood naked in the shower?
- What did the Nazis eat for breakfast?

From *King of the Jews,* a 1979 novel by Leslie Epstein about the *Judenrat* within the Polish ghettos: "*I am a dog, a dog,* Leibelshofter had said. But everyone knew he had been mad. No, no cure for Judaism. It was a sentence for life."

I have read that one of the children who survived the ministrations of Josef Mengele, the Auschwitz doctor who was obsessed with twins, upon whom he performed fastidious experiments, wishes nothing more in adulthood than to find Mengele, to be in his company. The ravaged self looks for sustenance from those who have ravaged it. Even within death camps there are havens, or the insinuating irony of a haven: Mengele's "hospital," wherein resided a form of malign beneficence.

What becomes difficult to define is the process whereby the Nazis became internalized as part of the apparatus of self-loathing. Although I don't think the enormity of the Holocaust was ever lost on me, at some moment in time the historical reality became overwhelming evidence, a shadow identity tagging along, obscuring the light. At various points I wonder, disloyally, what it would be like to grow up without an awareness of "the Jewish problem," what it would be like not to have to take in an event so vast and so pernicious it remains obdurately uninstructive.

Can there be "a Jewish problem" without the hostile prompting of circumstance? Is it possible to feel inordinately persecuted without the Nazis? By the age of ten, even earlier, self-loathing came off my skin like a stench. (I think of the skin of concentration-camp inmates, the fat content reduced into soap, a neutral sudsing bar purified of Jewish essence, capable of cleansing all unwanted smells.) Perhaps self-hatred is no more than a genetic mutation, DNA coding gone wrong, passed on from one generation to the next—Alois Hitler to Adolf, my parents to me—until the only way out is to dump the whole burden onto the shoulders of the next available victim. That process we define as "identification with the aggressor" is easier to classify than to track, much less understand, but what it seems to provide is an escape hatch from an intractable emotional agenda of humiliation and rage; it is a way of warding off the guard dogs that bark within the brutalized mind. For the act of displacing the Bad in oneself—involving both disassociation (from one's feelings of negative self-worth) and projection (of those feelings onto some other person or group)—someone's going to pay: If one can't kick one's father to death, 6 million Jews will do. My dreams of stopping Hitler from his dire deeds were also dreams of reparation, of saving my abject self. Spare me, spare my race, spare me from me. Who knows at what point within the developing personality the furies within become the furies without: *Juden Raus!* (Jews out!)

2

I cannot remember with any exactness how I first became aware of the Holocaust. Did it, for instance, impinge slowly or did it come as a flood, drowning out all prior views of the world? It seems to me that my earliest inkling was connected with a cousin who used to visit my family while still a bachelor. Although this cousin was not of particular interest, he came crowned with a halo: He had been in one of the "camps" as a young boy. Now he sat in our living room, and I occasionally sat on his lap and grilled him along with my siblings on the details. We asked him about his experience in the valley of death as though we were questioning him about a thrilling adventure, a lark, but that is the sort of evenhanded curiosity children have. We asked to see the number burned into the soft underside of his arm again and again. There must have been something titillating, even pornographic, about those blue digits tattooed on white flesh—a violent confusion of the usual, rigidly maintained categories of childhood. I knew that cattle were branded for purposes of identification, but I had never seen a person so branded. This numbered human arm was a glimpse of something wholly adult: human behavior that partook of the bestial. Although I always expected this cousin to show great emotion when recounting what he had been through, he seemed singularly muted, as though his responses had been overworked a long time ago.

However many inklings I had (and there were other cousins, other stories of harrowing escapes over barbed wire) didn't add up to an indelible impression—not, that is, until my mother showed me a pair of books she kept on a shelf in my father's study. She had purchased the books in Germany when she stopped there for a day or two in the early fifties on a European trip with my father. As my mother explained it, these books were photo albums of the war assembled for the benefit of Nazi documentation, as testament to the successful process of racial genocide. The photos were in black and white—shot without sentiment or judgment. What they presented was dramatic evidence of the camera's neutrality, but also—and this latter possibility suggested something too frightening to be fully grasped—of the neutrality of the recorded event itself.

An old frock-coated Jew whose beard was being clipped with a large pair of scissors stood with an air of passive pleading as a group of cackling SS officers watched; another old Jew, shorn of all dignity, danced a jig in the middle of the street to some invisible Nazi's command. I

looked at these pictures and felt the doctrinaire humiliation, the programmed dehumanization behind them. But what did the people for
whom the photographs were meant feel about these images? Nothing, it
suddenly became clear to me, was absolutely terrible; everything was
absolutely subjective, including the perception of evil. It was entirely
possible that the upstanding Germans, proud believers in the Aryan ideology, who observed these small tortures felt a kind of satisfaction, a
grim contentment at the settling of ancient scores. Anti-Semitism used
as a tool to redress the tyrant-parent within, the politicized healing of
private wounds: It made a horrible, rabid sense to me. Germans, as I
knew well from my own upbringing, are keen disciplinarians, intent on
instilling in their offspring a fear of their own childish willfulness and
an awesome reverence for adult authority. What greater pleasure, what
more ecstatic sense of reparation, than to see that parental model of
authority that the Nazis represented play childishly—*disobediently*—
with the natural order of things, vandalize and subvert the peace, bully
people who were smaller than they?

In my father's study filled with *s'forim,* his books of Jewish learning,
the realization dawned on me: The only road to safety was to identify
with the aggressor. Save your skin and join forces with the enemy, even
if the enemy happens to reside inside of you. What an ugly race Jews are,
I thought, looking at the photographs, turning resolutely away from
empathy and self-acceptance toward the open arms of mockery and self-
abnegation.

And so I was well on my way to embracing *Artfremd*—which was
what the Nazis had declared the Jew to be, in a word of their own devi-
ous coinage: inalienably alien. There I was, an Orthodox Jewish girl
engulfed by this dark clot of history, ready to sign up with the storm
troopers. Hitler would have been proud of me.

The trouble with imbibing the black draft of the Holocaust so early was
that it unfairly upped the ante: *How unbearable could anything be if it wasn't*

being in a concentration camp? As if it weren't enough that I reasoned this way myself and thus was constantly given to slighting my own adolescent misery, my mother used this logic as a constant pedagogic refrain. "Just imagine you're in concentration camp," she would blithely suggest to me about any situation I found unbearable. There were, admittedly, many, for whenever I went away from home for more than a night or two at a time, I experienced acute separation anxiety. I would find myself calling from sleep-away camp or my first trip on my own to Europe in a state of dazed panic, pleading to come home, only to be told that these discernible, enjoyable experiences that I was failing to enjoy were best viewed as a fore-taste of unknown horrors to come, pallid tests of my endurance, of my will to survive. *Just imagine you're in concentration camp:* It was my mother's unique form of tongue-in-cheek consolation, but against such consolation, what hope had my flimsy, self-indulgent despair?

If, in the course of my childhood, the Holocaust began to take on the quality of a fatal object lesson, it also threw up some less horrific sce-narios, intriguing possibilities for my further investigation. Chief among these was the example of Anne Frank: Her adolescent diary was found by a Gentile neighbor after the war and given to her father, Otto, the only surviving member of the family; it was published in 1947 to immediate acclaim. I read Anne Frank's diary when I was about ten or eleven, only a little younger than she was when she wrote it. I loved the way she addressed her diary by a name, "Kitty," as though it were a real person, a living and breathing companion. I started to keep a succession of abortive diaries myself; I gave them all names, in admiring emulation and in the hope that this gesture would keep me writing, but every name sounded hollow next to the vestal "Kitty."

There was another aspect of Anne Frank's diary that pleased me, an aspect that suggested my mother's lessons in the self-diminishing value of the Holocaust weren't necessarily the right ones to draw: The fact was that Anne Frank didn't in the least appear to think that the Holocaust—

although it howled like the hungriest of wolves right at her doorstep—devoured the intensity and dignity of all other, private experience. In the almost daily communications with her dear "Kitty," Anne's brooding, introspective nature was given free and writerly play. Her dissatisfactions with her mother; arguments with her older sister, Margot; sharp-tongued observations about the other family in hiding: These problems were important to her. The reality of her own mind was as valid as the life-threatening reality external to her mind. *How unbearable could anything be if it wasn't being in concentration camp?* I had before me now in Anne Frank's diary the glimmer of a different answer: You could be living right in the eye of the Nazi storm and still take your own little angst seriously. Better yet, you could emerge from the Holocaust a literary heroine! The thought was exhilarating.

3

Finally, last fall, I got to Germany. In my mid-thirties, a writer and editor, I attended the Frankfurt Book Fair for the first time. I was put up at the Frankfurter Hof, an icily run hotel considered to be one of the city's best. From the moment I arrived I felt on the alert—as though, more than forty years after the Holocaust, I might pass a half-open door along the hotel's wide and richly carpeted hallway and spot a decadent cocktail party of SS officers in full swing, their swastika patches winking out at me amid the tinkle of glasses.

The New York publishing world, which attends this international gathering en masse, is largely composed of Jews; many have been coming to the fair for years, seemingly without self-consciousness, with nary a wrinkle in their smoothly arranged professional identities. But then again, most of the Jews I have encountered since I began both writing and working in publishing are what I consider to be "closet" Jews—Jews with little or no background in Judaism and with a bemused, fiercely secularist attitude toward the many historical rituals that are the foundation of their religion. The extent of these Jews' evident disinterest in their own heritage puzzled me initially, just because they seemed so tolerant—so curious—about everything else, from Zen Buddhism to deconstructionism. Only the arcana of Jewish life struck them as humdrum. And the genuine Jewish "literati," the name-brand critics and writers I met in passing—their disregard for an almost six-thousand-year-old tradition was nothing short of dazzling.

I can't really claim, then, to have been surprised by the ease with which the Jews of publishing moved around a city that had once burned books written by Jews. (I knew there had been an organized protest within the past few years when a fair had been held on Yom Kippur. This quite estimable gesture seemed to have stood in for all assertions of racial pride past, passing, and to come.) What I was surprised by, rather, was how vigilant—on behalf of Jewishness, not only my own but the generic article—*I* felt. Everywhere I noted the brusque efficiency of a people who believed in imposing an ironclad sense of order—on their children, on their hotel guests, on their public transportation. The bellmen at the Frankfurter Hof could not be engaged in anything other than the most succinct dialogue about directions and restaurant reservations; they did not bend their ear to any attempt at friendly banter, nor did they crack an extra smile. I wondered, uneasily, whether they knew I was Jewish, that old stench coming off me.

At dinner one night with an executive from another New York publishing house, a Jew brought up in the Midwest who told me he had joined a synagogue and had recently been bar mitzvahed as part of a belated discovery of his roots, I referred in passing to my qualms. After dinner we began walking back to the Frankfurter Hof and found ourselves on a small back street. The street was empty, spotless, and suddenly it seemed full of menace. I made a nervous comment about there appearing to be no homeless in Frankfurt, or at least not anywhere I had been. "The homeless have been exterminated," my companion joked. And then he pointed at the small apartment building opposite us and asked me if I had noticed a woman standing by a window. "She looks," he said, "like a Nazi," only his tone wasn't jocular this time. I peered upward, and after several seconds I made out the figure of an elderly woman, holding a curtain back with her hand, staring down at us. Something about her face, about the hardness of her gaze, seemed unutterably hostile. "Maybe she's Ilse Koch," I said, referring to the lantern-jawed female SS officer who oversaw the women's barracks in Buchenwald.

On a cold and gray Saturday afternoon of my last day in Frankfurt, I set off with a colleague for the Israelitscher Friedhof at the far end of the city. I had with me a small index card on which my mother had written the address of the Jewish cemetery and drawn the triarch headstone that marked my great-grandfather's grave. The cemetery, my mother had warned, was hard to find and so were the individual graves; she had said to make sure to summon the old Jew who maintained the graves by ringing at the tiny gate to the right of the main entrance. The cemetery was kept locked, and this beadle was not only in possession of the key but would also be able to guide me to the spot where my great-grandfather was buried.

The sky seemed to darken even as we took the long taxi ride through neighborhoods that grew increasingly less affluent the farther we got from the hotel. There was a starkly concrete, postmodernist quality to the area the taxi finally stopped in—few visual adornments and a pervading atmosphere of urban gloom, like George Orwell's vision of the future. We alighted across the street from the cemetery and walked to the all-but-invisible gate. We rang and rang for the cemetery-keeper but he did not come: It was Saturday, after all, Shabbat, and I had known in the back of my mind that there was a good possibility he wouldn't be there. But it was the only opportunity in a frenetic week of appointments that I had, and I had somehow reasoned to myself that a Jewish cemetery in Frankfurt in the year 1988 wouldn't be closed in recognition of ancient laws.

I felt profoundly disappointed. I had imagined engaging in a long, gossipy dialogue with this keeper of old graves. My mother's family had been one of the most influential within the petit-bourgeois Orthodox community that flourished in Frankfurt until the early thirties, and I had pictured myself discovering all sorts of details about a bygone life that I had heard much about. I was disappointed, but I wasn't ready to give up. I suggested that we go into the small florist's across the street and see if there was any way we could obtain entry without the caretaker. Inside the flower shop I used my best garbled German to explain to the young boy who was wrapping flowers for a customer the nature of our expedition. Much to my surprise, he seemed to understand me and handed over a large key. In gratitude we bought several bunches of flowers—"to place on the graves," as my colleague suggested to me, although I in turn pointed out to him that this was a Christian rather than Jewish custom.

At last we found ourselves inside the cemetery proper. The wind had come up and the vista before us looked desolate. There were many more graves than I had envisioned—what looked to be acres of graves, erect and broken headstones stretching in every direction. I had expected a more modest expanse: If the Nazis had been too busy destroying living Jews to desecrate the burial place of dead ones, I still hadn't expected to find such a multitude of resting souls. I studied my mother's primitive illustration to see if it would help me, but the type of headstone she had drawn—like three, rather than two, Mosaic tablets—seemed to have its duplicate in every other row. The two of us started off for a section of the graveyard all the same; I had the name and the dates, and I was certain we'd stumble across it.

As the minutes passed and the wind moaned in the bare and wintry branches, my companion and I became absorbed in the graves, pausing to study dates and to decipher inscriptions. After a while we agreed to separate for efficiency's sake, and I soon found myself wandering around, lost in contemplation of the lives—many tragically brief—that the inscriptions attested to. I wondered what the furniture had looked like in the houses these men and women had lived in; what clothes they wore; how they felt about being Jewish. More than half of the epitaphs

were in German rather than Hebrew, which suggested that many of the
dead had been assimilated. There were headstones that marked empty
plots, with epitaphs that spoke of dearly loved kin who were deported as
late as 1944: These, I gathered, had been erected in memoriam after the
war. (The cemetery is still in use.) I became conscious of my very contemporary clothing, my jeans and sneakers and black leather jacket, so
different from the wardrobe these proper-sounding German women
would have been used to.

Somewhere among the stillness of the graveyard lay the bones of my
ancestor, a devout late-eighteenth-century Jew; I thought if I could find
him I would perhaps find a missing piece of myself, a way of casting off
the shadow identity of Jewishness for something more sustaining, something that would let in the light. When I came to the northernmost corner of the cemetery I suddenly realized I had no idea where my partner
in sleuthing was. I called out to him, but he didn't answer. All around
me was silence, and the impassive dignity of death. I looked around me
and felt a chill, a rustle of fear. What if my colleague wasn't able to find
me or I him? What if I was left here, locked in at evening's end with the
Jewish corpses of Frankfurt?

I gazed out into the haunted night and thought I saw someone moving toward me, a ghostly figure. "Control your imagination, girl," I told
myself firmly. And then, to distract myself from my growing panic, I
imagined that I was directing a movie, a gritty Fassbinder-like movie
about corruption and guilt, set in the Jewish cemetery. I quickly wrote
a script in my head, some vague story line involving an alienated American Jewish photographer who stumbles into this graveyard she hadn't
known of. I turned, readily imagining myself in the role, to the young
man coming toward me. He was of medium height, with piercing blue
eyes and a dark thatch of hair. He walked toward me, this angry young
painter and reader of Marx, in improbably tall and glossy black boots.
He took me in his arms and—in the magical way of cinema, where past
and present can be artfully cross-framed and all of life can be viewed as
a flashback—I found myself in the embrace of the young Adolf Hitler.

He played with my hair, the hair of a Jewess, the wrong color hair, not Aryan blond. I was about to talk him out of something enormous and evil when I heard someone shout my name.

The welcome figure of my colleague, in his navy-blue slicker, came toward me. The evening had settled in by now, and there was a light rain coming down. I reluctantly agreed that it was getting too dark to look anymore, although it seemed to me that my great-grandfather was expecting me. We placed the bunches of flowers on several graves, anonymous but somehow familiar, and then we left the cemetery.

These days I find myself dreaming less of Hitler. The grandiose fantasy of redeeming the man in the mustache and boots—and, in the process, myself—seems to have lessened its hold on my unconscious life. Part of me misses these dreams, and the wondrous sense of accomplishment they brought: There I was, the same girl who feared her own father, reversing the tide of history, demonstrating powers of understanding and persuasion that were unguessed at in my observable existence.

Perhaps the passing of these dreams suggests no more than that I have grown older and more resigned, that I have made some realistic accommodation with the forces that rage within and without. Just as there is no sign that the world has grown more fond of the Jews, so there is no sign that I will ever be free of a certain fascination with the darker impulses at work in myself and others. Still, I sense of late a slight shifting of the focus, a lifting of the onus of my own hostility. There is some kind of relief in being able to recognize the aggressor and then walk on. There is even more relief in being able to acknowledge that it is in the nature of evil to defy one's powers of comprehension, just as it is in the nature of one's enemies to remain implacable.

1989

Publication Credits

All of the pieces in this collection have been revised, more or less extensively, for their appearance here. The titles are frequently different from the original ones, and I consider these to be the final versions of the essays.

"On Not Becoming a Lesbian" is reprinted with the permission of Simon & Schuster from *Surface Tension: Lesbian and Straight Women Write About Their Relationships,* edited by Meg Daly. Copyright © 1986 by Meg Daly. First appeared in *Tikkun,* November–December 1995.

"Now, Voyeur: The Erotic Life of Movies" first appeared in *Premiere,* Winter 1991.

"Extramarital Cravings" first appeared in *The New Yorker,* December 27, 1993.

Excerpts from *Simple Passion* by Annie Ernaux, published by Seven Stories Press, New York. Reprinted by permission of the publisher.

"A Taste of the Stick: Joel and Hedda, 1988" first appeared in *Seven Days,* December 7, 1988.

"Desperately Seeking Torture: S&M on the Internet" first appeared in *U.S. News & World Report,* November 25, 1996.

"Spanking: A Romance" first appeared in *The New Yorker,* February 26, 1996.

"Ready, Willing & Wary" first appeared in *The New York Times Magazine,* July 16, 1989. Copyright © 1989 by The New York Times Co. Reprinted by permission.

"Secrets of a Pregnant Woman" first appeared in *New York Woman,* March 1990.

"The Knight in Shining Armani" first appeared in *The New York Times Magazine,* July 15, 1990. Copyright © 1990 by The New York Times Co. Reprinted by permission.

"My Kingdom for a Scarf" first appeared in *The New York Times Magazine,* May 5, 1991. Copyright © 1991 by The New York Times Co. Reprinted by permission.

"A Complicated Friendship: Remembering Diana Trilling" first appeared in *The New York Times Book Review,* November 17, 1996. Copyright © 1996 by The New York Times Co. Reprinted by permission.

"On Not Attending My College Reunion" first appeared in *Barnard* magazine, Summer 1991.

"Notes of a Lonely White Woman" first appeared in *Partisan Review,* Fall 1993.

"Dancing with My Daughter" first appeared in *Avenue,* March 1993.

"In the Country of Divorce," from *Women on Divorce: A Bedside Companion,* edited by Penny Kaganoff, copyright © 1994 by Daphne Merkin. Reprinted by permission of Harcourt Brace & Company. First appeared in *Harper's Bazaar,* October 1994.

About the Author

Daphne Merkin's work appears regularly in *The New Yorker, The New York Times Book Review,* and other leading periodicals. Her novel, *Enchantment,* won the Edward Lewis Wallant award. Born and raised in New York City, she is a graduate of Barnard College. She lives in Manhattan with her young daughter and is at work on a novel called *The Discovery of Sex.*